Education as social policy

SOCIAL POLICY IN MODERN BRITAIN

General Editor: Jo Campling

EDUCATION AS SOCIAL POLICY

Janet Finch

LONGMAN
London and New York

LONGMAN GROUP LIMITED
Longman House, Burnt Mill, Harlow,
Essex CM20 2JE, England.
Associated companies throughout the world

*Published in the United States of America
by Longman Inc., New York*

©Longman Group Limited 1984

First published 1984

BRITISH LIBRARY CATALOGUING IN PUBLICATION DATA

Finch, Janet
Education as social policy.—(Social policy in modern Britain)
1. Education sociology
I. Title.   II. Series
370.19   LC191

ISBN 0-582-29605-6

LIBRARY OF CONGRESS CATALOGING IN PUBLICATION DATA
Finch, Janet
Education as social policy.
(Social policy in modern Britain)
Bibliography: p.
Includes index.
1. Education—Social aspects—Great Britain.
2. Great Britain—Social policy.   I. Title.   II. Series.
LC191.8.G7F56 1984   379.41   83-785

ISBN 0-582-29605-6

Set in 10/11 pt Linoterm Plantin
Printed in Hong Kong by
Astros Printing Ltd.

CONTENTS

CONTENTS

This series, written by practising teachers in universities and poly-technics, is produced for students who are required to study social policy and administration, either as social science undergraduates or on the various professional courses. The books provide studies focusing on essential topics in social policy and include new areas of discussion and research, to give students the opportunity to explore ideas and act as a basis of seminar work and further study. Each book combines an analysis of the selected theme, a critical narrative of the main developments and an assessment putting the topic into pers-pective as defined in the title. The supporting documents and com-prehensive bibliography are an important aspect of the series.

Conventional footnotes are avoided and the following system of references is used. A superior numeral in the text refers the reader to the corresponding entry in the list of references at the end of each chapter. A select bibliography is found at the end of the book. A number in square brackets, preceded by 'doc', e.g. [doc 6, 8], refers the reader to the corresponding items in the section of documents which follows the main text.

Education as social policy is the first textbook which explores the English educational system in relation to social policy. In the British context, education is conventionally regarded as one of the major institutional areas of the welfare state, and is taught as such on social policy and administration courses. Yet, surprisingly there is no well-developed body of literature which treats education as part of the welfare state, to set alongside treatments from the perspectives of educationalists, of administrators, and of the major social science disciplines. The task of developing a specifically social policy per-spective on education therefore is long overdue.

The book develops a framework for studying education as social policy by looking both at social policy *in* education and *through* education. Studying social policy *in* education entails examining how the educational system has been shaped by the pursuit of various social policy ends within the educational context. Exploring social policy *through* education involves looking at ways in which the educational system itself has been used for social policy ends which are much broader than specifically educational goals. Throughout, simplistic accounts of these processes are rejected. Indeed a major theme of the book is that education cannot be seen just as an activity which benefits the recipients, or as an enterprise which merely serves the economy, the national interest or society's needs. Rather, it is argued that the tension between the interests of the individual and society has been a highly significant feature in shaping the often contradictory character of the educational system.

The book is structured around basic concepts with which social policy engages, and applies these to education. It utilises and evaluates a wide range of conceptual frameworks, reflecting both traditional social policy concerns (e.g. issues of redistribution; needs; welfare) and also issues raised by more recent neo-Marxist writings in social policy (e.g. concepts of reproduction; regulation; control). These are applied to the educational system through the use of specific, concrete examples e.g. the development of the school meals service; comprehensive reorganisation; the education of girls. Exploring these specific examples from the perspective of social policy in many instances sheds new light upon them, making them comprehensible in a different way than when they are considered purely in terms of the education system itself, and thereby generating important questions for discussion and further exploration.

Jo Campling

ACKNOWLEDGEMENTS

Many people have contributed, through discussion and argument with me, to the development of the ideas upon which this book is based, including successive groups of students who have taken my course on education and social policy at the University of Lancaster since 1976. For assistance in reading and commenting upon outlines and drafts, I would like to thank; Susan Clayton, Ian Dixon, Dulcie Groves, Felicity Harrison, Emma Redmond Pyle and Sally Tomlinson. My thinking has benefited especially from comments and suggestions made by Rosemary Deem, Dave Smith and especially Bob Burgess, who read the whole manuscript: I am grateful to these people for their enthusiastic encouragement during the preparation of this book. Finally, I would like to thank Sarah Bracewell, who typed the manuscript with characteristic efficiency, accuracy and interest.

We are grateful to the following for permission to reproduce copyright material:

George Allen & Unwin Ltd for Doc 45; Associated Book Publishers Ltd for Docs 1, 48, 51, 52; the Controller of Her Majesty's Stationery Office for Docs 2-4, 6, 8-19, 22-26, 29, 31, 38, 39, 41, 43, 49, 50, 56, 58; Mrs Nadine Marshall for Doc 35; National Council for Civil Liberties for Doc 55; Policy Studies Institute for Doc 60 from PS1 Discussion Paper No 3; Society of Teachers Opposed to Physical Punishment for Doc 59; Times Newspapers Ltd for Docs 21, 34.

Part one
ENGLISH EDUCATION SINCE 1944: A SOCIAL POLICY
OUTLINE

Chapter one
INTRODUCTION

This book has been written for students, teachers and others who want to think about education in the wider context of social policy and to learn something about how social policies have been pursued in and through education in Britain, especially since the end of the Second World War.

The approach differs, therefore, from books written by and for educationalists, or by those who study education from the perspective of a particular discipline, be it philosophy, sociology, history, economics or whatever. The perspective of social policy requires an approach which is wide-ranging and this means that there is no space here for a very detailed examination of particular issues, with careful weighing of all the evidence. Many interesting aspects of the educational system cannot be given detailed consideration because they do not relate directly to the context of social policy: the study of the cognitive development of children for example, or the organisation of teacher training. The aim is to offer a range of perspectives upon education which essentially raise questions rather than provide definitive answers, and to point the interested reader in appropriate directions for further study.

The point at which the discussion must begin is the question: why study education as social policy? To those born since 1944, education may seem part of the taken-for-granted world. However, an examination of the debates around the introduction and subsequent extension of compulsory education demonstrates quite clearly that it was intended to be the means of achieving social ends, and often social change. In the period immediately after the Second World War it was a fundamental part of the attempt at social reconstruction which gave rise to the institutions of the welfare state. Indeed it became the conventional wisdom in that period to regard the 1944 Education Act, along with the National Insurance Act and the National Health

Service Act, as one of the three 'pillars' of the welfare state. [1(p.87)]

The centrality of education in post war social reconstruction is one reason for examining it from the perspective of social policy, despite the fact that the study of the education service has developed in relative isolation from the study of other aspects of the welfare state. [2(p. 86)] More generally, it can be and has been used, as Silver has argued [doc 1] as a 'vital instrument of social policy by governments of all kinds – with varying degrees of commitment or reluctance, and with different and conflicting intentions'. The use of education for social policy purposes is very much a contested arena, where different ends can be pursued by a variety of means. Examining education in this perspective highlights aspects of the educational system – such as school meals or the educational welfare service – which otherwise often seem peripheral. They may be peripheral to the concern of educationalists, but they are central to an understanding of how education interlocks with other aspects of social policy in the context of the welfare state, most obviously with other policies which concern bringing up the young. At the same time, more obviously educational concerns – such as attempts to equalize access to education, and to produce more equitable educational outcomes, for children of different social backgrounds – are cast in a different light when placed in the broader context of a social policy programme designed to produce greater social justice by democratic reform.

The major themes developed in this book are derived from the study of social policy and then used to examine the particular field of education. These themes are taken from a range of approaches to social policy, as reflected in recent literature. Those approaches are somewhat disparate, because there is by no means a consensus about what social policy *is* and therefore what is the appropriate conceptual framework for studying it. The study of social policy (also called social administration) grew with the development of the welfare state, which it took as its main subject matter. Social policy of course is not necessarily confined to the actions of government. Welfare services can be provided by charitable bodies, by individuals caring for members of their family in their own homes, or on a commercial basis (private pension plans or private medical schemes, for example), but as far as education in the twentieth century is concerned, the state has been the major source of providing, funding and controlling it [doc 1].

Different views about what constitutes social policy derive essentially from varying ideological and political stances.[3] The predominant perspective in the study of social policy for many years was the social democratic, or Fabian socialist, emphasising government intervention to produce greater equality and social justice, through peaceful reform within the context of the prevailing capitalist economic structure. More conservative alternatives (called 'anti-collectivist' by George and Wilding) emphasize freedom and individualism and a necessary degree of inequality. Rather different accounts produced by Marxists and by feminists have gained momentum in recent years. These tend *inter alia* to emphasize the covert and more negative aspects of welfare, showing that apparently benign reform may in fact have the consequence of further disadvantaging those whom they purport to assist.[4]

This variety of standpoints gives rise to a range of concepts in social policy which prove useful in exploring features of the educational system. Variously, they suggest that social policy can be seen as action designed by government to engineer social change; as a mechanism for identifying human needs and devising the means of meeting them; as a mechanism for solving social problems; as redistributive justice; as the means of regulating subordinate social groups. Part Two of this book uses these conceptual frameworks to examine features of English education. Although they are disparate and in many ways conflicting, certain common themes are implied, and any discussion of education as social policy must address itself to these themes. They are, first: why does the state so significantly engage in the provision of education? Second, what kinds of social policy ends are being pursued through education, both overtly and covertly? Third, in whose interests are they being pursued and who actually benefits? Fourth, what kinds of outcomes ensue, both intended and unintended? Those four questions are implicit in much of the discussion of this book.

The major theme running through the book derives from the perspective implied by those questions. This theme is that, when one views the development of education as social policy in Britain, there is a fundamental tension revealed between education as an activity which offers benefits to individuals who receive it, and education as an activity which is designed primarily to meet 'society's needs' (however defined). This tension is apparent both in the intention of policy and its effects. To focus upon it involves rejecting two alternative views of the educational system, both of which are in fact too simple. They can be characterised thus:

1. Education is 'really' about opportunities offered to individuals, from which they derive personal benefits. Any demonstrable inequalities (e.g. of access) are simply unfortunate and can be eradicated.

2. Education is 'really' about moulding and controlling individuals in the interests of the economy, the state, or 'society'. The idea that

individuals actually benefit from it is merely an illusion, perpetrated to ensure co-operation.

There are some rather obvious problems with both of these approaches. The first, for example, is hardly credible when many children appear to derive so few benefits of any kind from their educational experiences, and when inequalities of access and outcome have proved so intractable. The second embodies a very simple and determinist version of the operation of power in social life, and treats 'society' as if it were a single entity with clearly identifiable interests, rather than made up of different individuals and groups with widely varying interests. However, it is useful in developing an analysis to retain these two characterisations as representing alternative versions of what and whom education is *for*. I shall refer to them as the 'individual's benefit' and the 'society's benefit' rationales.

In practice, education in Britain has exhibited a continual tension between these two. It often gives rise to incompatible ends being pursued at the same time. It is a major theme of this book that the shape of the educational system can be understood as a product of such conflicts and contradictions, and many illustrations will be offered in the course of discussion.

The plan of the book is as follows. Part One provides an outline of the English educational system and its development since 1944. It offers a chronological account of the development of education, highlighting features which are significant from the viewpoint of social policy. This is followed by a brief discussion of the administration of the system, examining certain aspects of what happens when policies are put into effect. Part Two uses concepts drawn from social policy to explore particular features of the educational system. Because these concepts provide the organising themes for the discussion, it often traverses the boundaries within which 'topics' are usually presented. So, for example, discussion of the work of the education welfare service appears in several different places, since aspects of their work are relevant to different themes. Also in Part Two, considerable use is made of case studies to illustrate particular discussions. These have been selected for their relevance to the themes, but often other case studies could have been chosen. The final chapter offers an evaluation of education as social policy.

NOTES AND REFERENCES

1. MARSHALL, T. H. (1965), *Social Policy*. Hutchinson: London.

2. WELTON, J. (1981), 'Two problems in the study of social policy with particular reference to educational administration', in P. Ribbins and H. Thomas (eds), *Research in Educational Management and Administration*. British Educational Management and Administration Society: Birmingham.

3. Useful discussions can be found in (a) GEORGE, V. and WILDING, P. (1976), *Ideology and Social Welfare*. Routledge & Kegan Paul: London: (b) MISHRA, R. (1977), *Society and Social Policy: Theoretical Perspectives on Welfare*. Macmillan: London.

4. FINCH, J. (1982), 'The sociology of welfare', in Burgess (ed.), *Exploring Society*. British Sociological Association: London.

Chapter two

EDUCATION AND SOCIAL POLICY SINCE 1944

This chapter offers a chronological account of a number of key events in the development of social policy in and through education in England in the period following the Second World War. It is divided into sections which coincide with historical 'periods'. Clearly these overlap, but (it will be argued) each one is characterised by predominant themes and concerns. These divisions help to give some shape to the discussion of very diverse features of educational provision, stretching over four decades. The last section is an outline of some major features of policy-making and administration in the education service.

The major events discussed in the text are summarised in Table 1:

Table 1. Education and social policy since 1944: major events

Date	Legislation and major official reports	Other reports and major events discussed in text
1943	White Paper: *Educational Reconstruction* Norwood Report: *Curriculum and Examinations in Secondary Schools*	
1944	Education Act 1944	
1945		Labour elected Implementation of Act begins
1951		Conservative government elected

Date	Legislation and major official reports	Other reports and major events discussed in text
1954	*Early Leaving*	
1958		White Paper: *Secondary Education for All: A New Drive*
1959	Crowther Report: *Fifteen to Eighteen*	
1960		Beloe Report: *Secondary School Examinations other than GCE*
1963	Newsom Report: *Half Our Future* Robbins Report: *Higher Education*	
1964		Labour government elected Ministry of Education re-titled Department of Education and Science
1965		Circular 7/65 Circular 10/65
1966	White Paper: *A Plan for Polytechnics and Other Colleges*	
1967	Plowden Report: *Children and Their Primary Schools*	
1968	Public Schools Commission (First Report)	Educational Priority Areas established Seebohm Report on local authority social services
1970	Public Schools Commission (Second Report)	Conservative government elected
1971	Education (Milk) Act 1971	
1972	White Paper: *Education: A Framework for Expansion*	School leaving age raised to 16

Date	*Legislation and major official reports*	*Other reports and major events discussed in text*
	Halsey Report: *Educational Priority* James Report: *Teacher Education and Training*	
1973		Russell Report: *Adult Education*
1974		Labour government elected House of Commons Committee: *Education Maintenance Allowances in the 16–18 Years Age Group* Circular 4/74 Local government reorganisation
1975	Bullock Report: *A Language for Life*	Sex Discrimination Act William Tyndale dispute
1976	Education Act 1976	Race Relations Act Tameside dispute House of Commons Committee: *Policy Making in the DES* Initiation of 'Great Debate'
1977	Green Paper: *Education in Schools* Taylor Report: *A New Partnership for our Schools*	Holland Report: *Youth and Work*
1978	Warnock Report: *Special Educational Needs*	
1979	Education Act 1979	Conservative government elected DES: *Local Authority Arrangements for the School Curriculum*
1980	Education Act 1980	MacFarlane Report: *Education for 16–19 Year Olds* White Paper: *Special Needs in Education*

Education as social policy

2.1 THE 1944 SETTLEMENT

1944 has been chosen for the starting point of this account because that was the date of the passing of the Education Act which laid the foundations of the contemporary educational system. Its major contribution was to attempt to put into effect the notion of 'equality of opportunity' through the provision of secondary education for all, but many other features of the Act have shaped the provision of education in England and Wales.[1] Although a number of subsequent Education Acts have modified certain features of the system, the 1944 legislation remains the basic framework.

From the point of view of social policy, the shape of the 1944 Act has to be seen partly as a product of the educational system which preceded it, but also very importantly as one aspect of postwar social reconstruction, although of course the Act was passed while the war continued. It was (as was noted in the introductory chapter) regarded as one of the main 'pillars' of the welfare state and – as will become apparent – was planned during the war as very much part of the anticipated reconstruction.

In an important sense the war itself can be said to have shaped the character of postwar reconstruction. Marshall has argued that war has predictable effects upon the way governments react to social problems, one of which is that they are obliged to assume heavier responsibilities for welfare.[2(pp.75–6)] So during wartime there is more intervention by government, and in situations where war involves the whole population (not just the armed forces) that intervention will have a very wide compass. The conditions in the Second World War were such, Titmuss has argued, that measures had to be developed which centred around the primary needs of the population irrespective of their social status (and to some extent of their wealth), thus universalising risks through public provision. Postwar social legislation was in part an expression of this wartime strategy to fuse and unify social life.[3a,b,c] As far as education is concerned, R. A. Butler, the government minister responsible for the Act, has claimed that the wartime evacuation of children from the cities had a particular impact, alerting the public to the continuing existence of the 'submerged tenth' of the population, and the fact that we were still 'two nations'. This was, he argued, the stimulus for 'rethinking the purposes of society and planning the reconstruction of a social system of which education formed an integral part'.[4(p.3)] As is apparent from Butler's approach, the whole idea of reconstruction is in fact a very clear example of the attempted use of social policy as social engineering (cf. Ch. 5).

More romantic accounts of wartime Britain tend to accept with uncritical enthusiasm its supposed egalitarian character, in which all risks were willingly 'pooled and shared'. In so far as hierarchies of privilege really were reduced, this was probably necessary to secure the active support of the whole population, essential to the success of the war effort. [3a(p.86)] It seems to have made possible a more overtly 'pooling and sharing' approach to postwar reconstruction. The dominant themes of the postwar legislation which established the welfare state clearly derive from this approach: collective responsibility, free and universal services, benefits provided as a right. These were precisely the kind of principles which can be seen translated into the educational context in the 1944 Education Act and the White Paper *Educational Reconstruction* which preceded it in 1943.[5]The general orientation and principal recommendations of the White Paper are set out in docs 2 and 3.

The character of the 1944 Education Act thus has to be seen partly as a product of postwar reconstruction when, for the first time, social policy measures were being welded together into a more coherent whole which could legitimately be referred to as a 'welfare state'.[2(p.77)] At the same time, many features of the system after 1944 were recognisable as continuations of, modifications of, or in some cases reactions against, prewar educational provision. The single most important departure from previous practice was the provision of secondary education for all. This had been a central demand of the Labour party in prewar years and was recommended in the 1943 White Paper. By conceding it at the stage of the White Paper, it can be argued, a major area of potential controversy was removed from the educational reconstruction. [6(p.58)] One particularly important continuation from the prewar position was that the actual provision of education was left in the hands of the local authorities, as it had been since 1902: while there were some changes in powers and duties, the basic administrative structure remained (see sect. 2.6). Finally, important modifications occurred in the area of religious education and the position of the churches in the educational system. These are discussed below in more detail.

What were the most important features of the Act itself? The 1943 White Paper had proposed fundamental changes in both the structure and content of education, especially at the secondary level, and these were implemented in the Act. In terms of structure, education was to be organised in 'three progressive stages', known as primary, secondary and further education [doc 4]. This section in fact was modified in 1964, to allow for middle schools to develop between the primary and secondary 'stages'.

In terms of content, the central aim of the elementary code – efficient instruction in the three Rs – would be replaced by an education system which aimed to offer education suited to individual 'abilities and aptitudes' [doc 4]. The White Paper [5(para.27)] was quite clear what this meant: 'The keynote of the new system will be that the child is the centre of education and that, so far as is humanly possible, all children should receive the type of education for which they are best adapted.' This emphasis upon the child as the centre of the educational process had been foreshadowed in several postwar reports, including the Norwood Report on the secondary school curriculum, published in 1943.[7]

Many of the individual provisions of the Act can be seen as measures which secure either one or other of two particular social policy aims: to ensure access to education on a more equal basis for all children, and therefore greater social justice: and to use the education system to promote the wider welfare of the child (not only intellectual development) (cf. Ch. 3 and 5). Within the Act itself, the removal of fees for all types of schools was a measure essential to securing the major aim of access to secondary education for all. The school-leaving age was raised to fifteen, thus ensuring a longer period of schooling, and the White Paper envisaged that it would be raised to sixteen at a later date. Access was also to be facilitated by the provision of transport to and from school [doc 4], a feature of the system which the government tried unsuccessfully to alter in 1979 (see sect 2. 5 below).

The principle of access was taken to mean that access to *suitable* education should be ensured, expressed essentially in the notion of 'abilities and aptitudes'. This of course immediately raises the issue of how individuals are to be chanelled into 'appropriate' types of education, especially since the Act also envisages that (under normal circumstances) children will be educated 'in accordance with the wishes of their parents' [doc 4]. It was from this section of the Act that the system of 'tripartite' secondary education developed. That was a system of secondary education based upon three different types of schools – grammar, technical and secondary modern – for which children were selected at the age of eleven. It is important to note that the Act itself did not require such a system, and when comprehensive reorganisation began, no legislative change was necessary. Indeed, the White Paper had specifically recommended that children should not be classified at the age of eleven on the basis of a competitive examination but by their school records and reports, supplemented where necessary by an intelligence test; and that the choice of secondary school should not be finally determined at the age of eleven, but subject to review thereafter.[5(para.27)] It did assume that there would be different types of schools, although it envisaged that they could be combined on one site. [5(para.31)] The main features of the system which actually developed will be discussed in the next section, since they are a consequence of the way in which the Act was applied in the immediate postwar years.

Measures to ensure the wider welfare of children through the educational system included the provision of full medical and dental inspections and treatment. Also, local authorities were required to provide meals, milk and 'other refreshments' for pupils in schools and colleges [doc 4]. Local authorities had been given permissive powers to provide meals and milk for the first time in 1906, and to undertake medical inspections and treatment in 1908. Under the 1944 Act, these were statutory duties. Indeed they were regarded as part of the comprehensive attack on poverty which was a central theme of postwar reconstruction. [8(pp.206-9)] However, along with the transport provisions, meals and milk were to become a controversial issue again in the late 1970s, in the wake of public expenditure cuts (cf. sect. 3.2 and 4.1.5). The Act also included measures to control the employment of young people under school leaving age, and laid upon the local education authority the duty of enforcing these (cf. sect. 3.1).

So the themes of access and welfare are apparent in many provisions of the 1944 Act, and imply that the legislation embodies the principle that the prime purpose of education is to benefit those who receive it. At the same time there was a very clear sense that national needs were to be promoted through social reconstruction. This is apparent from the opening paragraph of the White Paper [doc 2], and this dual purpose was made quite explicit by Butler himself. When discussing what had been his own ideas (as opposed to those of his civil servants) for educational reform, he asserts [4(p.6)]:

the aim should be elementary education up to eleven and secondary education for all after that age. Educationally after the war, Britain had to be one nation, not two. So there must be an education system providing a 'training suited to talents' of each individual. This would have to be combined with a more expert training for industry, with a revived system of apprenticeship, and with a practical form of continued education.

Finally, the Act laid down a framework within which the educational system was to be organised and administered. At central government level it created a Ministry of Education and gave the Minister certain apparently vague but nonetheless important powers:

'to secure the effective educational service in every area' [doc 4]. The actual running of the education service was to remain administratively in the hands of local authorities and professionally in the hands of teachers, in 'partnership' with central government. The nature of the relationship between central and local government in the provision of education has been important in shaping the character of the system. At the level of the individual school or college, each institution had to have a body of governors (called 'managers' in primary schools until 1980) (cf. sect. 2.6 below).

An important part of the settlement which led to the Act concerned the position of schools which previously had not been directly under the control of the local authorities. First, the position of private schools was a contentious issue as far as the Labour Party was concerned. However, it was dealt with by setting up a separate commission, the Fleming committee. No significant action was taken to alter the status of independent schools, and the Labour party did not press the point. As Butler puts it in his own account [4(p.22)]: 'though, the Labour members breathed a certain amount of ritual fire and fury about social exclusiveness, and privilege, the appointment of the Fleming committee had temporarily removed the fuse. Or, to use a railway metaphor, the first-class carriage had been shunted onto an immense siding.' The whole incident confirmed Butler in his view that there could be 'no practical solution to the problem of the public schools, since they were *sui generis*'.

The second major sector, on which significant progress *was* made, consisted of the church schools. Their position in relation to state education had been problematic since the early nineteenth century.[9] Briefly, the Church of England (as the established church) had always claimed a privileged position in relation to education, not only in its own schools but in those provided from public funds. Other denominations had fundamental objections to this. The settlement in 1870 (when the principle of elementary education for all was introduced) had acknowledged this by ensuring that schools provided by the schools boards would have religious education of a strictly non-denominational character. In the twentieth century, all denominations experienced severe financial difficulties in funding their own schools, and especially in providing new ones, and turned increasingly to the state for assistance. By the 1940s these difficulties were becoming acute. Meanwhile there was considerable pressure, especially in rural areas where often parents had no choice but to send their children to their local church schools, to reduce the dominance of the religious input with its frequent alliance, as Butler points out, with

Tory politics via the local squire.[4(p.9)]

Negotiations with church leaders occupied a considerable amount of time for Butler and his civil servants in the period which preceded the Act, and undoubtedly were the most politically delicate aspects of the 1944 settlement. The churches could not be ignored because of their significant contribution to the provision of education and because of the politically powerful lobbies they could muster. Agreement was finally reached on a scheme which created two categories of 'voluntary' – controlled and aided – schools which could draw upon state funds. The 'controlled' schools were in many ways indistinguishable from the local authority's own 'maintained' schools. The local authority became responsible for all funding and for the appointment of almost all teachers in 'controlled' schools, and for the appointment of the majority of the school governors. Religious education was to be taught according to the local authority's 'agreed syllabus'. This 'controlled' status met the needs of Church of England schools, but the Roman Catholic church opted for the alternative 'aided' status, which meant that they could continue to provide instruction in Roman Catholic doctrine by Roman Catholic teachers.[9(p.114)] Aided status meant that the local authority would be responsible for the running expenses of the school and for teachers' salaries but the school governors would retain responsibility for 50 per cent of the cost of repairs and new buildings. The church would have a majority on the governing body, would retain the right to appoint and dismiss teachers, and would continue religious education of a denominational character.

This arrangement did have the effect of stemming many of the previous difficulties between the churches and the state over the provision of schooling although it did not entirely avert financial difficulties, and further provisions in 1959 and 1967 set the funding of church schools on an even more generous basis. [9(pp.119-24)] The 1944 settlement had very clearly cemented the relationship between church and state in the matter of schooling. At the same time as it changed the English educational system from largely church-administered to largely state-administered, the Act also significantly strengthened the impact of religion upon schooling.[10] This can be seen clearly in the fact that religious education, plus a daily act of worship, became compulsory in the local authority's own schools for the first time in 1944 [doc 4]. The 1943 White Paper had enthusiastically advocated universal and compulsory religious education in schools, on grounds of the national interest[5(para.36)]: 'There has been a very general wish, not confined to representatives of the churches, that religious education should be given a more defined place in the life and work of the schools, springing from a desire to revive the spiritual and personal values in our society and in our national tradition.'

These sentiments were very much reflected in the debates when the 1944 Act was passing through Parliament. These debates had a strongly religious flavour, with only two MPs expressing an alternative view that 'education has nothing to do with the next world . . . therefore the Church should have nothing to do with schools'.[10(p.172)] Only an understanding of the long-standing importance of the 'religious' question in education in Britain can make some sense of one aspect of the legislation which otherwise seems quite bizarre: under the 1944 Act, the only compulsory subject which must be taught in all schools is religious education.

The 1944 Act, whilst clearly a product both of the social policy which developed during the war and of the education system which had existed before the war was, in a very real sense, a 'new' settlement in education. It represents, argue the authors of *Unpopular Education*, a considerable degree of agreement over both ends and means in educational policy, and its initiation of universal secondary education constituted a major victory for the Labour movement.[6(p.59)] R. A. Butler's own assessment of the Act can be found in doc 5. He emphasises that, whilst it was not a completely fresh start, the Act did cut through the principle of inferior education for the poorer classes, and gave every child a genuine opportunity for secondary education. At the same time, he recognises that some of the aims of the Act could be easily subverted. In particular, equality of opportunity would remain an empty phrase if children continued to enter schooling from backgrounds of deprivation, and to go into blind-alley jobs. In identifying these issues, Butler prefigures the kind of debates which were to become important in the 1960s (see sect.2. below), and also underlines the intimate links between education and other aspects of social policy. The changes which are necessary to secure the full effects of the Education Act may entail, Butler implies, major initiatives in other areas of social policy amounting to a comprehensive programme of social engineering (cf. Ch. 5).

2.2 1944–59: THE SYSTEM ESTABLISHED

The fifteen years following the passing of the 1944 Act essentially were a period of consolidation of the potential gains from the legislative change and a period when the new system of secondary education based upon the Act was firmly established. Towards the end of the 1950s, however, evidence about the reality of the new system began to build up, and the pressure for change – which was so important in the early 1960s – began to gather momentum.

The principal task in the years immediately following the 1944 Act was to develop a system of 'secondary education for all' which would fulfil the aspirations of the Act; in particular, the aim that each pupil would be educated according to his or her own abilities and aptitudes. It fell to the Labour government elected in 1945 to supervise the implementation of the Act, although it had been passed by the wartime coalition government. The Ministry of Education had worked on plans for implementation before Labour came into office, and these were not altered substantially. Essentially the plans were based upon the 1943 Norwood report, which envisaged three distinct and different types of curriculum for different 'types' of pupil. This could best be implemented by developing three distinct and separate types of school: grammar, technical and secondary modern.[7(p.14)] The Ministry's view of how such a system would cater for different 'types' of children was set out in their document called *The New Secondary Education* [doc 6]. Selection for different types of school would be made at the age of eleven. In practice, this usually meant a competitive examination, in which a 'pass' secured a grammar school place; and the offer of a place at a secondary modern could hardly be interpreted other than as a 'fail'.

Although the secondary modern school subsequently became the object of considerable criticism, it is important to remember that, at this stage in the late 1940s, it was possible to see it as innovative and exciting, offering a distinctive form of secondary education to many children who had no access to grammar school, and who hitherto had only the option of remaining in the elementary schools. However, the idea of the secondary modern school was not a totally new development. As early as the 1880s, Higher Elementary schools were provided in some large towns, to offer some post-elementary education. By the time of the publication of the Hadow report in 1926, several types of 'post-primary' schools were being developed, including nonselective central or 'modern' schools. The crucial difference after 1944 was that, as the Spens report had advocated in 1938, they became full secondary schools, no longer run under the elementary regulations.[11]

It fell to the Labour government elected in 1945 to implement the tripartite system of education, despite the fact that a resolution had been passed at the party conference in 1942 favouring 'multilateral' schools. Barker attributes their failure to alter the policy when they came into office to the long-standing ambivalence within the party towards the issue, and the fact that there was a strong element of loyalty to the grammar schools, which had provided the channel for working-class boys to become socially and occupationally mobile. There was, however, considerable debate within the party during the postwar Labour government and by 1951, when they left office, they were finally committed to the principle of comprehensive secondary education.[12(pp.83-96)]

In fact, during the 1950s, although the tripartite, selective system was consolidated as the main form of secondary educational provision, several local authorities did experiment with provision which was comprehensive in character. Certain local authorities, including most importantly the London County Council, intended from the end of the war to reorganise their secondary education along comprehensive lines as soon as was practicable; and their first purpose-built comprehensive was opened at Kidbrooke in 1954. Several local authorities (including notably Manchester and Swansea) were in conflict with the Ministry of Education over their comprehensive reorganisation plans in the 1950s.[13(Ch.5)] Some authorities who wished to reorganise were favouring fully 'comprehensive' schools (that is, with common teaching and minimal internal selection) rather than 'multilateral' schools, which combined distinct grammar, technical and modern 'streams' under the same roof. One highly innovative experiment during this period, introduced by Leicestershire in 1957, entailed a 'two-tier' system in which all children went to comprehensive schools at the age of eleven and then were offered the choice of transferring to an upper (grammar) school at fourteen, with the proviso that parents would then undertake to keep them at school until sixteen.[14(Ch.5)]

One important aspect of critical appraisal of the 1944 Act which began during this period was concern about whether the aim of equality of opportunity was being realised, especially through the new system of secondary education. The whole debate about equality of opportunity and the tripartite system is discussed in detail in Chapter 5. During the 1950s the issues began to take shape. In this period, Room has suggested, doubts centred on: first, whether the concept of 'ability' could be used and tested and whether it could really be said to reflect three 'types' of pupils who could be channelled into different types of schools; second, whether the grammar schools would ever cease to be regarded as superior to and more desirable than the rest, while they continued to give access to the most prestigious occupations.[15(p.130)]

The first of these two issues – the concept of ability – was fundamental to the operation of the tripartite system, which entailed selection for different types of school at the age of eleven. If such a process was also to give the appearance of granting equality of opportunity to all children, from whatever backgrounds, then it had to be based on the principle of inherent or natural ability. The most important way in which this was implemented in the selection procedures was through the widespread use of intelligence testing. If one can maintain a faith in the IQ test as a mechanism for identifying the inherent ability of any child, then its use can be justified as part of a selective process which nevertheless ensures equal opportunities. During this period, psychologistic testing achieved a primacy which can be attributed in part to its use during the war and the credibility which it achieved then. The use of assessment procedures of this type in the armed forces and elsewhere had made them familiar and accorded them a certain legitimacy. [6(p.61)] Nevertheless, the use of intelligence testing as part of a selective educational system began to be challenged from the mid-1950s onwards, given impetus by the publication of Brian Simon's critique in 1953 and an NFER study in 1954. [16a,b] Simon showed that there was plenty of evidence that children could be coached for intelligence tests and that their test scores could be improved by such tuition. This clearly undermined any notion of constant measurable intelligence.

The second line of criticism – about the comparative prestige of the three sectors of the tripartite system – is important because of the express intention of those who designed the new system of secondary education that all three sectors should be accorded 'parity of esteem'. In *The New Secondary Education*, the Ministry promoted the idea that this could be achieved by raising the prestige of the technical and modern schools to that of grammar schools. Banks' critique, published in 1955, showed very clearly why this was not possible: it was difficult for the secondary moderns to live down the tradition of the elementary school; they would always bear the mark of failure while the abler pupils were being creamed off to the grammar schools; they could draw little prestige from the manual occupations which most of their pupils entered. [17(p.214)] Yet despite these cogent criticisms which gained ground during the 1950s, the government's White Paper in 1958[18] still saw the promotion of the secondary moderns to a position of real parity of esteem as the way forward. At the same time it gave little encouragement towards extending the 'experiments' in comprehensive education. Evidence about the incapacity of secondary moderns to develop parity of esteem fed the fears (which had always been present in sections of the Labour party) that in practice the 'new' secondary education would be not much different from the old. Secondary moderns, like the elementary schools, would merely provide a purely vocational education for the working classes. Indeed, the situation could be regarded as somewhat worse after 1944, since the system of selection was even more firmly established.[12(p.92)]

Underlying the criticisms of the concept of ability and of parity of esteem was the recognition that the promised equality of opportunity was not being realised, especially in the sense that the grammar schools still predominantly tended to recruit pupils from middle-class homes while most working-class children were going to secondary moderns, and sometimes to technical schools, although these were not well developed in many areas.[17(Ch.11)] Considerable evidence about the class-related nature of the selection process began to be amassed in this period[19a,b] and there is a sense in which these outcomes can be seen as an inevitable consequence of the way in which the Act itself was formulated and implemented. As Halsey and his co-authors in a later study have pointed out, there was no way under the Act of dealing with potential conflict between parents' wishes for their children's education and their children's aptitudes, nor conflicts between both and resources. The effect was that the supply of grammar school places in different areas was largely determined by historical accident, being as low as 10 per cent of the school population in some areas and as high as 45 per cent in others.[20(p.28)] Meanwhile, middle-class parents were far more effective than the majority of working-class parents in ensuring that their own children would succeed in the competitive entry to the grammar schools (cf. sect. 5.2.3 and 6.2.4).

One important government report published during this period merits attention in the context of the present discussion. This was *Early Leaving*, published in 1954.[21] Its terms of reference were to investigate what factors were influencing pupils who left school at the statutory leaving age, whether it was desirable to encourage a greater proportion to stay on, and how such an increase might be secured. It therefore afforded an opportunity for some critical appraisal of the working of the 1944 Act, although from a very specific perspective. The report itself expressed considerable concern about the numbers leaving school early who might benefit from a further period of full-time education, including many in the secondary modern schools. It identified the pupil's home background as important in the decision to leave early and recommended very practical remedies about extending maintenance allowances to enable pupils from poorer families to stay on without subjecting the family to financial hardship. The theme of the importance of home background was to be a constant one in many subsequent reports and research findings, as will become apparent in the next section. *Early Leaving*, however, did not simply 'blame' the wastage of talent upon the pupil's family. It recommended remedies in the form of the development of sixth form courses in secondary modern schools and increased transfer to grammar schools at the age of fifteen.

One interesting aspect of *Early Leaving* is that it took seriously the issue of gender as well as that of class. Girls were particularly likely to leave school at the earliest opportunity, it concluded, and attributed this to a number of factors: parents were less willing to make financial sacrifices to enable their daughters to stay on; girls more than boys were likely to leave because of petty irritations with the school (for example, regulations about uniform); and schools themselves were offering rather different sixth form courses to boys and girls, with boys unlikely to be offered a general course, and girls having less access to science facilities (cf. sect. 5.3.2). On the latter point, the report recommended that the situation should be rectified for both boys and girls, so that all individuals would be more able to choose courses suited to their needs and interests.

The issues identified in *Early Leaving* reflect the fact that, as Deem puts it, the benefits of the 1944 Education Act in practice were small for working-class boys, and even smaller for working-class girls. The allocation of resources in the secondary schools quickly took on a pattern which favoured boys, with girls' schools having minimal scientific and technical provision.[22(pp.131-44)] The Norwood report had regarded boys' interests as being dominated by their future occupational roles, but girls' interests as dominated by their future roles as wives and mothers and had considered that their education quite properly should be oriented differently, especially in secondary modern schools [23(pp.142-7)] (cf. sect. 6.2.3). This approach set the tone for developments after 1944, given impetus at the ideological level by the publication in 1948 of Newsom's book *The Education of Girls*, which takes an uncompromising position that girls must be educated to be women, to fulfil their biological destiny, rather than to compete with men [doc 7]. By contrast with all this, the rather modest proposals in *Early Leaving* begin to look decidedly radical.

The period between 1944 and the end of the 1950s can be seen as essentially one of consolidation, but also a time when the beginning of the important challenges to the operation of the Act were developed. Meanwhile, the system was established on a basis which, far from radically implementing the policy of equality of opportunity for all and carrying forward the momentum of the postwar social reconstruction, tended to confirm the status quo. This is true in terms of both class and gender. By and large, the 'new' structure of secondary education served to enable the more privileged to ensure that their children secured similarly advantaged positions; and the content of the curriculum, plus the way in which schools were resourced, continued to ensure that boys and girls were mostly being prepared for very different types of adult life. The issues of class began to be challenged long before those of gender. Indeed, it is interesting to note that, whilst the 11+ examination was rapidly becoming the target of criticism because it covertly favoured middle-class children, the fact that it also quite explicitly favoured boys received very little attention. It was in fact widely used to reduce the number of girls securing grammar school places. As Deem has argued, in the period after 1944 girls consistently demonstrated their superiority over boys in the primary schools, and more girls than boys passed the 11+ examination. The results, however, were weighted differently, to ensure that the numbers proceeding to grammar schools were more equal – boys thus obtained more places than their performance merited [22(p. 135)] It is important to recognise therefore that, within an education system based overtly upon the principle of equal opportunities, there was not simply an implicit but also an active pursuit of inequality.

2.3 1959–64: ACHIEVEMENTS QUESTIONED

The Conservative government was elected for a third successive term of office in 1959. The same year also saw the publication of the Crowther report, one of the three important reports on education published between then and 1964, when a Labour government was returned to office. The other two reports – Newsom and Robbins – were published in 1963. From the perspective of social policy, the educational scene during these five years was dominated by the publication of these three reports on the one hand; and on the other hand by the build-up of evidence about the operation of the educational system established after 1944, especially the apparent failure of the new system of secondary education to effectively promote equality of educational opportunity across social class lines. This period, therefore, was characterised by a questioning of post war *achievements*, both in official reports and elsewhere, but not fundamentally a questioning of the postwar *aims*. The issue was how equality of opportunity could be more effectively established, not whether it was a goal still worth pursuing. Issues about the concept of equality of opportunity are discussed in some detail below (cf. sect. 5.2.2). In this section, attention will be concentrated first upon the content of the three major reports and their implications and, secondly, upon some main themes in academic studies of education produced during this period.

2.3.1 The Crowther report

The terms of reference given to the Crowther committee encapsulate perfectly the twin aims of education, as benefiting both the recipients and 'society'. The committees was asked to:

> consider, in relation to the changing social and industrial needs of our society, and the needs of its individual citizens, the education of boys and girls between fifteen and eighteen, and in particular to consider the balance of various levels of general and specialised studies between these ages and to examine the inter-relationship at various stages of education.

The report which it produced, entitled *Fifteen to Eighteen*[24] included a lengthy discussion about the 'changing world' in which education had to operate, a review of the development of secondary education for all (and of the secondary modern school in particular) and recommendations about sixth forms, county colleges, technical training, the organisation of school and the supply of teachers. Its primary concern was with those young people whom the earlier report *Early Leaving* had identified as a cause for concern; namely those who were capable of benefiting from education beyond the statutory leaving age but were not receiving it. The report recommended that the school-leaving age be raised to sixteen and that county colleges be created to offer compulsory part-time education to those below the age of eighteen who had left school. Both measures had been envisaged in the 1944 Act, and Crowther regarded their full implementation as an essential first step towards providing a 'satisfactory education system for teenagers'. The 1944 Act had been a 'bold act of faith', and it was time to confirm both of these provisions on the 'agenda of educational advance' [doc 8]. Additional recommendations for improving education for this age group included the development of sixth form work, especially to include courses of a general as well as a specialist nature; the development of a coherent national system of technical and vocational education; improvements in the supply of teachers, the quality of their qualifications, their training and their pay; and the development of extended courses in secondary modern schools, including the introduction of a new system of external examinations below the level of GCE. This last issue was important because only a minority of secondary modern schools were offering extended education, therefore many young people quite simply were not being offered the *opportunity* to stay on. If the rate of those receiving full-time education after the statutory leaving age was to be significantly increased, developments in this sector would be crucial.

The Crowther report was well received but the government took very little action upon its recommendations. [25(pp.13–22)] The school-leaving age was not raised to sixteen until 1972. The proposal about county colleges has not been put into effect as national policy. The most important specific response to Crowther concerned the development of extended education in secondary modern schools. The Beloe committee was set up to consider the question of examinations. Its report led to the development of the Certificate of Secondary Education (CSE): while the GCE would continue to serve the needs of about 20 per cent of the school population, who were capable of attaining four or more passes at this level, the CSE would be for the next 20 per cent, who would be capable of four or more passes in the new examination, and for a further 20 per cent who would be able to attempt individual subjects. [26] The introduction of this plan was highly successful in terms of the increased number of individuals leaving school with some sort of external examination certificate. The numbers rose from 51 per cent of school-leavers in 1967 to 88 per cent in 1980. [27]

Quite apart from its specific recommendations, Crowther was important in the way in which it constituted – and to some extent reformulated – the terms in which debates about education were handled. Its focus was still essentially the issue of access to education, in a context which emphasised individuals' rights and needs regardless of parental income. However, there was an explicit (and to some extent a new) emphasis upon education as a national investment. This is apparent, for example, in the report's argument for raising the school-leaving age [doc 9]: while maintaining that the 'real' reason is that the young need to go on learning and that there is a collective obligation to provide them with the facilities for doing so, the case in fact is presented in terms of national needs. The whole chapter is entitled 'The school-leaving age and the national interest', and the case is argued on the grounds of a waste of talent which the country can ill afford.

The report envisaged that the 'national interest' would be served by extending educational opportunities in the 15–18 age group. This was not simply an economic issue: it was also a matter of suitably preparing the young for adult life in a society which, according to the report, had significantly changed since the end of the war. The work of schools, it argued, was being profoundly affected by demographic change, especially earlier marriage, greater affluence among the young, a general questioning of conventional morality, and the increase in juvenile delinquency which, the report noted, was reaching a peak in the last year of compulsory schooling. It urged schools therefore to take a much more active role in guiding young people on moral issues, in counteracting the undesirable effects of 'mass media', in stemming the tide of juvenile delinquency, and in the preservation of the family in the future, because 'we can be content with nothing less' [doc 10] (cf. sect. 6.4.4).

2.3.2 The Newsom report

Four years later, the Newsom report, *Half our Future*,[28] picked up some of the same themes. This report also concerned the later years of secondary schooling but, whereas Crowther had concentrated principally upon those who could benefit from education beyond school-leaving age, the Newsom committee was asked to consider the education of pupils between the ages of thirteen and sixteen who were of average or less than average ability. The most important theme running through the report was that these young people should receive a greater share of the nation's educational resources, since they were currently being rather ill-served. Again, the case for this was argued most importantly on grounds of the wastage of talent which 'the country cannot afford', and which might well give rise to frustrations showing themselves in 'apathy or rebelliousness' [doc 11]. Yet when it came to discussing the objectives of education for these pupils, the report made much of issues of personal fulfilment [doc 38]: young people need to learn basic skills because otherwise they will be 'cut off from whole areas of human thought and experience'; they need to develop capacities for judgement, enjoyment and curiosity; and it is important to foster the capacity to do 'something worthwhile for its own sake' as a principle aim of education (cf. sect. 4.1.3).

Specific proposals for expanding the educational opportunities available to 'Newsom children' included a strong recommendation (echoing Crowther) that the school-leaving age should be raised at the earliest opportunity; that there should be curriculum developments to foster both the teaching of basic skills and the development of personal talents; that there should be improvements in teacher training and in buildings as a matter of urgency; that schools should resist pressures to become too examination-oriented, and that examinations certainly should not dictate the shape of the curriculm for these pupils; that schools should encourage the spiritual and moral development of young people, partly through the medium of religious education; and that further studies should be made of how to improve the performance of those young people whose material and social circumstances seemed to be preventing them from realising their full potential. In focusing on aspects of home and social background, the Newsom report articulated more explicitly concerns which had been apparent both in *Early Leaving* and in Crowther, and about which considerable evidence was then being gathered by academics. Its discussions of education in the slums foreshadows the much more thorough and systematic analysis of the Plowden report four years later: seriously inadequate buildings; high staff turnover; a high percentage of pupils leaving early; home environments not conducive to the educational development of young people. The report recommended [doc 12] that schools in the slums be given special treatment – not because less able pupils in these schools are essentially different from elsewhere, but because they might need additional assistance and a different range of experiences to be able to benefit fully from their schooling.

The responses by government to the Newsom report was no more positive than it had been to Crowther.[25(pp.71-81)] The urgency of its recommendations to raise the school-leaving age had little effect; improvement in school buildings (to say the least) was patchy, and often took place as a consequence of comprehensive reorganisation rather than as a direct concern with 'Newsom' pupils; even then, these pupils did not always have an equal share of resources.

Taken together, the Newsom and Crowther reports can be seen to have developed some themes which are important from the point of view of education as social policy. First, they helped to crystalise an understanding of the barriers to realising equality of opportunity. Both reports (especially Newsom) helped to highlight issues of home circumstances, parental attitudes and environmental factors in the comparative under-achievement of working-class children. In formulating the issues in this way, they were reflecting the general tenor of the debates being conducted in academic circles, and which were taken much further by Plowden and the policy initiatives which followed it. The dominant understanding of educational inequality in Newsom and Crowther was that it was 'an unfortunate by-product, residue or anachronism which, with the right kind of interventions, could be controlled, if not abolished'.[6(p.120)]

Second, the two reports shifted the predominant understanding of what constitutes individual capacity, at least as that was understood in official reports. In contrast with the dominance of the notion of fixed and measurable 'abilities' in the earlier postwar period, Newsom stated quite firmly that 'intellectual talent is not a fixed quantity with which we have to work, but a variable that can be modified by social policy and by educational approaches'.[28(para.15)] Crowther had taken a somewhat less radical stance which still broadly accepted the idea of testing abilities but recognised that the outcome of conventional tests might be to waste a great deal of 'native intelligence'.[24(para.543)]

Third, the two reports both identified a specific area of concern in issues related to the 'moral development' of the young (cf. sect. 6.4). Reflecting a more general social policy concern, 'youth' *per se* was identified as a potential social problem area, with issues of crime, sexuality and spending being especially prominent.[6(pp.117-18)] In most cases, the 'youth' which gave cause for concern implicitly was male, working-class and lacking in qualifications; but issues of sexuality applied very much to girls as well. The Crowther report explicitly charged the education service with helping to preserve family life [doc 10] and Newsom took a very firm, conventional line on sexuality, urging that 'religious instruction has a part to play in helping boys and girls to find a firm basis for sexual morality based on chastity before marriage and fidelity within it'.[28(p.58)] It is clear that girls are not merely included in this but in many ways are the prime targets, since both reports saw the main task of educating girls (especially working-class girls) as educating them for marriage and motherhood, rather than for the labour market.[23(pp.149-52)] Concern with the moral development of the young, although presented in terms of benefits to young people themselves, looks very much more like an exercise in their regulation and control in which education can play a key part.

2.3.3 *The Robbins report*

The third of the major educational reports published in the 1959–64 period was the Robbins report on higher education.[29] Both the impetus for the report and its subsequent application contrast sharply with Crowther and Newsom. The committee was set up essentially to recommend plans for an expansion in higher education which was already being regarded as economically necessary.[30(p.127)] Since its task was to plan the expansion of higher education, the discursive consideration of the nature of education and its application (which characterised both Crowther and Newsom) was missing from Robbins, although it included a substantial research input.

The report argued that there existed large untapped reservoirs of young people capable of undertaking higher education, especially girls. It therefore recommended an expansion of places in higher education, increasing the proportion of the relevant age group who received it from 8 to 17 per cent, thus fishing more extensively in the pool. This would mean an increase of places from 216,000 in 1962/63 to 560,000 in 1980/81, thus enabling the 'Robbins principle' to operate; that is, that 'courses of higher education should be available to all who are qualified by ability and attainment to pursue them and who wish to do so'. The report recommended that this expansion should be facilitated by the immediate foundation of six new universities and by the designation of the existing Colleges of Advanced Technology as technological universities. It regarded the creation of new types of higher education institution as unnecessary, and recommended the integration of teacher-training colleges with universities. Its view of the curriculum in the expanded provision was that there should be an expansion of broader (rather than very specialised) degree courses and that some priority should be given to technological education.

As the implementation of these proposals took place under the Labour government elected in 1964, they will be discussed in more detail in the next section. Broadly, the expansion took place, but not quite in the way which Robbins intended. The enthusiasm of both parties for an expanded system of higher education is interesting in the context of the tension between the 'individual's needs' and 'society's needs' rationales. In a sense, it fed into both agendas. On the one hand, expanded higher education meant increased educational opportunities. This meant that those in the 'pool of ability' whose class or gender had hitherto kept them out of higher education might be drawn in. On the other hand, the report was quite clear that its recommended expansion was justified on the grounds of national economy. Its first justification for the provision of higher education was formulated quite specifically in these terms [doc 13], and it claimed to be convinced that the increased expenditure 'will be remunerative both in its absolute effects on the general productivity and in helping to maintain our competitive position in the world at large'. [29(p.241)] The same could hardly be claimed about Newsom children, although it could perhaps be argued (less convincingly) about those who were the concern of Crowther. By contrast, the apparently unequivocal case in economic terms for expanding higher education led to a very different outcome for this report.

Before leaving the 1959–64 period, it is important to note some of the main features of the evidence being built up from academic sources, especially about the ineffectiveness of measures purporting to ensure equality of educational opportunity. These debates were of great significance once Labour came back into power.

From a number of studies produced during this period, principally by sociologists of education, two influential ones are used here to illustrate the kind of debates which were being pursued. In the 1950s, criticism of the secondary education system had concentrated upon the process of selection and the tripartite organisation itself. In the 1960s, attention was turned also to the content and organisation of education within the school itself. From the debates in the 1950s one might imagine that the issue was solely: who gets into a grammar school? For those working-class children who passed the 11+, one might conclude, everything was fine. That conclusion was seriously challenged by Jackson and Marsden's study of eighty-eight working-class children in grammar schools, published in 1962.[31] They showed very effectively that the culture of the grammar school actively discriminated against working-class entrants, who would find that they had to 'accommodate . . . to the prevailing middle-class values, or rub up against them'. The consequence was that they would either leave at the earliest opportunity, or they would survive within the grammar school but become alienated from their family and neighbourhood. The spotlight, therefore, was turned clearly upon the schools themselves as *producing* working-class failures, and this theme was taken up in important ways in the later part of the 1960s.

The other approach which gained momentum in the early 1960s can be illustrated by Douglas' important study *The Home and the School*.[32] Douglas also was concerned with working-class failure in school, but his work turns the spotlight upon the child and the family (rather than on the school) as a way of accounting for it. He showed that when, for instance, children of the same measured ability compete for grammar school places, those from 'satisfactory' homes had an advantage over the rest. 'Satisfactory' homes are identified partly in material terms: whether they are overcrowded, provided with basic amentities, afford children the chance of privacy, and so on. But 'satisfactory' homes also have certain cultural attributes; in particular, they contain parents who value education and who demonstrate this in the upbringing of their children. Again, the idea that failure in school can be attributed to factors quite outside the educational system itself was pursued throughout the 1960s in debates about educational policy and in certain specific initiatives.

What both these approaches share is the clear implication that the postwar educational system has failed to secure equality of educational opportunity for the working classes. The implication taken from that was that new methods of securing equal opportunities needed to be tried, and the elimination of selection from the educational system was a front runner. This was true especially within the Labour party, and there were strong links between the party and the academics who were producing the evidence during this period, an alliance which directly influenced Labour's policy when they came back into office.[33a,b] Finn and his co-authors have argued that it produced a particular set of questions which were shaped by the Fabian end of the Labour party, in which the occupational hierarchy, and the system of social stratification based upon it, was taken as given. The issue was merely: who gets access to different positions? Comprehensive education was seen as a major means of modifying patterns of access. This represents, they argue, a very significant shift in the way in which the Labour party understands both inequality and social change. From the prewar emphasis upon the need to redistribute resources widely and across a whole range of social and economic areas, the emphasis had moved to the technical and organisational problems of education, treated as a discrete policy area, and to the culture of the working classes and its alleged deficiencies.[33a(pp.159-67)] Whatever the significance of these themes for the development of the Labour party itself, they were of considerable importance in terms of educational policy when Labour returned to office, as will become apparent in the next section.

2.4 1964–72: EXPANSION AND BEYOND

The next period selected for consideration begins with the election of a Labour government in 1964 and ends in 1972, the year of publication of the White Paper called *A Framework for Expansion*, which ironically effectively marks the end of the expansionist phase. Although this period was predominantly characterised by expansion on many fronts, there were signs of the contraction to come, especially from the late 1960s onwards. These trends were accelerated by the election of a Conservative government in 1970, in which Margaret Thatcher was appointed Secretary of State for Education and Science.

The educational issues which characterise this period can be seen as a mixture of continuities which will be familiar from the discussion of the earlier periods, and certain specific commitments of the Labour party on returning to office. The most important of these were, first, to complete the educational programme of 1944, especially by raising the school-leaving age to sixteen; second, to tackle the public schools; third, to abolish selection at 11 + and to press ahead with comprehensive reorganisation of secondary education. These represent, argue the authors of *Unpopular Education*, a consolidation of educational issues around questions of *access* to education, and gave rise to policies which essentially stressed the social *distribution* of benefits and privileges.[6(p.72)] However, in many cases these policies built upon expansionist measures already prepared by the Conservatives, even if they broke with the latter in their more explicit attempts to create greater social equality in and through education.[34(p.37)]

Policies pursued in this period covered the whole range from preschool to higher education. It is important, however, not to assume that they represent a well planned and integrated attempt to pursue explicit objectives. In fact the changes introduced were partial and uneven, and not always pursued with unambiguous commitment when it came to resource allocation.

2.4.1 Comprehensive reorganisation

Many of the developments during this period can be seen as variations on the theme of equal opportunities (cf. sect. 5.2.2), but some of the variations represent important modifications of earlier strategies which increasingly were seen to have failed. Under the general heading of 'equal opportunities' it is useful to consider the progress made on comprehensive secondary reorganisation and the publication of two major reports: the Plowden report on primary education, and the two reports of the Public Schools Commission.

The background to comprehensive reorganisation has been discussed in the previous section. When Labour returned to office they acted upon their stated intention to proceed with reorganisation by issuing Circular 10/65, which 'requested' local authorities to produce plans. The reason for this non-directive 'request' was that the legal distribution of powers between central and local government seemed to prohibit a firmer stance (see sect. 2.6). The consequence of placing the onus upon the local authorities to take the initiative was that plans for reorganisation were presented and implemented in a patchy way, depending primarily upon the enthusiasm of each LEA for the reorganisation. That enthusiasm was, not surprisingly, closely related to the political complexion of the authority. Most of those LEAs which made no response to the Ciruclar (or who delayed) were Conservative-controlled, while most of those which responded quickly and positively were held by Labour. There were some, however, (of which Bath is a notable example) where the Circular itself was an important stimulus to producing plans for reorganisation, plans which were unlikely to have been contemplated without it.[35(pp.28-9)] In the following year, Circular 10/66 reinforced the likelihood of reorganisation by warning LEAs that building grants from central government could be refused if the proposed building did not accord with the general intention to introduce comprehensive secondary education.

Labour's policy in this period must be considered as having achieved some considerable success which only really bore fruit after they left office, as the plans were gradually implemented. However, a brake was applied to further development when the Conservatives returned to office in 1970. One of the early acts of the new government was to withdraw Circulars 10/65 and 10/66 and replace them with 10/70, which indicated that schemes for secondary education need no longer follow comprehensive principles but instead were to take general educational considerations into account, along with local needs and wishes and the 'wise use of resources'. Despite this, LEAs (including some Conservative-controlled) continued to present comprehensive plans and some were approved, although central government used its powers in a number of cases to refuse permission for some grammar schools to be included in the schemes.[35(p.30)] This reinforced the likelihood that 'comprehensive' education could (at least in some areas) be an empty label, especially if grammar schools were still creaming off the most academically able pupils at the age of eleven. In so far as comprehensive reorganisation was seen as a strategy designed to make a reality of the equal opportunities which the 1944 Act had intended to implement, the retention of grammar schools seriously undermined its potential. Moreover, the seesaw effect of central government's stance (continued throughout the 1970s – see following sect.), made the uneven implementation of schemes inevitable, and effectively recreated the kind of territorial injustice which had been one of the main arguments against the selective system: just as a child's access to grammar school had varied according to the LEA in which he or she lived, so now access to comprehensive education varied on the same basis.

2.4.2 The Public Schools Commission

The setting up of the Public Schools Commission represents another of Labour's commitments when they returned to office. The Commission produced two reports: the first, in 1968, was on independent boarding schools, after which the Commission was reconstituted with modified terms of reference and produced a second report in 1970 on independent day schools.[36a,b] The government's approach to this Commission is an example of the development of quite explicit social engineering stategies in the field of education during this period – that is, strategies in which government actively intervenes to produce social change through social policy measures (cf. Ch. 5) The terms of reference given to the Public Schools Commission denote an apparent intent to reduce the 'divisive influence' which such schools exert. The terms of reference in fact *assume* that the public school will be integrated with the rest of the school system, and the Commission was apparently being given the task of devising the *means* to this integration: 'The main feature of the Commission will be to advise on the best way of integrating the public schools with the state system of education.' However, by the same token, since integration was apparently assumed, abolition was ruled out. In other words, the Commission was not being given the option of recommending that the independent sector *per se* should be totally abolished. This reflects the classic ambivalence within the Labour party towards the public schools, which had been apparent in the negotiations for the 1944 settlement (see above, sect. 2.1).

In the event, the Commission reflected this ambivalence by recommending (in its first report) that independent schools should continue to exist, albeit with modifications in their tax and other financial privileges, and that they should be integrated with the state system by making over up to half of their places to assisted pupils in need of boarding education. In so doing, they did not reject the argument that the privileged position of such schools, and the benefits which they confer upon those whose parents can afford to send them there, are morally unjustifiable. On the other hand, they did reject the more radical options of treating this sector much more punitively [doc 14]. The emphasis of the proposals was upon the slow and gradual change in the intake of pupils from the maintained sector, in recruiting from a wider ability range, in increasing the number of places for girls in this sector, and in the sharing of facilities and resources with maintained schools. A good deal of the Commission's argument hinged upon their assumption that there was a considerable unmet 'boarding need' among pupils in maintained schools, which the independent sector could supply. As well as the traditional use of boarding schools by parents who live abroad, or who are frequently geographically mobile, the Commission believed that 'boarding need' covered many children whose 'home circumstances are seriously prejudicial to the normal development of the child'. It cited quite explicitly instances such as children who had been received into the care of the local authority because their family circumstances were deemed unsatisfactory. 36a(para.153-4)

This assumption about unmet boarding need was challenged by Vaizey in his important dissenting note to the Commission report [doc 15]. Vaizey argued that there was no real evidence of such unmet need. In his view, the Commission had failed to grasp the key issues about abolition of the public schools and instead had produced a very strange compromise, which attempted to solve the problems of the social divisiveness of such schools simply by filling the beds in them with different bodies.

The second report of the Commission was in some ways more brave. It concerned the day sector of independent education. Many of these schools were financed under the 'direct grant' system; that is, the schools received a grant from central government, in return for which they made available between 25 per cent of their places (without fees) to pupils who had spent at least two years in a maintained primary school. For many years this had been regarded as the classic route through which very able children of the working classes could receive a good grammar school education; but the mid-1960s, it was becoming apparent to many people that in practice the direct grant system principally enabled middle-class children to attend independent schools at public expense.[37(p.41)] The Commission confirmed that this essentially was the case: it found that only one in thirteen pupils attending such schools came from the homes of semi-skilled or skilled workers. It recommended that direct grant status should be ended and that these schools should be encouraged to participate in local plans for reorganisation in the state sector, as appropriate. Those who could not or would not do so would have to become fully independent.

The response of the Labour government to these reports demonstrates, as Corbett puts it, the insurmountability of Labour's problems with the public schools.[37(p.39)] The route of integration was never taken as a serious policy option. The government did take some action to reduce the financial privileges of public schools but this was reversed by the Conservatives. When re-elected in 1974, Labour did, however, implement the recommendation that direct grant status should be ended. The effect of this, however was simply to expand the independent sector, since the great majority of schools opted to become fully independent rather than come into the state system.

Later, the 1980 Education Act effectively reintroduced something equivalent to direct grant status (see following section).

2.4.3   The Plowden report

The third event of this period which was important in relation to general issues of equal opportunities was the Plowden report on primary schooling.[38] This had been set up with very wide terms of reference: 'to consider primary education in all its aspects and the transition to secondary education'. As the report itself pointed out, major policy issues since the Second World War had mainly concerned secondary schooling and higher education. The report was based upon extensive research and much careful argument, and made a cogent case for the importance of 'good' primary education, especially to those 'deprived' children who formed a major focus of its considerations [doc 16]. It can in fact be seen as continuing and expanding upon many of the themes in the Newsom report, especially by identifying specific areas (called 'the slums' in Newsom) where educational resources should be concentrated, and by its major argument that the most significant factor in a child's educational performance is the attitude of its parents to education. Plowden's emphasis upon the *cultural* barriers to a child's capacity to make full use of educational opportunities contrasts with the predominant approach in the immediate postwar period (in *Early Leaving*, for example), where the barriers were assumed mainly to be material and financial.

Specific recommendations of Plowden included measures to encourage more parental involvement in children's education; improved health, welfare and social work services attached to schools; improvements in class size, teacher training and remuneration; the encouragement of child-centred methods of education. In view of its potential for overcoming educational handicaps, the expansion of nursery education was to be a priority and the aim should be to provide enough places by 1981 for 50 per cent of three year olds and 90 per cent of four year olds. Above all, Plowden's strategy depended upon its innovative idea of the creation of educational priority areas in those geographical locations where children could be identified as suffering especially from educational handicaps associated with social, cultural and environmental factors. In those areas, additional educational resources should be committed initially to bring the standard of schooling up to the average and then 'quite deliberately, to make them better' [doc 17]. This explicit espousal of the principle of positive discrimination in favour of the most deprived social groups represents a most important initiative in social policy, and a very explicit recommendation that government should act in a highly interventionist manner to produce significant social change. These issues are discussed in some detail below (sect. 5.3.1).

In the context of the late 1960s, Plowden represents an imaginative development of, rather than a significant departure from, the prevailing educational climate. The Newsom report had already begun to move very much in the same direction. The Public Schools Commission (reporting a year later) also concerned itself with the educational needs of socially 'deprived' children. The Seebohm report on the personal social services,[39] also published in 1968, was prepared to make very close links between the welfare of children and their education, and envisaged a social work service based in schools (cf. sect. 3.3). Further, although the principle of positive discrimination in a sense was new, it was also quite consistent with the long-standing concern about educational opportunities for working-class children. In a sense, it simply offered a different *method* for pursuing their claims, and one which linked well with social policy initiatives in other fields, especially anti-poverty programmes. Within Educational Priority Areas (EPAs) especially, it envisaged that strategies could be developed for forming close links with the local community through the development of community schools in which facilities would be used by a variety of groups and would therefore be playing a part in general community regeneration.

The government accepted the report's advocacy of positive discrimination and committed £16 m. over two years for rebuilding programmes in such areas, which was actually a very limited resource allocation in relation to the total educational budget. LEAs were asked to bid for part of this allocation in respect of areas which they believed suitable for designations as EPAs. In the event, the money was shared between 150 building programmes in 51 local authorities. The government also accepted Plowden's recommendations that special payment should be made to teachers in EPA schools, and 572 schools initially were recognised for this purpose. [40(p. 38)]

A major initiative was set up jointly by the Department of Education and Science (the new name for the Ministry from 1964 onwards) and the Social Science Research Council. This was a £175,000 action research programme to study and develop policies for EPA areas. This programme was put under the direction of A. H. Halsey, and five areas were designated to take part. The programme developed rather differently in each area and the six volumes which report the

results of these projects make fascinating reading.[40] The main conclusions on the viability of EPAs are summarised in document 18.
Broadly, they supported the Plowden position on educational priority
areas, and especially endorsed its faith in both nursery schooling and
the idea of the community schools as a means for improving educational standards in these areas, provided they formed part of a more
extensive community development programme. One important
problem, however, concerned the identification of areas suitable for
such treatment. Although the Halsey report broadly accepts the EPA
as an administratively viable unit, it does recognise that it entails
considerable problems. The Plowden report had recommended that
resources be concentrated in certain geographical areas, but the
criteria for identifying such areas principally entail characteristics of
individuals and families (e.g. overcrowded housing, a high proportion
of single-parent families, and so on). It is therefore quite easy to see
that the idea of an EPA may well turn out to be a blunt instrument,
since not all families who meet these criteria of deprivation will live in
the designated areas. None the less, the consequences of Plowden
have had profound effects upon social policy in the educational sphere
and beyond.

2.4.4 *Racial and ethnic minorities*

During the 1964–72 period, the question of the education of children
from different racial, ethnic and religious backgrounds entered policy
debates for the first time, because of the increased migration of
families from various parts of the Commonwealth [doc 19]. With
hindsight, this clearly also presented issues of equal opportunities,
but at the time it was not predominantly treated in that way. In 1965
the government issued Circular 7/65, which aimed to 'consider the
nature of the educational problems that arise' from having Commonwealth immigrants, children in schools, and to give advice. This
Circular is characteristic of the approach to this issue during the
1960s. First, it is taken for granted that such children need to be given
'a knowledge and understanding of our way of life' and of 'social
habits and customs in this country': they must, in other words, learn
to become like the white population as quickly as possible. Second,
the major problem for the schools is seen as language: that is, teaching
English to children whose first language is something else. The way in
which language teaching was introduced tended to ensure that pupils
attained sufficient command of English to cope minimally in the
classroom, rather than achieving their full educational potential, and

ignored the linguistic problems of children of West Indian origin, many of whom speak English of a non-standard form. Other than in the specific area of language, the characteristic approach to racial diversity in schools was low-key: a kind of approach to policy which Kirp has described as 'inexplicit' and 'doing good by doing little'.[41a,b]

A study undertaken during this period, under the auspices of the National Foundation for Education Research,[42] indicated that by 1970 there, were about a quarter of a million children on school rolls (out of a total of seven and a half million) whose parents were 'new commonwealth' immigrants – that is, principally blacks from the West Indies or Asians from India and Pakistan. These pupils were concentrated mainly in inner and outer London, the West Midlands, West Yorkshire and South Lancashire, with considerable concentration also within each LEA. [42(pp. 19-22)] Townsend's study again reflects the concentration upon teaching English as a second language as the major focus at this stage, with comparatively little attention given to questions about whether ethnic minority children were achieving their full potential at school or how far the schools themselves needed to adapt to accommodate the cultural diversity now represented within them.

These broader questions began to be asked from the late 1960s onwards. The whole range of issues about the education of immigrants' children, as represented in policy debates up to the late 1970s, has been usefully summarised by Rex and Tomlinson [doc 20]. Whatever advances were made subsequently, the context for dealing with these questions was set in the mid 1960s. As Rex and Tomlinson argue, questions of how to ensure equal opportunities in education for these children were not given priority. Instead decisions taken were often unplanned and unco-ordinated, and debates structured in such a way as to be essentially racist in character, thus ensuring that children from ethnic minorities were very unlikely to be accorded equal opportunities in practice.

2.4.5 *The expansionist phase in higher education*

New initiatives to improve educational opportunities during this period took place in the context of an atmosphere which essentially was expansionist, but towards the end of the period (and especially after the re-election of the Conservatives in 1970) began to show signs of contraction. Kogan argues that the general expansionist atmosphere of this period was characterised by an optimism and a faith in the potential of education for promoting personal wellbeing and social advance, and in its potential for manipulating the life chances of individuals without too seriously altering the whole fabric of the distribution of social and economic resources.[34(p.41)] In other words, education seemed to provide a way towards a more just society by peaceful and relatively painless means.

The most spectacular example of expansion during this period undoubtedly is to be found in higher education, although the example of comprehensives and the initiatives following Plowden have a similar flavour. The recommendations of the Robbins report had been immediately accepted by the Conservative government but a general election followed quickly and it fell to the Labour government to implement the expansion, which it needed to do as a matter of urgency if the postwar bulge in population was to be accommodated in higher education.[43(p.231)] In the event, the expansion as implemented departed quite radically from the Robbins' plan. Instead of relying solely upon the creation of new universities as the means for increasing the numbers in higher education, there was the proposed creation of new institutions (a development specifically precluded by Robbins) called polytechnics which in the government's view were the way of achieving the best results bearing in mind the demand for higher education, the needs of industry, the availability of residential provision, and the desirability of achieving a balanced provision of different fields of study in different areas of the country. [44(para. 11–12)] Thus the expansion of places in higher education took place in the framework of the newly created 'binary system', with universities remaining as autonomous bodies established by royal charter, and the polytechnics developing as the highest level institutions within the public sector controlled and financed by the local authorities, with considerable grant input from central government. In addition, there was the creation of the Open University to serve the needs of adults for part-time study to degree level (especially working-class adults, as it was hoped at the time) by the new and adventurous means of using television and radio as principal teaching mediums (cf. sect. 4.1.4).

The expansion which took place during this period radically changed the shape of higher education. As Robbins recommended, the Colleges of Advanced Technology were accorded university status, several completely new universities were created, making a total of forty four universities in all in the whole United Kingdom. As the 1966 White Paper made clear, the government's intention was to designate a limited number of polytechnics, to be based upon institutions already carrying out higher degree work, and these would become points of development for higher education in the public sector. Eventually thirty polytechnics were designated.

So a considerable expansion did take place, as Robbins had recommended but in so far as this expansion was intended to ensure that opportunities for higher education would be spread more representatively among the population, especially the working classes, the policy must be deemed a resounding failure. Farrant, writing in 1981, showed that the class composition of university entrants had scarcely changed over twenty-five years; indeed, in the late 1970s, the proportion of middle-class entrants actually seemed to be increasing.[45(p.60)] Meanwhile, the development of the polytechnics out of the former colleges of further education actually served to reduce the numbers of working-class students in these institutions, especially through the reduction in part-time courses, while continuing the traditional trend in FE of offering few opportunities to women students.[46(pp.78-82)]

Expansion had been one of the major means by which, it was assumed, educational opportunities could be extended. Towards the end of this 1964–72 period the climate of expansion began to come to an end. At the same time there began a much more serious questioning of whether the creation of equal opportunities (in the terms in which that had been traditionally understood) was viable economically, or even desirable. Those on the political left began to look more closely at the operation of the educational system, and to question whether it was really a coincidence that the working classes seemed systematically to lose out whatever modifications were made. At the same time, those on the political right began to go on the offensive and to attack more explicitly the kind of egalitarian aims which they saw as embodied in various educational reforms of the 1960s, especially comprehensive reorganisation (cf. sect. 5.2.2). However, it is important to note here they do represent a recognisable break-up of the apparent consensus which had characterised the major participants in educational debates in the earlier period. At the same time, the climate of expansion became more difficult to sustain as cuts in public expenditure began to be implemented.

An early victim of these cuts was the stated intention of the Labour government to raise the school-leaving age to sixteen. Just before the Conservatives left office in 1964, they announced that they would implement this from 1970. In the event, the Labour government postponed its implementation to 1972. The return of the Conservatives in 1970, with Margaret Thatcher in charge of education, denoted a further change in direction, although it was still possible to think to some extent in expansionist terms (see the following section). There was, however, a clear willingness to make reductions in the education service, if that seemed necessary to meet public expenditure targets. This is seen most explicitly in the 1971 Education (Milk) Act, which removed the right to free milk from all children over the age of seven, except from those in special need. This symbolic act by 'Thatcher the Milk Snatcher' can indeed be regarded as an indication of what was likely to follow.

2.5 1972–80: CONTRACTION AND THE NEEDS OF THE ECONOMY

1972 has been chosen as the date at which to begin the discussion of this last period, because it is the date of publication of the White Paper, *A Framework for Expansion*. The account ends with the major event of the passing of the 1980 Education Act (although some comments are made upon developments in the early 1980s), because this again represents a decisive shift in the social policy agenda in education.

In the 1940s, education was very clearly part of a wider programme for social reconstruction. So too in the later part of the 1970s education was caught up in a rather less explicit – but nonetheless extremely important – restructuring of the welfare state. It can be argued that this denotes a decisive breakdown in the social democratic consensus, and the character of that change is discussed in this section. [33a(pp.187–93)]

This restructuring was related of course to cuts in public expenditure consequent upon successive economic crises; but the way in which those cuts were implemented helped significantly to reshape the character of welfare during this period. The case for seeing these changes as a restructuring is set out very clearly by Gough,[47(Ch.7)] and some of its implications for education are discussed in Chapter 6. Briefly, Gough argues that social policies in various fields (including education) increasingly were designed to adjust the labour force and the potential labour force more effectively to the changing needs of the capitalist market. This involves the creation of greater 'efficiency' within the services themselves, the shaping of the services to give greater control over the population (providing work incentives and encouraging labour discipline) and a pressure for the 'reprivatisation' of social services; that is, a switch of emphasis from state-provided services to greater reliance on private provision, albeit often with state subsidies. This section discusses developments in education during the period 1972–1980, and shows that many of these processes are apparent in this area of social policy.

1970 to 1980 was a decade which saw a decisive shift away from access to educational opportunities as *the* social policy issue in education. As Silver puts it, faith in the earlier interventionist strategies crumbled. The centre of the stage, which had previously been held by the 'reforming egalitarian', was claimed by the two opposing groups: those who were developing radical critiques of schooling as a process of control, in the service of capitalism; and those who presented (from the liberal centre to the right) critiques which actively opposed social engineering and promoted issues of standards and the content of education. [30(pp.36–7)] By the end of the decade, the concerns of the latter group were very much on the political agenda at national level.

There were, however, some important events in the 1970s which essentially were a continuation of the 'access agenda'. In particular, comprehensive secondary reorganisation accelerated, despite lack of encouragement by the Conservative government. In 1974, when Labour returned to office, 62 per cent of secondary pupils were in comprehensive schools. At this point, Labour determined to press ahead with full reorganisation and issued Circular 4/74, which reaffirmed the objectives of 10/65, this time 'requiring' rather than 'requesting' LEAs to produce plans. The stronger tone was thought necessary because, by this stage, a number of LEAs who had not produced plans definitely did not wish to do so. When this Circular was issued, out of a total of 105 LEAs (after local government reorganisation in 1974), 67 expected to complete their reorganisation by 1980, 37 were committed in principle to reorganisation, and 7 refused to commit themselves unless the law was changed to require them to do so. [48] The consequences of central government's attempt to 'require' recalcitrant authorities to reorganise were that it was eventually established that the Secretary of State was exceeding his legal powers; but only after a court case was brought by Tameside LEA, which went to the House of Lords (see next section).

This meant that reorganisation could only be accomplished through legislative change, so the government passed the Education Act 1976, which required LEAs to 'have regard to the general principle that [secondary] education is to be provided only in schools where the arrangements for admission are not based (wholly or partly) on selection by reference to ability or aptitude'. This change was designed to deal with the handful of local authorities who refused to reorganise. For the rest, the government's objectives were already well in hand since, by the time this Act was passed, the proportion of pupils in comprehensive had risen to 75 per cent. Further progress, however, was to be short-lived. One of the first acts of the Conservative government elected in 1979 was to repeal the 1976 Education Act, thus ending (at least for their term of office) any prospect of universal comprehensive secondary education. An opportunity to extend the comprehensive principle into education for sixteen to nineteen-year-olds was missed when the MacFarlane committee recommended that arrangements for this age group should simply vary with local needs (a characteristic arrangement in the English system, rather than recommending the option of 'tertiary' colleges, which provide the whole range of academic and vocational courses in one institution.[49]

Two other important pieces of legislation should be mentioned in the context of the continuing issue of equal opportunities in education. The Sex Discrimination Act 1975 and the Race Relations Act 1976 – the latter of which to some extent consolidated earlier legislation – both had the effect of making unlawful direct acts of discrimination in education against women and ethnic minorities. At the same time, they specifically allowed certain types of positive discrimination in favour of these groups. Their impact upon education was hardly instant and startling. A cynical interpretation would be that they were never meant to be more than token gestures; although even if this is true, they do at least have the merit of making more difficult the most overt discriminatory acts. It is certainly the case that by the time this legislation was passed the circumstances were not auspicious for capitalising upon it.[22] Public expenditure cuts were well under way and the dominant political agenda in education was already moving strongly away from issues of access and equal opportunity to issues of the content of education.

Issues about the content of education – both the content of the curriculum and the standards achieved – had been raised in the Black Papers from the late 1960s onwards. These were a series of publications, [50a-e] emanating from the political right, which played a significant part in shifting the terms of educational debate in the 1970s. They challenged a number of issues which had constituted the social policy agenda in education in the previous decade; especially whether it is justifiable to attempt to create equality through education and to eliminate selection. Instead, they substituted a concern about *what* is taught, standards of basic literacy and numeracy, the need to foster 'excellence', and the importance of discipline and of inculcating moral values in the young. The quality of argument and the intellectual content of these documents is scarcely impressive, and Wright has produced a very convincing critique of them.[51] This, however, in no way prevented their having an important impact. Margaret Thatcher, in response to right-wing criticism that standards were falling, set up the Bullock Committee to investigate literacy. Their report was low-key from the point of view of social policy, since many of its recommendations in fact were aimed at individual teachers and their classroom practice, rather than at the DES or local authorities.[52] The Labour party, whose own position was already being seriously undermined – as has already been noted, eventually took up a number of the Black Paper themes, thus achieving a new consensus about what constituted major policy issues in education. The most important manifestation of this was the initiation by James Callaghan, as Prime Minister, of the Great Debate on education.

2.5.1 The Great Debate

In a speech made at Ruskin College in October 1976, in which James Callaghan declared that public interest in education was legitimate, strong and ought to be satisfied, he called for a great debate on education to begin. This speech had been forecast in advance as a major intervention, and the origins of the initiative lie partly within the Labour party and partly within the DES. Hopkins' account[53(pp.101-3)] places the initiative firmly with Callaghan himself and his concern both that education was becoming an important political issue and that Labour's former policies – designed to ensure equal opportunities – had conspicuously failed. At the same time, the DES had its own concerns and played a major part in formulating the terms in which the 'debate' was to be conducted. Callaghan asked the Ministry to prepare a memorandum for his use, and the *Yellow Book* which they produced (written mainly by the Inspectorate) formed the basis of the Ruskin speech [doc 21]. In his speech, he argued that schools were in danger of concentrating too much upon the preparation of pupils for a 'lively, constructive place in society', and of underemphasising preparation 'to fit them to do a job of work'. Following this speech, the DES organised a series of regional conferences, with invited audiences only, through which the debate would be started. The document which they produced as the basis of these conferences (called *Educating our Children: Four Subjects for Debate*) shows clearly that they were picking up on the kind of agenda which right-wing critics had been promoting since the early 1970s. The four subjects were: the school curriculum; assessment and standards; education and training of teachers; school and working life. These same four subjects appeared as major headings in the Green Paper produced in

1977, which was meant to be the government's reflections upon the debate.[54] Additional headings in the Green Paper were; transition between schools; special needs of minority groups; schools and the community (for some of these themes, see doc 22). From that point onwards, the 'debate' and its consequences became somewhat fragmented into discrete areas of policy; but in the area of curriculum, a direct line of action can be seen. Circular 14/77 requested local authorities to answer a detailed questionnaire about curriculum arrangements in their school, and the results of this were published in 1979. The Inspectorate produced their own comments upon this document in 1980 and the DES formulated a response in the following year.[55a-c] The issue of producing a 'core' curriculum for all schools remained very much on the agenda.

From the point of view of education as social policy, three important features of this series of events and reports are apparent. First, questions concerning the *content* of education are given primacy, and questions concerning access are very peripheral. Second, a major impetus behind the debate was the assertion of greater control by central government over the practice of schooling.[56(pp.222-6)] Sofer sees the core of the Great Debate as being about power and, specifically, about the DES trying to marshal public opinion behind its attempt to take more control over the curriculum. To this end, the Green Paper emphasises issues such as arrangements for transition between schools, co-ordination and record keeping, and a nervousness about variety in education – all of which points towards more centralised control.[57a(pp.145-61)]

Third, a major preoccupation of the Debate was the relationship of education to the economy. This is particularly important in the light of the tension being explored in this book between education for the 'individual's needs' and education for 'society's needs'. If one studies the documentation associated with the Debate, both themes are apparent; where the balance is tipped, it is always in favour of 'the economy', which is clearly established as the major *raison d'être* of schooling.[57a(p.155)] The authors of *Unpopular Education* see the Green Paper as decisive in this regard:

> The Green Paper formally set the seal on the school-work bond as the rationale for schooling: the subordination of schooling to the requirements of industry was complete. Gone were the references to any egalitarian ambitions for schooling – instead the definition of education's effectivity was the extent to which schools were able to match the stipulated requirements of industry.[6(p.226)]

The Great Debate therefore was decisive in confirming three shifts in the terms set for the formulation of policy within education. The first of these – access to content – has already been discussed. The increase in centralised control will be considered in the next section. The shift towards the primacy of the economy has to be set in the context of rising youth unemployment during the late 1970s (cf. sect. 6.3.2). Government initiatives designed to deal with this were channelled mainly through the Manpower Services Commission from 1974 onwards, and this meant that the DES was not directly involved. However, the way in which initiatives were formulated very much concerned 'education', since the problem was said to be that young people lacked training in skills and attitudes appropriate to the workplace, a view endorsed in the Green Paper [doc 22]. This all links very clearly with the claim that the welfare state was being restructured in the late 1970s so as to adjust the labour force to the changing needs of a capitalist economy.

2.5.2 *Contraction in higher education*

The shift of emphasis from education for the individual to education for the economy was paralleled in the 1970s by an equally important shift from expansion to contraction as the basic premise upon which resources for education were planned. At the beginning of this period, the 1972 White Paper had appeared still to be operating within an expansionist framework, especially since it resolved to expand nursery education to meet the Plowden targets within a decade.[58] This commitment was, however, very quickly overtaken by public expenditure cuts.

The contraction which took place in the education service was related to cuts in public expenditure on the one hand and to falling school rolls on the other. The total number of pupils in maintained schools had grown steadily from under 5 million in 1944 to 8.5 million in 1977. From this point it declined to 7.8 million in 1982, and this decline was expected to continue until the late 1980s, when the projected figures are around 6.7 million.[59] The effects of this are obviously felt in different parts of the education system at different times.

The first important impact in policy terms was felt in the teacher-training sector. The James report on teacher education, published in 1972,[60] was in fact still working within expansionist assumptions. The committee recommended radical changes in the organisation of the content and location of teacher-training courses but appeared to make the assumption that numbers in training would go on expanding (as they had done during the 1960s), or at least remain steady. But even as early as 1967, the DES's own *Statistics of Education* were predicting that there would be a surplus of teachers, in relation to the size of the school population, by the late 1970s. In the event, the changes in teacher education which actually occurred represent the first large-scale contraction in education since the end of the war. In the following year the government issued Circular 7/73, which made reference to a reduction of teacher-training numbers from 114,000 to 60–70,000. By 1975, this had been translated into proposals for the actual closure or merger of colleges: 13 were to be closed completely; 40 to be merged with polytechnics and 6 with universities; 50 would be merged with colleges of FE or with other teacher-training institutions. Subsequently these actual numbers were modified somewhat and the total output of teachers was again revised downwards, but the basic pattern was implemented during the late 1970s.[61a,b]

Higher education as a whole is particularly vulnerable to public expenditure cuts, since it is not provided statutorily for all citizens. It is therefore open to governments to reduce the number of places available. This is precisely the effect of changes introduced in the financing of universities from 1981 onwards, when the University Grants Commission implemented cuts which were to have the effect of reducing the overall size of the student body by 3–5 per cent by 1983–84, the year in which the eighteen-year-old age group would reach its peak. This effectively abandons the Robbins principle and provides from public funds only the amount of higher education which 'the country can afford'. This was a major theme of the eloquent critique provided by Neil Kinnock, speaking for the Labour party, in the House of Commons debate on the day in November 1981 when the Association of University Teachers organised a mass lobby of parliament [doc 23]. He argued that the Conservatives' view of education directly conflicts with the interests of working people and favours those who can afford to purchase privilege.

At the level of schools, the most significant event in the contraction of the system was undoubtedly the 1980 Education Act. This Act contained many important provisions, covering a wide range of issues. From the point of view of the present analysis, the most significant concerned school meals, school transport, and the new scheme for assisted places at independent schools. Clause 22 had the effect of repealing section 49 of the 1944 Education Act, which laid upon LEAs the statutory duty to provide meals for all children who wished for them [doc 4], and replaced this with the discretionary powers to make provisions if they thought fit, and to fix a scale of charges (whereas previously charges had been fixed by the DES). The only pupils for whom the statutory duty to provide meals was retained were those eligible for free meals – who were to be defined as children from families receiving supplementary benefit or family income supplement. The effect was to give LEAs the option of reducing their education expenditure by significantly reducing the scale of their school meals provision (cf. sect. 3.2). Proposed changes in school transport would similarly have enabled education authorities to save money, this time by introducing charges for transport to many children who had previously been entitled to free provision (cf. sect. 4.1.5). In the event, this clause was defeated when the Bill reached the House of Lords and no change was introduced. The grounds of opposition make fascinating reading in the light of the 1944 settlement, which was explicitly being challenged. Opposition was led by the Duke of Norfolk, defending the interests of Roman Catholic and rural schools, and Lord Butler, defending the integrity of the Education Act with which he had been associated. He argues that agreements which he had made in the 1940s should be honoured, and that transport was a vital part of this [doc 24].

The 1980 Education Act did not directly implement the contraction of educational provision, but it did decisively redefine the educational task in such a way as to make contraction easier. In particular, provision such as school meals and transport were defined as peripheral to the 'real' tasks in the classroom, and thus a luxury which could no long be afforded. At the same time as these items were being regarded as frills to be cut out, the 1980 Act also strengthened the provision of private schooling by introducing the Assisted Places Scheme. This provided for the Secretary of State to reimburse fees 'for the purpose of enabling pupils who might otherwise not be able to do so to benefit from education at independent schools'. Past experience, however, would lead one to suppose that many beneficiaries of such a scheme would be middle-class children, as under the direct grant system. Thus the contrasting effects of different parts of this legislation was stark. As one Labour member put it in the House of Commons debate[62]: '[This is] a class-biased Bill which, far from increasing educational opportunities, will remove them. It is intolerable that in the same Bill which deprives working-class children of assistance with transport costs and school meals we find proposals that must give additional educational privilege to the very section of the community that already has it.'

The actual implementation of public expenditure cuts in the

education service has to be done in a fairly indirect way, because of the division of powers between central and local government in the provision of education in Britain (see sect. 2.6 below). Greater centralised control over local authority funding, implemented through Local Government Act 1980, facilitated cuts from central government's point of view. This entailed the introduction of a 'block grant' system of channelling money from central government to local authorities, which involves the DES in negotiating what LEAs 'ought' to be spending on various educational items. The way in which the system operated previously left greater autonomy to local authorities to define what their 'needs' were in resource terms.

The effects of successive cuts have varied widely between different local authorities. The most authoritative accounts of the effects of the cuts have been produced by Her Majesty's Inspectorate (see next section), whose annual reviews of local authority provisions were made public for the first time in 1981. The review published in 1982 shows clearly that most schools were increasingly relying on contributions from parents and upon money-raising activities to provide items such as books, equipment and financing for a whole range of school activities which previously would have been funded by the local authority. Their summary of the position is given in document 25. They show that, while all schools and pupils are affected to some degree, some are more easily able than others to mitigate the effects of cuts. The consequence is that the gap is widening in the educational experience offered in schools serving affluent and poor areas.

This observation provides an interesting, if depressing, contrast with the concerns of the 1940s, with which this chapter began. In the wartime context, the emphasis of social policy in education was to equalise opportunities, to pool resources and to share them equitably, and to eliminate (as far as possible) the relationship between a child's financial circumstances and the educational opportunities offered to him or her. By 1981, government policy was actively reinforcing these divisions in education and in a very real sense was responsible for discriminating *against* the poor (cf. sect. 6.2.2) in the provision of educational opportunities.

2.6 A NOTE ON POLICY-MAKING AND IMPLEMENTATION IN THE ENGLISH EDUCATIONAL SYSTEM

This section is about some key features of the making and implementation of policy in the English educational system. The discussion of these essentially 'administrative' aspects of policy is fairly brief, since the main focus of this book is the *content* of policy rather than its formulation. The purpose here is to sketch in sufficient of an outline to enable readers to make sense of the discussions of the material in the rest of the book.

Although issues of social policy sometimes get discussed as if policies are unproblematically 'made' at central government level and then passed down straightforwardly to the grass roots, the processes entailed in making policy and implementing it are both complex and diffuse. Policy-making sometimes does involve formal, overt decision-making, which is then universally applied; as for example, when governments pass legislation laying statutory duties upon other bodies. In many cases, however, legislation and official policy documents often reveal little about the character of the educational facilities or educational experiences provided for children in a given locality. 'Policy' gets interpreted and often significantly modified when put into practice, and its interpretation and implementation is almost always open to local pressures, governed by the local distribution of resources, and so on. Further, 'policy' does not always begin at the top, that is, with central government. In many cases it is effectively created *through* the practice of education in schools and classrooms and through pressure-groups activity by parents, by teaching unions, and so on. This 'inexplicitness' in policy-making has been characteristic, for example, of the handling of issues related to race and schooling in Britain (see above sect. 2.4).

These approaches operate in a context in which specific powers and duties are allocated to different parties in the educational system. The English system is characterised by a division of powers and duties which ensures that 'policy' is both made and implemented at three different levels: central government, local government and the individual school or college.

2.6.1 Central government

Central government plays a fairly limited part in the actual provision of education in Britain, since the running of the service is in the hands of local authorities (see below). Under the 1944 Act, the Minister of Education is accorded the apparently rather vague responsibility to: 'secure the effective execution by local authorities, under his control and direction, of the national policy for providing a varied and comprehensive educational service in every area' [doc 4].

To assist him or her, the minister has a government department, which was given the status of a full ministry after 1944 and retitled

Department of Education and Science in 1967. Like other government departments, the DES is divided into different administrative branches, specialising in different features of the educational service. [63a-c] The day-to-day work mostly entails the administration of policy in the sense of implementing decisions already made at national level, through working with local authorities, teachers' unions, other ministries, or dealing with complaints for example from parents or MPs about the actions of a specific local authority. However, the DES clearly has an actual and potential role in the formulation of new policy. The ministry was active, for example, in the development of the tripartite system in the 1940s, and in defining the content of the Great Debate in 1976.

In the early 1970s, the DES was the object of considerable criticism about the way in which it operated, first in a document produced by the Organisation for Economic Co-operation and Development, then in three well-publicised articles in *The Times Higher Education Supplement* by Lord Crowther-Hunt (a former junior minister), culminating in an investigation by a parliamentary select committee reporting in 1976. [64a,b] This committee essentially upheld the earlier criticism, endorsing the view that there was a lack of long-term planning within the DES, that outside interest groups were insufficiently involved in planning, and that its affairs were conducted with excessive and unnecessary secrecy. To some extent, these criticisms were subsequently overtaken by events, with successive rounds of public expenditure cuts making the concept of 'planning' look rather different. More recent criticisms of the DES have indicated that there has been an increase (unwelcome to some parties) in centralised control within the education service, in which the Great Debate marked a fairly decisive shift (see sect. 2.5 above). The DES has, it is said, 'harnessed the economic pressures for educational change in a way which suited its aspirations'. [56(p.224)]

A section of the DES which deserves special mention is Her Majesty's Inspectorate (HMI). The first schools' inspectors were appointed in 1839 to monitor the use of government money given to schools. They have developed into a very prestigious body who jealously guard their independence from the DES, whilst working closely with civil servants and ministers. Their traditional inspection role to some extent has given way to a more complex definition of their work, which stresses advising as well as monitoring and evaluating. [65a-c] They have also become involved in general evaluations of the educational service, producing, for example, major reports on primary and secondary education in Britain and evaluations of the effects of spending cuts upon educational provision in local authorities (see sect. 2.5 above).

In the context of policy-making in the diffuse sense in which it is being used here, it is interesting to consider the question: who actually runs the ministry – politicians or civil servants? Many accounts of policy-making concentrate upon the activities of politicians, and sometimes seem to imply that individuals are totally responsible for a specific policy change. The 1944 Act, for example, is routinely referred to as the 'Butler' Act, as if it was Butler's personal creation. In fact it was a product of prewar educational reports, plans already being worked on by civil servants, and some very hard negotiations with church leaders as well as Butler's personal contribution (see sect. 2.1 above). Clearly, in formal terms, politicians are responsible for decisions made and actions taken as part of the democratic processes of government, and in that sense they hold the power. On the other hand, they cannot possibly acquaint themselves with all the details of what happens in their ministry and thus are bound to rely heavily upon civil servants, who usually work at the DES for far longer periods than the average minister's term of office. Two fascinating accounts of being a minister of education have been given by Anthony Crosland and Edward Boyle, in interviews with Maurice Kogan.[66] It seems clear from these accounts that although a minister will always have the power of veto over policies of which he or she does not approve, where a minister has not taken a specific interest in any given aspect of policy, civil servants are always ready with their 'own' policies and plans. Kogan[66(p.41)] quotes a senior DES civil servant as claiming: 'I can honestly say that there is not one new policy in my sector of responsibility that I have not either started or substantially contributed to over the last twenty years.'

2.6.2 Local government

In the English system education is actually provided at the level of local, not central government. This arrangement originated with the state's growing involvement in education in the nineteenth century. The 1870 Act accorded responsibility for the provision of schools (in areas where insufficient were being provided by voluntary bodies) to locally elected School Boards. In 1902, their functions were given over to those local authorities which are designated Local Education Authorities. This arrangement continued under the 1944 Act, although there was a significant change in the identity of those local authorities designated LEAs. After 1944, LEAs were county councils and county borough councils, thus eliminating many of the smaller LEAs and transferring their functions to larger authorities. In particular, the so-called Part III Authorities (which had had responsibility for elementary education only) were abolished. [3b(pp.9-11)] Since local government reorganisation in 1974, LEAs have been the county councils in non-metropolitan areas (that is, the larger authorities in this two-tier system), and the metropolitan district councils (the smaller authorities) in the six metropolitan counties. London has a distinctive arrangement: in outer London, the borough councils are the LEAs, but the inner London boroughs have a combined LEA – the Inner London Education Authority – which exercises the function *only* of an education authority and no other functions of local government. Altogether, this makes a total of ninety-six LEAs in England and eight in Wales.

The LEA is responsible for providing a whole range of services: statutory schooling, nursery schools, further and adult education, special schools and higher education (apart from the universities, which are funded separately by the DES through the University Grants Commission). They also have statutory duties and permissive powers to provide a wide range of facilities which serve all the schools in their locality: for example, advisory services, teachers' and resource centres, and a whole range of welfare services associated with education (cf. Ch. 3). As well as the direct provision of their own 'maintained' schools and colleges, they also have a responsibility for various aspects of the service provided in voluntary aided and controlled schools, in ways which are discussed in relation to the 1944 settlement (see sect. 2.1 above). [67a,b]

Local authorities can use money from the rates to fund the education service. In practice, however, a substantial and growing proportion of the resources needed comes from central government, mainly through the mechanism of the Rate Support Grant (RSG). The proportion of LEA expenditure coming from central government rose from 54 per cent in 1967/68 (when RSG was introduced) to 61 per cent in 1980/81. [63c(p.59)] Although central government in many ways is the paymaster, the DES in practice has had little control over the ways in which LEAs actually spend this money, once allocated. Legislative change in the Local Government Act 1980 made possible a new method of calculating RSG, which gives the DES more control over defining what a local authority 'ought' to be spending on different items and gives central government greater control over the implementation of public expenditure cuts. [68a, b]

Local authorities carry out their duties as LEAs through an

administrative structure whose main decision-making body is the education committee, which LEAs must appoint under the 1944 Act and whose composition is subject to approval by the Secretary of State. It includes elected members of the local authority itself (who must form a majority on the education committee) and co-opted members who represent various interested parties, typically the churches, teachers' organisations and others who are deemed to have special knowledge of the educational needs of the area. Although the size of education committee varies considerably in different local authorities, most find it necessary to delegate a good deal of their detailed work to various sub-committees, typically covering areas such as schools, further education, finance, buildings and special services.[69a,b]

The actual implementation of the local authority's policy and the running of the service are in the hands of the professional and administrative staff of the LEA, as well of course as the teachers in the schools. The 1944 Act says that all LEAs must appoint a 'fit person' as the chief administrator, but makes no further specifications. This person is usually called the Chief Education Officer (CEO). Typically he or she has a background in teaching as well as experience in educational administration, and combines responsibility for the day-to-day administration of the service with being the professional advisor to the LEA, supported by a staff of administrators, advisors and local inspectors (separate from HMI). The CEO is obviously in a very powerful position to influence the formulation of policy, as is clear from interviews conducted by Maurice Kogan with three former CEOs.[70] In these accounts, the relationship between education officers and elected members in local government emerges as somewhat different from that between civil servants and ministers in central government, although clearly there are some similarities: the greater continuity of service among the officials than among the politicians, for example. However, in local government, the CEOs interviewed by Kogan firmly maintained that they expected to be able to make professional and administrative decisions (within very broad guidelines laid down by their committees) and would not expect councillors to take part directly in running departments, as ministers at least in theory could do. On the other hand, at local government level virtually all decisions of any importance are discussed in committee, whereas in central government, many decisions are taken within the DES of which the minister in practice has no knowledge.[70(pp.43-5)]

The relationship between central and local government in the provision of education and its control is a complex and delicate balance whose character can be seen most clearly in situations where it is contested. The Tameside dispute in 1976 was one such instance. The dispute concerned the comprehensive reorganisation of secondary education, the background to which has already been outlined. By the mid-1970s, only a small number of LEAs had failed to produce plans for reorganisation, and most of these definitely did not wish to reorganise, despite the wording of Circular 4/74 which 'required' them to do so. Tameside LEA was prepared to challenge in the courts the legal right of the Secretary of State to make this requirement, after the return to power in 1975 of a Conservative controlled council committed to retaining selection. When the case eventually went to the House of Lords, the judgment was that the minister had indeed been exceeding his powers. The case hinged on the interpretation of section 68 of the 1944 Act which enables the minister to take action if he or she believed that a local authority is acting 'unreasonably' in the exercise of its duties [doc 4]. This had been invoked by the ministry to oblige Tameside to reorganise, but the Lords' judgment was that the circumstances did not constitute 'unreasonable' action. The result was that Tameside did not have to reorganise. Central government always can have the last word, however, because it has the power to change the law, as was done in the Education Act 1976 which made it a legal requirement to reorganise along comprehensive lines. The Tameside case illustrates very clearly the nature of the local–central government relationship in the provision of education. LEAs have considerable autonomy which they do indeed exercise against the wishes of the DES on occasion; but central government holds both the purse-strings and the ultimate sanction of legislative change.

2.6.3 The individual school

The third level at which policy is both made and implemented is the individual education institution. At this level there are two important parties to the process; the teachers – especially the headteachers – and the governing body.

Under the 1944 Act, all schools have to have a board of governors (called managers in primary schools until 1980). The powers and duties accorded to this body look quite extensive, in that the model 'articles of government', prepared by the ministry in 1945 and adopted by most LEAs, accord them 'general oversight of the conduct and curriculum of the school'. The practice of appointing governing bodies in fact has a long history both in the public schools and in the voluntary and maintained sectors.[71a-c]

The LEA appoints members of governing bodies, so practice varies somewhat, but usually a considerable number of appointees are either serving councillors or members of the party in power in the local authority (and sometimes, members of opposition parties), along with a smaller number of governors who are said to be politically 'neutral' individuals representing various community interests. From the mid-1960s onwards, some LEAs began to appoint small numbers of serving teachers, parents and even pupils to the governing bodies of their 'own' schools.

The Taylor committee, reporting in 1977, recommended radical changes in both the composition and the powers of governing bodies, including the proposal that they should have more active control of the curriculum, that some financial decisions should be devolved from the local authority to governing bodies, and that there should be some training for school governors. The composition of boards of governors, they recommended, should operate on a four-equal shares principle, with 25 per cent of places being taken by representatives of each of the following groups: the LEA, teachers, parents, and 'community' representatives. The Taylor proposals have never been implemented, although the 1980 Education Act made a new requirement that the governing bodies of maintained and voluntary controlled schools should include at least two elected parent governors and at least two elected teacher governors (one in the case of schools with less than 300 hundred pupils).

Even if the Taylor proposals were to be fully implemented, they would not necessarily secure the greater degree of grassroots democratic control of education which the committee seemed to favour. In a study of governing bodies in Sheffield, where arrangements roughly similar to Taylor had been introduced in the early 1970s, Bacon found that the incorporation of both teachers and parents onto governing bodies made relatively little difference to the way they operated. Teachers tended to be loyal to the position of the head: to do otherwise might be to place their own employment situation in jeopardy. Parents, on the other hand, often came on to governing bodies with little knowledge of the operation of the educational system, and were heavily reliant upon the 'professionals' for guidance about procedures and powers. The net result was, if anything, to strengthen the position of the headteacher and the clerk to the governors (usually an employee of the LEA), who were the knowledgeable and longstanding members with the power to define legitimate topics for discussion and to make formal recommendations.[71c]

The relatively weak position of the governing body within a particular school has to be understood in relation to the peculiarly strong and autonomous position of the headteacher in the English education system. The 1945 model articles of government, again building upon practice which had developed in the public schools and later been transplanted into the state system, accords to the headteacher control of 'the internal organisation, management and discipline of the school'. This means that the division of powers between head and governors on paper is unclear. In practice, the head is responsible directly to the LEA who is his or her employer, and the governors stand (perhaps rather uneasily) to one side of this structure of responsibility and authority as a quasi-independent body. Fenwick and McBride argue that the Taylor committee tried to change this by inserting the governors into the hierarchy of authority.[63c(p.139)]

The strong and autonomous position of the headteacher to some extent is based on custom and tradition, but it is also reinforced by quite concrete powers over deployment and promotion of staff, use of buildings, making school rules, and some parts of the school's budget.[72a-c] Coupled with these wide-ranging administrative powers, heads are also meant to be the professional leader of their teaching staff, a function which they exercise with a wide variety of leadership styles.[73]

This brief account of the three levels at which policy is made and implemented has concentrated principally upon the formal distribution of powers and duties; but the formulation and outcome of 'policy' in any given instance may also be shaped by interventions from other sources. At central government level, for example, decisions taken in the Treasury may sometimes be more important than those taken in the DES, especially in an era of public expenditure cuts. Media interventions, which focus public attention on a particular aspect of educational provisions at a given time, can significantly influence decisions taken within the formal structure. Pressure groups and interest groups of various sorts (representing teachers or parents, for example) sometimes make quite successful interventions in the policy-making process. For example, the National Union of Teachers was active in the 1980s and 1970s in pressing for comprehensive plans to be developed at local level, and in pressing for them to be approved by the DES after the Conservatives had returned to office in 1970.[74]

Parents are a group whose potential capacity for intervening successfully has been increased since 1980. Under the 1944 Act they have the duty to ensure that their children receive full-time education, and the LEA has the duty, wherever possible, to ensure that children are educated in accordance with the wishes of their parents [doc 4]. The 1980 Act accorded them the right of representation on governing bodies for the first time. Probably much more important in terms of the impact which parents *actually* are likely to have upon the educational process are the provisions within the Act which require schools to make available to parents more detailed information about secondary schools and accord them strengthened rights over the choice of their child's school. The likely consequence of such measures is that some schools will develop a reputation as highly desirable. This effectively will act as a self-fulfilling prophecy, since more middle-class parents (whose children continue to produce better results in terms of measured academic outcomes) will opt for them. This is a good example of how the shape of educational provision can be significantly changed without any 'policy' in the formal, overt sense, being made or implemented. Similarly teachers, by their actions in the classroom and through their exercise of professional judgements, routinely make and implement social policy in and through education.

The complexities of the relationships of power and control between different parties to educational policy-making and implementation were well illustrated by the dispute at the William Tyndale junior school in London in 1975. Accounts of these events have been given by two journalists, by the teachers who were at the centre of the dispute, and in the Auld report, the official ILEA enquiry into the case. [75a-c] Briefly, the dispute was about the way the school was organised and the 'informal' style of education being offered. Complaints from parents and from some members of staff occasioned several governors to become involved, then subsequently officials and elected members of the LEA. The episode was well publicised in the media, which linked it with the themes of the Black Papers (see sect. 2.5 above). Finally, after a formal enquiry set up by the LEA, four of the teachers, including the head, were dismissed.

There are many fascinating aspects to this case but, from the point of view of issues of power and control within the educational system, perhaps the most interesting is that the whole affair was protracted and confused. Teachers, parents, governors and inspectors all held differing views about what constitutes satisfactory education and who should ultimately decide what goes on in the classroom. The complexities of the division of powers and responsibilities within the English system assume – and to some extent require – that there is broad consensus between parties for most of the time. Where the different parties do *not* agree (as in the Tyndale case) there is certainly no easy mechanism for resolving the issue and the disruptive consequence can be fairly spectacular. Ultimate power of course is held by those bodies (usually either the LEA or the Secretary of State) who have the legal powers to dismiss teachers, modify the character of schools, and so on. The most important lesson to be learned from the Tyndale case (in relation to the material discussed in Part Two of this book) is that one can never assume that policy in education is unproblematically 'made' and then straightforwardly 'happens' at grassroots level. The many steps between, say, the passing of a piece of legislation in Parliament and what actually happens in the local primary school on a Monday morning, leaves ample room for 'policy' to be interpreted, adapted, fought over and sometimes effectively ignored. Social policy in education (as in other fields of welfare) is very much a contested arena.

NOTES AND REFERENCES

1. The discussion in this book is confined to England and Wales, since both Scotland and Northern Ireland have educational systems with a separate history and character. A useful introductory account of regional variations can be found in BELL, R. and GRANT, N. (1977), *Patterns of Education in the British Isles*. Allen & Unwin: London.

2. MARSHALL, T. H. (1965), *Social Policy*. Hutchinson: London.

3. (a) TITMUSS, R. (1968), *Essays on the Welfare State*. Allen & Unwin: London. Discussions of the impact of the war specifically upon education can be found in; (b) DENT, H. C. (1944), *Education in Transition*. Routledge & Kegan Paul (RKP): London: (c) GOSDEN, P. (1976), *Education in the Second World War: a Study in Policy and Administration*, Methuen: London.

4. BUTLER, R. A. (1973), 'The politics of the 1944 Education Act', in G. Fowler, V. Morris, and J. Ozga, (eds), *Decision-Making in British Education*, Heinemann/OU: London.

5. BOARD OF EDUCATION (1943), *Educational Reconstruction*, Cmd. 6458. HMSO, London.

6. CENTRE FOR CONTEMPORARY CULTURAL STUDIES (1981), *Unpopular Education: Schooling and Social Democracy in England since 1944*. Hutchinson: London.

7. SECONDARY SCHOOLS EXAMINATIONS COUNCIL (1943), *Curriculum and Examinations in Secondary Schools*, The Norwood

Report. HMSO: London.

8. GOSDEN, P. (1976) *Education in the Second World War: A Study in Policy and Administration*. Methuen: London

9. MURPHY, J. (1971), *Church, State and Schools in Britain 1800–1970*. Routledge & Kegan Paul (RKP): London.

10 CANNON, C. (1970), 'The influence of religion on education 1902–1944', in, P. Musgrove (ed), *Sociology, History and Education*. Methuen: London

11. CONSULTATIVE COMMITTEE TO THE BOARD OF EDUCATION (1926), *The Education of the Adolescent*, The Hadow Report; and (1938), *Secondary Education*, The Spens Report. HMSO: London. For discussion see: TAYLOR, W. (1963), *The Secondary Modern School*. Faber & Faber: London.

12. BARKER, R. (1972), *Education and Politics 1900–1951: A Study of the Labour Party*. Clarendon: Oxford.

13. FENWICK, I. (1976), *The Comprehensive School 1944–1970* Methuen: London.

14. RUBENSTEIN, D. and SIMON, B. (1969), *The Evolution of the Comprehensive School 1926–1972*. RKP: London.

15. ROOM, G. (1979), *The Sociology of Welfare: Social Policy, Stratification and Political Order*. Blackwell: Oxford.

16. (a)SIMON, B., (1953), *Intelligence Testing and the Comprehensive School*. Lawrence & Wishart: London; (b) NATIONAL FOUNDATION FOR EDUCATIONAL RESEARCH (1954), *The Appraisal of Intelligence*. Methuen: London.

17. BANKS, O. (1955), *Parity and Prestige in English Secondary Education*. Routledge & Kegan Paul: London.

18. MINISTRY OF EDUCATION (1958), *Secondary Education for All: a New Drive*. Cmnd. 604, HMSO: London.

19. See especially: (a) FLOUD, J., HALSEY, A. and MARTIN, F. (1956), *Social Class and Educational Opportunity*. Heinemann: London; (b) HALSEY, A., FLOUD, J. and ANDERSON, C. (eds) (1961), *Education, Economy and Society*. Free Press: New York.

20. HALSEY, A., HEATH, A. and RIDGE, J. (1980), *Origins and Destinations: Family, Class and Education in Modern Britain*. Clarendon: Oxford.

21. MINISTRY OF EDUCATION (1954), *Early Leaving*, A Report of the Central Advisory Council for Education. HMSO: London.

22. DEEM, R. (1981), 'State policy and ideology in the education of women 1944–1980', *British Journal of the Sociology of Education*, Vol. 2, No. 2.

23. WOLPE, A. M. (1974), 'The official ideology of education for girls',

in M. Flude and J. Ahier (eds), *Educability, Schools and Ideology*. Croom Helm: London.

24. MINISTRY OF EDUCATION (1959), *Fifteen to Eighteen*, The Crowther Report. HMSO: London.
25. For discussion of what happened to the report's recommendations, see ROGERS, R. (1980), *Crowther to Warnock*. Heinemann: London.
26. SECONDARY SCHOOLS EXAMINATIONS COUNCIL (1960), *Secondary School Examinations other than G.C.E.*, The Beloe Report. HMSO: London.
27. DEPARTMENT OF EDUCATION AND SCIENCE (1982), *Data on School Leavers 1979/80*. DES: London.
28. MINISTRY OF EDUCATION (1963), *Half Our Future*, The Newsom Report. HMSO: London.
29. COMMITTEE OF HIGHER EDUCATION (1963), *Higher Education*, The Robbins Report, Cmnd. 2154. HMSO: London.
30. SILVER, H. (1980), *Education and the Social Condition*. Methuen: London.
31. JACKSON, B. and MARSDEN, D. (1962), *Education and the Working Class*. Routledge & Kegan Paul: London.
32. DOUGLAS, J. (1964), *The Home and the School*. MacGibbon & Kee: London.
33. (a) FINN, D., GRANT, N. and JOHNSON, R. (1977), 'Social democracy, education and the crisis', in Centre for Contemporary Cultural Studies, *On Ideology*. Macmillan: London; p. 165; (b) HALSEY, A. (1982), 'Provincials and professionals', *Times Higher Education Supplement*, 25 June, pp. 10–11.
34. KOGAN, M. (1975), *Educational Policy Making*. Allen & Unwin: London.
35. JAMES, P. (1980), *The Reorganisation of Secondary Education*. NFER: Slough.
36. *Public Schools Commission* ((a) 1968 and (b) 1970). HMSO: London.
37. CORBETT, A. (1978), *Much Ado About Education*, 4th edn. Macmillan: London.
38. DEPARTMENT OF EDUCATION AND SCIENCE (1967), *Children and Their Primary Schools*, The Plowden Report. HMSO: London.
39. DEPARTMENT OF HEALTH AND SOCIAL SECURITY (1968), *Report of the Committee on Local Authority and Allied Personal Social Services*, The Seebohm Report, Cmnd. 3703. HMSO: London.
40. DEPARTMENT OF EDUCATION AND SCIENCE (1972), *Educational Priority*, The Halsey Report, Vol. 1. HMSO: London.

41. (a) KIRP, D. (1979), *Doing Good by Doing Little: Race and Schooling in Britain*. University of California Press: Berkeley; (b) see also REX, J. and TOMLINSON, S. (1979), *Colonial Immigrants in a British City: a Class Analysis*. Routledge & Kegan Paul: London, p. 169.

42. TOWNSEND, H. E. R. (1971), *Immigrant Pupils in England: the L.E.A. Response*. NFER: Slough.

43. LAYARD, R. and KING, J. (1973), 'The impact of Robbins', in G. Fowler, V. Morris, and J. Ozga (eds), *Decision Making in British Education*. Heinemann/OU: London.

44. DEPARTMENT OF EDUCATION AND SCIENCE (1966), *A Plan for Polytechnics and Other Colleges*, Cmnd. 3006. HMSO: London.

45. FARRANT, J. (1981), 'Trends in admissions', in O. Fulton (ed.), *Access to Higher Education*. Society for Research into Higher Education: Guildford.

46. PRATT, J. and BURGESS, T. (1974), *Polytechnics: A Report*. Pitman: London.

47. GOUGH, I. (1979), *The Political Economy of the Welfare State*, Macmillan: London.

48. DEPARTMENT OF EDUCATION AND SCIENCE (1977), *The Growth of Comprehensive Education*, Report on Education No. 87. DES: London.

49. DEPARTMENT OF EDUCATION AND SCIENCE (1980), *Education for 16–19 Year Olds*, The MacFarlane Report. DES: London.

50. COX, C. and DYSON, B. (eds) (n.d.), *Fight for Education: a Black Paper*. Critical Quarterly Society: London; (b) COX, C. and DYSON, A. (eds) (1969), *Black Paper Two*. Critical Quarterly Society: London; (c) COX, C. and DYSON, A. (eds) (1970), *Goodbye Mr. Short: Black Paper Three*. Critical Quarterly Society: London; (d) COX, C. and BOYSON, R. (eds) (1975), *Fight for Education: Black Paper 1975*. J. M. Dent & Sons: London; (e) COX, C. and BOYSON, R. (eds), *Black Paper 1977*. Temple Smith: London.

51. WRIGHT, N. (1977), *Progress in Education*. Croom Helm: London.

52. DEPARTMENT OF EDUCATION AND SCIENCE (1975), *A Language for Life*, The Bullock Report. HMSO: London.

53. HOPKINS, A. (1979), *The School Debate*. Penguin: Harmondsworth.

54. DEPARTMENT OF EDUCATION AND SCIENCE (1977), *Education in Schools: a Consultative Document*, Cmnd. 6869. HMSO: London.

55. (a) DEPARTMENT OF EDUCATION AND SCIENCE (1979), *Local*

Authority Arrangements for the School Curriculum. HMSO: London; (b) DEPARTMENT OF EDUCATION AND SCIENCE (1980), *A View of the Curriculum*, HMI Series No. 11. HMSO: London; (c) DEPARTMENT OF EDUCATION AND SCIENCE (1981) *The School Curriculum*. HMSO: London.

56. SALTER, B. and TAPPER, T. (1981), *Education, Politics and the State*. Grant McIntyre: London.

57. (a) SOFER, A. (1978), 'Educational arguments in 1977', in M. Brown and S. Baldwin (eds), *The Yearbook of Social Policy in Britain 1977*. Routledge & Kegan Paul: London, pp. 145–61. See also: (b) LAWTON, D. (1980), *The Politics of the School Curriculum*. Routledge & Kegan Paul: London.

58. DEPARTMENT OF EDUCATION AND SCIENCE (1972), *Education: a Framework for Expansion*, Cmnd. 5174. HMSO: London.

59. DEPARTMENT OF EDUCATION AND SCIENCE (1982), *Pupils and School Leavers: Future Numbers*, Report on Education No. 97. DES: London.

60. DEPARTMENT OF EDUCATION AND SCIENCE (1972), *Teacher Education and Training*, The James Report. HMSO: London.

61. (a) RAGGETT, M. and CLARKSON, M. (eds) (1976), *Changing Patterns of Teacher Education*. Falmer Press: Brighton; (b) HENCKE, D. (1978), *Colleges in Crisis*. Penguin: Harmondsworth.

62. Mr David Stoddart, *Parliamentary Debates (Commons)*, Vol. 973, 5 Nov. 1979, col. 107.

63. Accounts of the organisation of the DES and how it operates can be found in; (a) FOWLER, G. (1974), *Central Government of Education*, Open University Course E221, Unit 2. OU Press: Milton Keynes; (b) DEPARTMENT OF EDUCATION AND SCIENCE (1977), *How the Department of Education and Science is Organised*. HMSO: London; (c) FENWICK, K. and MCBRIDE, P. (1981), *The Government of Education*. Martin Robertson: London, Ch. 2.

64. (a) ORGANISATION FOR ECONOMIC CO-OPERATION AND DEVELOPMENT (1975), *Educational Development Strategy in England and Wales*. EOCD: Paris; (b) HOUSE OF COMMONS EXPENDITURE COMMITTEE (1976), Tenth Report: *Policy Making in the Department of Education and Science*. HMSO: London.

65. (a) BLACKIE, J. (1970), *Inspecting the Inspectorate*. Routledge & Kegan Paul: London; (b) GATHERER, W. A. (1975), 'Control and guidance: the role of the inspectorate', in M. Hughes (ed.) *Administering Education*. Athlone Press: London; (c) HOUSE OF COMMONS SELECT COMMITTEE ON EDUCATION AND SCIENCE

(1968), *H.M. Inspectorate*. HMSO: London.

66. KOGAN, M. (1971), *The Politics of Education*. Penguin: Harmondsworth.

67. Accounts of the responsibilities and operation of LEAs can be found in: (a) REGAN, D. E. (1977), *Local Government and Education*. Allen & Unwin: London; (b) Fenwick and McBride (1981), *op. cit.*, Ch. 3.

68. (a) LIPSEY, D. (1980), 'Councils of despair', *New Society*, Vol. 53, No. 924, pp. 211–12; (b) Salter and Tapper (1981), *op. cit.*, pp. 106–9.

69. (a) BIRLEY, D. (1970), *The Education Officer and His World*. Routledge & Kegan Paul: London; (b) FOWLER, G. (1974), *The Local Authority*, Open University Course E221, Unit 5. OU Press: Milton Keynes.

70. KOGAN, M. (1973), *County Hall*, Penguin: Harmondsworth.

71. For discussion on the history of governing bodies and their operation since 1944, see: (a) BARON, G. and HOWELL, D. (1974), *The Government and Management of Schools*. Athlone Press: London; (b) DEPARTMENT OF EDUCATION AND SCIENCE (1977), *A New Partnership for our Schools*, The Taylor Report, HMSO: London; (c) BACON, W. (1978), *Public Accountability and the Schooling System*. Harper & Row: London.

72. For discussion of the headteacher in English schools see: (a) RICHARDSON, E. (1973), *The Teacher, the School and the Task of Management*. Heinemann: London; (b) MUSGROVE, F. (1971), *Patterns of Power and Authority in English Education*. Methuen: London; (c) PETERS, R. (1976), *The Role of the Head*. Routledge & Kegan Paul: London.

73. KING, R. (1973), 'The headteacher and his authority', in G. Fowler, V. Morris and J. Ozga (eds), *Decision Making in British Education*. Heinemann/OU Press: London.

74. KOGAN, M. (1975), *Educational Policy Making: a Study of Interest Groups and Parliament*. Allen & Unwin: London, Ch. 7.

75. (a) GRETTON, J. and JACKSON, M. (1976), *William Tyndale – Collapse of a School or a System?* Allen & Unwin: London; (b) INNER LONDON EDUCATION AUTHORITY (1976), *Report of the Public Enquiry into the William Tyndale Junior and Infants Schools*, The Auld Report. ILEA: London; (c) ELLIS, T., MCWHIRTER, J., MCCOLGAN, D. and HADDOW, B. (1976), *William Tyndale; the Teachers' Story*. Writers and Readers Co-operative: London.

Part two
SOCIAL POLICY ISSUES AND THE EDUCATIONAL SYSTEM

Chapter three
EDUCATION AND WELFARE

3.1 EDUCATION AND THE WELFARE STATE

To begin the second part of this book with a consideration of the 'welfare' aspects of education is to begin with issues which most books on the education system relegate to a minor subsection. But the explicit 'welfare' concerns embodied in education demonstrates clearly that it always has been an integral part of social policy, and they provide a useful starting point for examining those aspects of education which overtly serve 'individual' needs.

Historically, welfare provisions connected with education can be seen as important aspects of the developing welfare state. For many years the education system in general, and schools in particular, have provided the setting for activities whose concerns go well beyond the narrowly educational. The provision of school meals and a school health service, for example, were introduced in the early twentieth century as permissive powers which LEAs could exercise if they wished. This was regarded as a milestone in social policy as well as education and a great victory for the working classes because, 'it implied acceptance by the community of responsibility for poverty'.[1(p. 282)] Under the 1944 Act, where promoting the wider welfare of the child is a prominent theme (cf. sect. 2.1), provision of meals and a health service is a statutory duty. The duty in respect of school meals was considerably restricted in 1980 (cf. sect. 2.5).

Concern for the wider well-being of children (not merely for their intellectual development) in a sense is fundamental to the whole rationale for an education system which is not simply universal but also compulsory in character. To express it crudely, if education is good for children, then a responsible government is quite justified in forcing them to undergo it whether or not they themselves (or their parents) wish it. From this perspective, compulsion can be seen as the act of a benign state expressing a collective commitment to the well-being of all citizens.

The issue of child employment and its relationship to compulsory education provides a good illustration of this. Concern about child labour and continuing pressure to restrict it is a recurring theme in discussions of nineteenth-century social policy.[2(Ch. XIV)] Historically, moves to make education compulsory were intimately linked with the desire to restrict children's participation in employment.[3(pp. 19-34)] Thus education was seen very much as an alternative to paid work, and one which was greatly preferable in the child's own interests. The introduction of the principle of universal elementary education in 1870 by no means disposed of the child-labour issue, since the 'half-time' system, which allowed older children to work half-days and be at school half-days, remained common in certain parts of the country well into the twentieth century.[1(pp. 138-42)] The effective separation of children from economic production in their 'own' interests is somewhat double-edged: it can be seen either as a liberal advance which freed children from the obligation to work[1(p. 142)] or as part of the process of removing from children the opportunity to support themselves and obliging them to rely either on parents or on the state for support.[4] The continuing restriction upon the employment of young people under school-leaving age remains closely linked to the educational system. Under the 1944 Act, local education authorities have the statutory duty of enforcing the provisions about the part-time employment of young people between the ages of thirteen and sixteen, and this system is commonly policed by the education welfare service.[5(Ch. 4)]

The operation of certain aspects of child care legislation is another area which demonstrates the continuing close links between the education service and other statutory agencies whose concern primarily is with the welfare of children. Under section 1(2) (e) of the Children and Young Persons Act 1969, a local authority may start legal proceedings if a child is not 'receiving full-time education suitable to his age, ability and aptitude' and the child is also deemed to be in need of care and control. Such court action may result in the receipt of the child into the care of the local authority, or the granting of a supervision order. In this instance, non-attendance at school acts as the trigger for the state to intervene in a particular family (cf. sect. 6.4). The supervision of the child will subsequently be handled by the social services department, not by the education welfare service, who seldom have any involvement in such situations beyond the preparation of school reports. [5(p. 48)]

Within the education system itself, certain aspects in particular embody a wider welfare orientation: the school health service, the school meals service, the school psychological service and the education welfare service. Within the individual school the development of pastoral care and counselling services can be seen as part of the same process, although the nature and extent of the welfare tasks of the school would not necessarily be a matter of consensus among teachers.[6 a, b] The rest of this chapter will be concerned with these more explicitly welfare services, and will explore what this overt concern with the wider welfare of children means in practice.

3.2 EDUCATION AS A VEHICLE FOR WELFARE

In the case of several of the welfare services, the education system acts principally as a vehicle through which the wider welfare of children is addressed. With the exception of the school meals service, these services are not located within schools themselves but are centralised within the local education authority or its districts and have little direct connection with educational activities within the school: schools simply provide the site upon which welfare interventions with individual children take place. Such interventions explicitly extend beyond those matters of intellectual development which are the principal concern of teachers, and tend to be located in wider issues of social policy. This is illustrated in the Plowden Report [doc 26], which sees the school meals service in the context of child poverty and the school health service as a branch of preventive medicine, designed to ensure that children 'function normally and live and grow in harmony with their environment'. A brief outline of the operation of the main welfare services will be given before moving on to discuss the issue of whether the education system provides a suitable vehicle for ensuring the wider welfare of children.

The school health service is the one welfare service accorded a statutory responsibility for all schoolchildren. Like the school meals service, it was first introduced following three government reports which demonstrated the poor physical health of many schoolchildren.[7] The Liberal government passed the Education (Aministrative Procedures) Act 1907, which gave local education authorities the statutory duty to arrange for the medical inspection of children in elementary schools and the power to provide health services for them. The fact that the provision of services was only a permissive power (not a statutory duty) meant that services were uneven throughout the country, and women especially in the Labour government were active in pressing home the point that medical inspection was of little value if not followed by proper treatment.[8(pp. 42-4)] The provision of treatment was made a statutory duty under the Education Act 1918. The administration of the school health service remained the responsibility of LEAs until 1974, when it was transferred to the reorganised National Health Service. Although concerned with the health of all children, one of its major areas of work has concerned the identification of handicap and the assessment of suitability for special education.[9]

By contrast, the school psychological and child guidance services have no specific basis and deal with only a small minority of schoolchildren. Both services have developed essentially to enable the local education authorities to fulfil various statutory duties laid upon them by the Education Act 1944, including the assessment of the provision of education for 'maladjusted' and other handicapped children.[10(pp. 353-4)] Educational psychologists who work within the school psychological service are concerned with assessing the educational capacities and potential of individual children, while the interdisciplinary teams who work in child guidance are concerned often with much wider issues, and may well work with the child's family as well.

In the child guidance setting, education and child care services are closely interwoven, and the links became more explicit after 1944.[11(Ch. 2)] On the one hand, education provides the setting for identifying individual children who display and present various difficulties and who are then handed over to a child guidance team to 'treat'. On the other hand, the child guidance service has traditionally used remedial education *as* a treatment. In this setting, 'backwardness' has been regarded as either a symptom or a cause of emotional disturbance,[11(pp. 36-7)] and therefore an appropriate response is remedial teaching under the guidance of an educational psychologist, accompanied by social work intervention in the child's family who frequently are seen as the root cause of the child's problems.[12(Ch. 7)]

There are thus two models of the basis of welfare concerns within the educational setting: the school health service is concerned with ensuring the basic well-being of all children, while the psychological and guidance services are concerned with only a small minority of children with special needs. Other welfare services tend to approximate more closely to the latter than the former. The education welfare service itself, discussed in the next section, while potentially concerned with any child, in practice deals only with those whose absence from school or other kind of special needs (e.g. financial) have brought them to the attention of the headteachers, or of pastoral care staff in comprehensive schools.

The pursuit of these twin aims (ensuring the well-being of all children and catering for the special needs of a minority) has been a continuing tension in the development of the school meals service. School meals will be considered here in more detail than the other services for three reasons: its historical importance in the development of social policy; the significant changes which have occurred in this service since 1980; and because it affords the opportunity to consider the question – how effective is the education service as a vehicle for ensuring the wider welfare of children?

In one sense, the introduction of school meals is a prime example of the identification of a social problem – in this case the poor physical health of schoolchildren – and the use of the educational system as a vehicle for solving it (cf. sect. 4.2). From the very beginning, however, there was disagreement about whether the provision of meals should be a selective service – offered only to children of proven poverty – or whether it should be universally available to all schoolchildren, either on the grounds that a universal service is the only way to ensure that all the hungry are fed, or in recognition that the provision of food at school may be a service welcome to many families, for reasons other than poverty. After the passing of the Education (Provision of Meals) Act 1906, women in the labour movement were especially active in arguing the case, first that the powers of local education authorities to provide meals should be strengthened from permissive to statutory, and second that meals should be available to all children, on the grounds that this would be a service to working mothers, many of whom would gladly pay for them [doc 27].

The Education Act 1944 embodied the principle of universality in the provision of school meals [doc 4], by laying upon local authorities the statutory duty to make available for every child a dinner 'in every respect suitable as the main meal of the day', but elements of selectivity were retained in that a charge would be made except where parents could not afford to pay. Since 1980, however, the process has been reversed, by legislation which enabled savings in public expenditure to be made on 'peripheral' areas of education (cf. sect. 2.5). Under the Education Act 1980, the statutory obligation to provide school meals was removed from LEAs, except that they had to retain a free service for children whose families depended on supplementary benefit or family income supplement. If they did provide meals for other children, they were to be free to fix their own charges, and national standards for the nutritional content of meals were abolished.

This represents a reversion to an extreme selectivist position, where state intervention in ensuring that children are well fed is treated as appropriate only in the case of the poorest families, and a retreat from the view that an important function of the education system is to be a vehicle for securing children's welfare.

Does the school meals service provide an effective way of securing the welfare of children, either in its more generous form between 1944 and 1980 or in its attenuated and limited form thereafter? The answer to this question turns very largely on the balance between the principles of universality and selectivity in the administration of the service. From the mid-1960s onwards, concern was expressed in various quarters about the low level of take-up of free school meals, a phenomenon characteristically associated with selective and means-tested services.[13(Ch. 1)]

A major reason commonly suggested for low rates of take-up is the stigma associated with claiming a benefit designed only for the poor. In the case of school meals a variety of stigmatising practices exist, even within the classroom, through which 'free dinner' children can be identified.[14] Indeed, the DES itself was sufficiently concerned about this matter to issue Circular 12/67, asking LEAS to identify and cease such practice. It was the recognition of these possibilities which led Bradshaw and Weale, on the basis of a study undertaken for the Child Poverty Action Group, to argue that: 'Means-tested exemption from charges for school meals is not a satisfactory way of helping poor families. There will always be problems of stigma and non-take-up associated with it.'[15(p. 22)]

The most thorough exploration of these issues is to be found in Davies,[13] where he uses the example of school meals specifically to examine the arguments around universality and selectivity. He compared the situation in local authorities where the take-up of free meals was above average and those where it was below average, and concluded that lack of knowledge about the service and the extent to which local authorities promoted it were as important as was stigma as an explanation of the reasons why eligible families were not claiming free meals. On the other hand, stigma was still important, and was more likely to be experienced by people living in an area where the level of take-up was low.[13(Ch. 5)]

Although it is important not to over-simplify the issue of stigma, it is clear that (for whatever combination of reasons) where free meals are available only to a section of the poorest families, many children do not actually receive them – selective concentration upon those most in need does not guarantee that even they will receive the service.

Further, the strengthening of the principle of selectivity since 1980 has served to exclude children who previously would have received free meals. The criteria of eligibility have changed so that in many local authorities fewer children are now entitled to free meals than before the 1980 Act. Indeed, 35 per cent of LEAs now restrict entitlement to children whose families receive family income supplement or supplementary benefit, [16(p. 32)] whereas regulations previously in operation allowed free meals to children whose family income was somewhat above this level. On the whole, the LEAs which allow the fewest free meals also have the highest charges. The effect of these changes, as reflected in the 1981 census of school meals, is first a widening gap between the quality and scope of the service in different LEAs. Secondly, it is becoming more clearly a 'second class stigmatised service', because overall since 1979, 1.25 million fewer children are taking *paid* meals so that the proportion taking *free* meals has increased to almost one quarter of all meals provided. [17(pp. 91–2)]

In the case of school meals, the education service has in practice been a rather ineffective means of securing children's welfare. This need not necessarily be so: because education is compulsory, it provides access to all children and therefore has the potential of being a very important means of securing their welfare. To put it at its simplest: if *all* pupils were given good school meals, that might well be an excellent means of promoting the physical health of the school population. Its universal coverage could be an appropriate basis for the provision of a universal service. The introduction of an element of selectivity into the administration of school meals undermines precisely that potential, since concentrating selectively upon the poor seems inevitably to mean that some of the target population are missed.

3.3 THE EDUCATION WELFARE SERVICE

The education welfare service is, as its title implies, a specialist welfare agency working within the context of education and, as Jenny Shaw has pointed out, it is the last sizeable agency to retain the term 'welfare' in its title. [18] Its origins and major work, however, concern the enforcement of compulsory school attendance, and problems associated with the double-edged nature of 'welfare' are particularly apparent in its operation. The rationale given by education welfare officers (EWOs) for enforcing attendance is essentially one which focuses upon the needs of the child, the argument being that a child cannot be benefiting from education if he or she is not at school. [5(p. 64)]

The public image of the EWO is very different, however.[19(Ch. 2)] The work of the 'kid-catcher' or 'school board man', from the Education Act 1870 onwards, has been seen essentially as one of policing the compulsory system and enforcing attendance if necessary. Attendance still forms a major part of the EWOs' work [5(Ch. 4)] and it will be discussed more fully in relation to issues of control in the education system in section 6.4.2. This section concentrates upon the EWOs' other, more obviously welfare work, and especially considers the issue of how it relates to the provision of a social work service in the school setting.

Apart from enforcing attendance, EWOs make arrangements for school transport (especially for children in special schools), become involved in placing children in nursery schools and special schools, in regulating child employment, and in arrangements for obtaining free school meals, clothing and educational maintenance grants. The range of work as seen by the local Government Training Board's important review in 1973 (the *Ralphs Report*) is set out in document 28. MacMillan suggests that the EWOs' work can be divided into three broad categories: allocation and support duties, in the fields of nursery education, handicapped children and school placement; provision duties, in respect of clothing and meals; and regulation duties, in respect of attendance, child employment and neglect.[5(pp. 125-6)] One of the most important issues within the service in recent years has been the question of whether it should become more explicitly a social work service. The issues raised will be considered here through a series of linked questions, which for the purposes of this analysis will be considered separately.

First, is there a case for a social work service in the education setting? That such a case exists was strongly promoted by a series of government reports in the 1960s: the Newsom and Plowden reports both supported it, as did the Seebohm report on the personal social services. The Newsom report's discussion of 'education in the slums' argued that the problems of health, poverty and delinquency found there 'make a good case for the employment of a trained social worker'.[20(para. 70)] Several years later, the Plowden report spelled out the case more fully [doc 29], seeing social work as the means of dealing with those features of a child's family setting which were preventing him or her from achieving full potential at school. The following year, the Seebohm report gave support to this case and took the view that truancy *per se* should be the trigger for social work intervention [doc 58]. It recommended that such services should be integrated with Social Services Departments.[21(para. 226)] Thus the central rationale reflected in government reports is that a school social work service in some form is needed to identify and deal with these problems, especially those which relate to home settings and which are preventing children from benefiting from education.

Second, are education welfare officers already providing a social work service in schools? Here there is considerable difference of view, and probably the answer depends upon how one defines social work. On the one hand the Ralphs report established that over 70 per cent of the work of the EWOs was 'work of a social nature', and argued that this should be recognised in the training offered. This should be a social work training which also gives a sound knowledge of the educational context. [22(paras. 130–3, 175)] On the other hand, it can be argued that much of the work of EWOs is more to do with the administration of the education service than with social work,[5(p. 97)] and EWOs themselves mostly want to retain a clear identification with the education service.[5(p. 59)]

Third, should a school social work service be a development of the education welfare service or quite separate from it? While there would seem rather obvious advantages in building upon a service which already exists, there are some strong arguments for keeping social work quite separate from education welfare. These centre upon the EWOs' work of enforcing school attendance, and raise in particularly acute form the general problem which social workers face when they have to combine in one job both coercive and benevolent activities.[18] The Ralphs report itself was highly ambivalent on this issue since, although it took the view that EWOs *are* social workers, it also identified a deep divide between the characteristic approach of the EWO and of the social worker, when working with the same child.[22(paras. 70-1)] Nowhere is this more apparent than on the issue of attendance, which forms the statutory core of the EWO's work. As MacMillan argues [doc 30], education welfare officers are likely to line up with teachers on this issue, believing that their primary task is to get a child back to school. Social workers meanwhile are more likely to emphasise medium or long-term casework with pupils and their families, in order to understand the underlying reason for the absence (cf. sect. 6.4.2). They may regard EWOs as too eager to push a child back into what may be an unsatisfactory, even repressive, experience, whilst EWOs regard them as simply making excuses for recalcitrant children and their families. With such fundamentally different approaches, there clearly are problems about using the education welfare service as a base from which to develop school social work.

Finally, should the education welfare service be located in the social services department? The Seebohm report set out the case for this on five grounds [doc 31], which amount to advocating a full integration with education welfare. These include the view that a child can be dealt with most effectively when seen in the context of family and neighbourhood, and that work would be less fragmented, more effective and more personally satisfying if social work in schools came under the umbrella of the social services department. This implies that education social work is, as Lyons puts it, a 'legitimate sub-division of social work' and should be based in social services area offices.[23(pp. 37-8)] The Association of Directors of Social Services (perhaps not surprisingly) 'believes wholeheartedly in the need for a social work service to schools to be professionally based in social services departments'.[24(para. 75)] The Ralphs report remained agnostic on the question of integration.[22(para. 176)] Education welfare officers themselves strongly opposed the idea of being transferred to social services. Although some local authorities did make the transfer, the education service as a whole was hostile and most authorities took the opportunity of local government reorganisation in 1974 to return the education welfare service to the education department.[5(Ch. 8)]

Issues about the operation of the education welfare service and the potential for social work in schools focus attention upon the tensions between welfare and control which have been an important theme of this chapter. This issue will be considered more specifically in the next section, which examines the rationales which underpin the education-welfare link.

3.4 RATIONALES FOR THE EDUCATION – WELFARE LINK

It will be apparent from the preceding discussion that there are several different grounds upon which it can be argued that it is appropriate to address the wider welfare of children through the educational system. This section draws out those rationales more specifically and suggests that there are three main ones which, while certainly not mutually exclusive, can be treated as conceptually separate.

3.4.1 Education is a convenient setting because it provides universal coverage

Precisely because education is compulsory, it potentially gives universal coverage of all children. Schools, for example, can be used as a location for identifying children's medical needs, for ensuring that they are well fed and for enabling education welfare officers or social workers to identify problems in children's families which merit further attention. The emphasis of this argument is on convenience: schools provide a convenient location for these activities not because of their educational activities but simply because they supply a captive audience of the total child population.

Essentially there are two different types of activity implied by this rationale: surveillance and treatment. The fact that the education system has universal coverage of children gives opportunity for both, but treatment does not automatically follow from surveillance. For example, although the medical inspection of schoolchildren was introduced in 1907, provision of treatment was permitted only five years later and was not made statutory until 1918.[1(pp. 285-9)] So the case for monitoring and surveillance of children's health was accepted some considerable time before the case for providing health services: a sequence which must at least raise a question about whose interests were really being served. The opportunities for the surveillance of children provided by a universal education service are obvious; equally such a service provides considerable potential on the 'treatment' side, that is, for the positive promotion of children's welfare. However, as has been seen with the example of school meals, such potential can be significantly undermined by the introduction of selective elements into universally provided services.

If schools are merely providing a convenient location for welfare services, in principle it is possible to keep the provision and administration of such services quite separate from the educational activities of the school, as indeed most of the services are. However, it is very likely that teachers will be drawn into such activities, precisely because they are the people who do have the daily contact with children. They can be used, as one writer has put it, as the 'eyes and ears of the early warning system' which alerts the child care services of the possible need for intervention.[25(p. 103)] The Seebohm report argued strongly that teachers should have the prime responsibility for identifying children at risk and for referring them to the appropriate agency, when they wrote: 'We cannot over-emphasise our view that the role of the teachers is of prime importance. It is he or she who, seeing the child daily in class, is often the first to become aware that all is not well.'[21(para. 216)]

It can be claimed, however, that teachers have seldom been given much guidance in their training about the extent of their responsibilities in such areas, nor about claims which they can make on other professionals.[26(Ch. 1)] Moreover, some teachers would regard it as inappropriate and unethical for them to attempt to intervene in a child's family situation, and the dilemmas which they may face are well expressed by Fitzherbert [doc 32].

The problems of relying upon schools in general, and upon teachers in particular, for the surveillance of children at risk are well illustrated by the report into the circumstances leading to the death of Maria Colwell at the hands of her step-father despite the fact that teachers, social workers and education welfare officers had been concerned with the family for some time, and that Maria had been the subject of a care order of the local authority. The report describes the schools which she attended as an 'important link with the welfare chain' [27(para. 164)] and says of her teachers 'we are impressed by their sincerity and perceptiveness of Maria as an individual'; [27(para. 178)] yet their concern was not conveyed effectively and promptly to Maria's social worker, for a variety of complex reasons. Clearly there are issues raised here about communication and co-operation between different agencies, and there has been considerable discussion in recent years about notions of teamwork and inter-professionalism in such cases. [28a, b, c] However, underlying this issue are ethical and political questions about how far those whose prime task is to foster children's intellectual development can and should be drawn into the activity of monitoring family life, just because the education system happens to provide conveniently comprehensive contact with children (cf. sect. 6.4).

3.4.2 Provision of state education entails taking responsibility for the total well-being of children

The second kind of rationale for the education–welfare link raises rather similar issues about whether teachers' responsibilities stop at the classroom door, or at least the school gates. However, while the emphasis in the first rationale was upon schools simply as a convenient location for welfare interventions, the emphasis here is upon concern for the wider welfare of the child as central to the activity of educating. The argument essentially is that the imposition of compulsory education is an integral part of, and in a sense is justified by, the state's acceptance of responsibility for the total well-being of children. It is appropriate therefore for those wider concerns to be expressed by the provision of welfare services within the educational system. A further question is whether teachers themselves should be part of such services.

This rationale can be used to justify a range of activities, aimed either at the whole school population or at minorities within it. On the one hand, it can be used to support the provision of pastoral care services within schools which apply to all pupils (see below, final section for further discussion); on the other hand, it can be offered as a reason for providing services such as child guidance, on the grounds that securing the well-being of certain children requires that kind of specialist attention.

Major areas of debate about this rationale concern the relationship between parental responsibilities and state responsibilities Many people who originally opposed the introduction of school meals did so on the grounds that their provision would reduce parental authority and responsibility,[1(p. 280)] and arguments about the proper limits of state responsibility for children have pervaded policy debates about a whole range of child care services during this century.[29] However, as David has pointed out in relation to the measures introduced by the Liberal government in the early part of this century, the introduction of health and welfare measures in the educational setting involved the state in assuming some 'parental' responsibilities and also in imposing new standards upon parents, especially upon mothers, who were 'increasingly obliged to care for their children in particular ways and to co-operate with the state in rearing the country's children.'[30(p. 50)]

The issue, in other words, cannot be seen simply as a question of how far a benign state can justifiably encroach upon parental rights in the interests of individual children. It is also a matter of how far an apparently benign concern for a child's well-being can mask attempts to impose particular patterns of childrearing upon parents in the interest of some much more general goal. In the case of the material reviewed by David, it is in the interests of 'national efficiency'. This provides a good illustration of how an aspect of education which seems to quite clearly focus upon 'individual needs' in practice can contain important elements of 'society's needs'.

3.4.3 Welfare interventions are necessary to ensure that education takes place efficiently

This third rationale again sees concern for a child's wider welfare as an integral part of education, but accords it a very specific role which is both instrumental and subordinate. The argument essentially is that, if all children are to benefit to the full from educational opportunities, it may be necessary in some cases to provide certain services which facilitate this.

The argument that teachers cannot teach starving children was central to the introduction of the school meals service, as it was to the provision of clothing grants, to ensure that no child 'is unable by reason of inadequacy of his clothing to take full advantage of the education provided at school' (Education Act 1944, sect. 51). As has already been noted, the education welfare service offers this as the major rationale for their activities.

This rationale accords welfare an instrumental and subordinate role in facilitating efficient and effective education. If interpreted broadly, it can also be used to justify an almost endlessly expanding range of activities. A narrow interpretation would emphasise the identification and removal of specific barriers to children's learning, whilst a broader interpretation would seek in addition to create the conditions conducive to learning within the school, in the child's family, and in the community. A very clear example of both kinds of interpretation is given in the Plowden report's discussion of social work services in schools ˉdoc 29ˊ. On the one hand, barriers which prevent consistent attendance must be removed. On the other hand, conditions conducive to learning can be fostered by the development of 'general family casework'.

Again, this justification for welfare, while apparently focusing upon the individual child, can be seen as embodying other interests. Providing health services, school meals and so on may indeed benefit children, but it also ensures a more efficient and healthier workforce. That point certainly was not lost on those who supported the introduction of such services: as David has argued, the health of the nation was a more pressing concern for the Liberal government than the education of children. [30](p. 49) In these circumstances, 'welfare' interventions may have the production of a healthy workforce as a major rationale and the effectiveness of education simply as a subsidiary benefit.

3.5 DOUBLE-EDGED WELFARE: BENEVOLENCE AND CONTROL

The theme that welfare measures are often double-edged has been present throughout this chapter. In this concluding section I will explore more specifically what that means, and discuss three examples which should help to clarify it.

Several of the activities reviewed in this chapter can be seen as implying both a concern to benefit the young and a desire to control them. The tensions generated when both are present in one set of activities can be seen very cearly in the work of the education welfare service. Education of course is not unique in this respect: rather similar tensions can be seen in other sectors of the welfare state which deal with the young. Sometimes the welfare and control elements can directly conflict, in that they suggest opposite courses of action. A good example of this can be found in the response of the education service to schoolgirl pregnancies. The study by the National Council for One Parent Families [doc 33] shows that, in terms of the welfare of the individual, all the arguments are in favour of keeping the school-girl mother in school for as long as possible before the birth and facilitating her rapid return after it. However, concern for the 'moral standards' of the school and above all a desire to ensure that others are not contaminated, suggests her exclusion. In other words, the school's role in controlling the lifestyle of young people and imposing upon them a particular moral order (cf. sect. 6.4) runs completely counter to the welfare of the individual in this instance. The likely outcome of such conflicts between considerations of control and welfare is suggested by the fact that, on the evidence of the National Council survey, some education authorities are more ready to exercise their powers to exclude pregnant schoolgirls from school on medical grounds than they are to make alternative arrangements for their education.[31(para. 86)]

The same kind of questions, about whether issues of welfare or of control are the major concern of the education service, are raised in relation to the second example: educational provision in Community Homes with Education (CHEs). These homes are provided and administered as part of the child care (not educational) system, under the Children and Young Persons Act 1969, and cater for children and young people deemed to be in need of care, treatment and control of a type which can best be provided on a residential basis. Ostensibly, the provision of education within these establishments is part of their 'treatment' programmes, for the benefit of individuals. In practice, the educational experiences offered are very limited in character. An HMI survey of these establishments in 1977 was very critical of them on grounds which included the low overall standards of educational provision, high turnover of staff (many of whom were not qualified for such work), the lack of social educational programmes and the low priority given to careers education. In all these respects, girls' CHEs were worse provided than boys'.[32] This suggests that those features of educational provision which might most clearly serve the needs of individuals were (to say the least) under-emphasised, in a context where other features of CHEs are clearly concerned with control.

The fact that 'welfare' activities are often mixed with 'control' elements does not necessarily negate the benevolent aspects, but it does make welfare double-edged. This is illustrated in the third example: the provision of pastoral care in secondary schools. The development and institutionalisation of the academic and pastoral as two separate but linked elements within secondary schools has occurred in the wake of comprehensive reorganisation and the creation of large secondary schools.[33a, b] The overt aims of pastoral care systems are to create a sense of security and identity for pupils and to enable teachers to get to know them as individuals and to help with any problems they may have. [33b(p. 22)] The most common ways of organising pastoral care are the house and the year system, within which there are divisions into form or tutor groups.[34(Ch. 13)] Thus pastoral care in a sense aims to be a welfare system within the school which gives universal coverage, and represents the most systematic way in which teachers engage with the wider well-being of pupils, supported sometimes by a specifically appointed school counsellor.[35a, b]

The overt focus of this system is individual welfare but the reality is often very different. Galloway sees two possible dangers in many schools' pastoral care: either they are in danger of 'enveloping an essentially human activity in a pseudo-psychological mystique' or of 'placing a respectable label on an old fashioned lecture'. [36(p. 2)] Most of the available evidence suggests that the latter is more likely than the former. As Dooley has pointed out, the concept of 'pastor', with its religious connotations is inseparable from notions of authority.[37] Since the immediate concern of teachers is to manage large numbers of children, it is hardly surprising if many pastoral care systems effectively become disciplinary systems, in which even welfare issues are handled in purely administrative terms. [33a(pp. 263-5)] The pastoral 'care' which is produced may well be experienced as control rather than welfare by its recipients and, as Lang has highlighted [doc 34], the major purpose of such arrangements may appear to be to facilitate the administering of punishments.

Whether or not one regards the double-edged nature of welfare as regrettable, there is a sense in which it is inevitable within the educational system. One important reason for this is that schools are legally 'in loco parentis'. This is the basis upon which teachers and others within the educational system act to secure the welfare of children (cf. sect. 6.4.3). The legal meaning of 'in loco parentis' was established by a series of judgments in the courts, the most important of which was the Cockburn judgment which indicated that 'A parent when he places his child with a schoolmaster delegates to him all his own authority so far as it is necessary for the welfare of the child.' [28c(p. 6)] This formulation perfectly encapsulates the tension between welfare and control: the *welfare* of the child is secured by the exercise of *authority*. This chapter has demonstrated how that tension is replicated in many different ways in the provision of welfare in the educational setting.

NOTES AND REFERENCES

1. SIMON, B. (1965), *Education and the Labour Movement 1870–1920*. Lawrence & Wishart: London.
2. PINCHBECK, I. and HEWITT, M. (1973), *Children in English Society*, Vol. 2. Routledge & Kegan Paul: London.
3. BALL, N. (1973), 'Elementary school attendance and voluntary effort before 1870', *History of Education*, Vol. 2, No. 1, pp. 19–34.
4. FITZ, J. (1981), 'Welfare, the family and the child', in *Education, Welfare and Social Order*, Open University Course E353, Block 5, Unit 12. OU Press: Milton Keynes.
5. MACMILLAN, K. (1977), *Education Welfare*. Longman: London.
6. (a) CRAFT, M. (1980), 'School welfare roles and networks', in, M. Craft, J. Raynor, and L. Cohen (eds), *Linking Home and School*, 3rd edn. Harper & Row: London; (b) JOHNSON, D., RANSOM, E., PACKWOOD, T., BOWDEN, K. and KOGAN, M. (1980), *Secondary Schools and the Welfare Network*. Allen & Unwin: London.
7. These reports were: *Royal Commission on Physical Training in Scotland. 1903; Interdepartmental Committee on Physical Deterioration, 1904; Interdepartmental Committee on Medical Inspection and Feeding of Children Attending Public Elementary Schools, 1905*.
8. FERGUSON, S. (1977), 'Labour women and the social services', in L. Middleton (ed.), *Women in the Labour Movement*. Croom Helm: London.
9. For an outline of the work of the school health service see DEPARTMENT OF EDUCATION AND SCIENCE (1975), *The School Health Service 1908–74*. HMSO: London.
10. FITZHERBERT, K. (1980), 'Strategies for prevention', in M. Craft *et al.*, (1980) *op. cit.*, pp. 353–4.
11. SAMPSON, O. (1980), *Child Guidance: its History, Provenance and Future*. British Psychological Society: London.
12. PETRIE, C. and CONOCHIE, D. (1975), *Child Guidance*. Macmillan: London.
13. DAVIES, B. (1978), *Universality, Selectivity and Effectiveness in Social Policy*. Heinemann: London.

14. FIELD, F. (1974), *The Stigma of Free School Meals*. Child Poverty Action Group: London.
15. BRADSHAW, J. and WEALE, J. (1978), *Free School Meals: Area Variations in Take-up*, Poverty Research Series No. 7. Child Poverty Action Group: London.
16. CHILD POVERTY ACTION GROUP (1981), *Poverty*, No. 49, August.
17. BISSET, L. (1982), 'Second-class fare', *New Society*, 15 April.
18. SHAW, J. (1981), 'Family, state and compulsory education', in *Education, Welfare and Social Order*, Open University Course E353, Block 5, Unit 13. OU Press: Milton Keynes.
19. CORRIGAN, P. (1979), *Schooling the Smash Street Kids*. Macmillan: London.
20. MINISTRY OF EDUCATION (1963), *Half Our Future*, The Newsom Report. HMSO: London.
21. DEPARTMENT OF HEALTH AND SOCIAL SECURITY (1968), *Report of the Committee on Local Authority and Allied Personal Social Services*, The Seebohm Report, Cmnd. 3703. HMSO: London.
22. LOCAL GOVERNMENT TRAINING BOARD (1973), *The Role and Training of Education Welfare Officers*, The Ralphs Report. Local Government Training Board: London.
23. LYONS, K. (1973), *Social Work and the School*. HMSO: London.
24. ASSOCIATION OF DIRECTORS OF SOCIAL SERVICES (1978), *Social Work Services for Children in School*. ADSS: London.
25. EVANS, N. (1977), 'The professional stance of teachers', in Department of Health and Social Security/Welsh Office, *Working Together for Children and Their Families*. HMSO: London.
26. FITZHERBERT, K. (1977), *Child Care Services and the Teacher*. Temple Smith: London.
27. DEPARTMENT OF HEALTH AND SOCIAL SECURITY (1974), *Report of the Committee of Enquiry into the Care and Supervision Provided in Relation to Maria Colwell*. HMSO: London.
28. (a) ROBINSON, P. (1976), *Education and Poverty*. Methuen: London, pp. 103–7; (b) Craft *et al.* (1980), *op. cit.*, Part VI; (c) MURGATROYD, S. (1980), *Helping the Troubled Child: Inter-Professional Case Studies*. Harper & Row: London.
29. PACKMAN, J. (1975), *The Child's Generation; Child Care Policy from Curtis to Houghton*. Blackwell: Oxford.
30. DAVID, M. E. (1980), *The State, the Family and Education*. Routledge & Kegan Paul: London.
31. NATIONAL COUNCIL FOR ONE PARENT FAMILIES (1979), *Pregnant at School*. National Council For One Parent Families: London.

32. DEPARTMENT OF EDUCATION AND SCIENCE (1978), *Community Homes with Education*, HMI Series No. 10. HMSO: London.
33. (a) BEST, R., JARVIS, C. and RIBBINS, P. (1980), *Perspectives on Pastoral Care*. Heinemann: London; (b) Johnson *et al.* (1980), *op. cit.*
34. BENN, C. and SIMON, B. (1970), *Half Way There*. McGraw Hill: London.
35. (a) HAMBLIN, D. (1974), *The Teacher and Counselling*. Blackwell: Oxford; (b) DAWS, P. (1980), 'The school counsellor', in M. Craft *et al.* (1980) *op. cit.*
36. GALLOWAY, D. (1981), *Teaching and Counselling: Pastoral Care in Primary and Secondary Schools*. Longman: London.
37. DOOLEY, S. (1980), 'The relationship between concepts of "pastoral care" and "authority" ', in R. Best *et al.*, *op. cit.*

Chapter four

EDUCATION: A SERVICE OFFERED FOR THE BENEFIT OF ITS RECIPIENTS

This chapter focuses on education for the 'individual's benefit', despite the fact that the discussion in earlier chapters makes it apparent that there are very good reasons for doubting whether any type of educational provision can be regarded as solely and unambiguously for the benefit of its recipients. However, some examples can be found of educational policy presented primarily in these terms and where there does seem to be a prima facie case for evaluating the provision as the action of a benevolent state, mindful of the 'good' of its citizens. Such sentiments are expressed in the 1943 White Paper on Educational Reconstruction [doc 2], when the purpose of educational reform was said to include: 'to secure for children a happier childhood and a better start in life; to ensure a fuller measure of education and opportunity for young people.'

In exploring a number of instances of this kind, this chapter sets out to examine whether, when such a perspective is embodied in policy and practices, the outcome actually *is* the provision of education solely for the benefit of its recipients. Material will be divided into two main sections: first, the idea of the right to education; second, educational provision as a response to individual need and social problems. As rationales for the provision of services, in some ways these do represent rather different types of social policy. None the less, they share a common focus upon the recipients of education (rather than, say, upon 'the needs of the economy') as the basis of provision.

4.1 EDUCATION AS A RIGHT

In this section we will consider those approaches to social policy which treat education as a valuable commodity, to which all individuals have a right. From this perspective, the distribution of educational resources according to accidents of birth and parental income leads to the denial of the natural rights of certain children.[1(pp. 63-4)]

The emphasis upon rights to services regardless of resources was prominent in social policy in the postwar reconstruction, when the foundations of the existing education service were laid (cf. sect. 2.1). Major writers in the social democratic tradition of social policy have argued that the creation of the welfare state at this time represented a significant shift away from the principles of the capitalist market as the basis for access to services, replacing it with a different kind of distributive system which accords rights of access to services according to need: 'The social policies (of the postwar welfare state) group and treat individuals not according to their economic power but according to their needs: the substantial dissolution of the cash nexus has proceeded, *pari passu*, with the increasing realisation of a 'needs nexus.' [2(p. 59)]

These principles appear to have been applied in distinctive ways to different services. In a sense, the principle of right was much more radical in its implications for access to health services, or to income support, than for education, because some education was already universally available, at least at elementary level. None the less, the 1944 Education Act was a point at which, as T. H. Marshall put it, 'respect for individual rights could hardly have been more strongly expressed' [doc 35]. The following discussion will examine the provision of education as a right by looking first at Marshall's notion of citizenship rights and then by examining the key assumption that education is a valuable commodity intrinsically of benefit to its recipients. Finally, the application of these ideas to the provision of education will be considered in relation to the specific example of adult education, and of aspects of education (especially school transport) designed to ensure maximum access to provision.

4.1.1 Citizenship as the basis of rights

In recent writings on social policy,[3a, b] the notion that citizenship is a proper basis for the provision of welfare derives from an essay by T. H. Marshall entitled *Citizenship and Social Class*.[4] In this essay (extract in doc 35) Marshall divides citizenship rights into civil, political and social rights, which together constitute 'a kind of basic equality associated with full membership of a community'.[4(p. 8)] The acquisition of social rights 'rounds off' civil and political rights and enables them to be exercised better.[3b(p. 22)]

What would be the major features of any social policy with this basis? In Parker's view, citizenship as the basis for services should mean that the distribution of resources is based on an agreed level accessible to everyone irrespective of bargaining power; that similar needs should receive similar treatment as a right (that is, with no discrimination against racial, political or social minorities); that no stigma should be attached to the use of public services and that the quality of public services is the best possible, given other claims on public resources.[3a(p. 145)] The notion of citizenship as the basis of the provision of social services has some strong and obvious attractions. Chief among these is its overtly egalitarian character, which breaks the link between access to services and ability to pay for them. A further attraction is that the use of state services will not be stigmatising to the users, although there are many reasons for questioning this claim.[5]

Marshall himself recognises that there are problems in applying the notion of citizenship to education. Although the policy embodied in the 1944 Act ostensibly bases educational provision on the notion of the right to be educated to the limits of one's own 'ability', such a goal is in fact impossible because education also prepares individuals for different positions in the occupational structure [doc 35]. If the principle of citizenship rights is to be applied without challenging the economic order, the aim of the right to unlimited education for every citizen cannot be sustained. Marshall deals with this problem via the notion of equal opportunities which, he argues, to some extent resolves the issue by acknowledging that citizenship rights in education means 'the equal right to be recognised as unequal'.[4(p. 67)]

Marshall therefore identifies the major criticism of the principle of citizenship as far as education is concerned: that citizenship rights are quite compatible with, and may even sustain, other forms of inequality. As Mishra argues [doc 36], this means that welfare is not necessarily an egalitarian measure in the sense, say, of reducing class inequalities. It may even reinforce underlying inequalities, if they affect an individual's capacity to make use of the services. This applies very clearly in the case of education where, for example, material poverty appears significantly to affect the outcome of a child's schooling (cf. Ch. 2 and sect. 6.2.2).

The right to education on the basis of citizenship may thus be accorded without making any change whatever to structures of social and economic inequality, or to an individual's position within them. This makes it a much less egalitarian measure than it first appears. Moreover, there are certain practical problems about operationalising the concept, because it is not easy to see what level of educational provision would be necessary to fulfil this particular 'social right'.[3a(p. 160), b(p. 26)]

The failure of the educational system after 1944 to tackle many fundamental inequalities can be seen in this context as a natural consequence of the principle of citizenship rights implicit in the 1944 Act. That principle accommodates, rather than challenges, underlying inequalities, so it is not surprising if policies based on citizenship do not produce fundamental social change. At the same time, it is important not to overlook the positive consequences of the citizenship principle. In particular, its potential for developing state services in a way which is not stigmatising to their users has been realised with some success in the widespread use of the state educational system in Britain.

The principle of citizenship offers one way of promoting policies which focus upon the 'individual's benefit' rather than 'society's benefit'; but in that respect it can be double-edged. In the same opening paragraph of the 1943 White Paper on education, which claims that the good of the individual child is to be promoted, it is also made clear that the development of education is seen as an investment in the youth of the nation, 'our greatest national asset' and the object of the proposals is 'to strengthen and inspire the younger generation' [doc 2]. Marshall himself recognised that the very fact that education is compulsory (not merely *available* to all) indicates that it is not solely for the benefit of the individual and that 'the duty to improve and civilise oneself is a social duty'. In this extended discussion of education, he emphasises that education is a right with a duty attached to it [doc 35].

So citizenship rights are mirrored by citizenship duties, and sometimes the latter are more prominent than the former. As the authors of *Unpopular Education* argue, in the 1930s there was a growth in movements which promoted education *for* citizenship (cf. sect. 6.2.5). In the 1940s this ideology helped to redefine the relationship between schooling and the economy, implying a curriculum which was social in character rather than narrowly technical as a preparation for 'responsible citizens and workers.'[6(pp. 53-61)] Even the notion of citizenship rights, which seems so clearly to focus upon the individual as the basis for educational provision, entails necessarily the notion of duties, which immediately introduces the theme of 'society's needs'.

4.1.2 Education: a valuable commodity

The use of 'citizens' rights' as the rationale for providing state education implies an assumption (not always spelled out) that education is an intrinsically valuable commodity, since it makes no sense to argue that anyone has a 'right' to something which is not worth having. Whether education *is* intrinsically valuable (or whether particular forms of it are and others are not) is of course a question open to challenge. The very fact that universally available education is also compulsorily administered indicates that its intrinsic value is not immediately apparent to all citizens. None the less, the idea that education is a valuable commodity is implicit in all arguments which focus on education for the 'individual's benefit' (not only those which explicitly espouse a notion of citizens' rights), and has been influential in the development of certain features of the British educational system. In the words of the Warnock report on special education, 'education . . . is a good, and a specifically human good, to which all human beings are entitled'.[7(para. 1.7)]

As was seen in relation to arguments about citizenship rights, the assumption of intrinsic value leads quite naturally to policy issues which focus upon the distribution of this valuable commodity, and upon the ease of access accorded to different individuals and social groups. Although implicit in the development of the education system after 1944 (and to some extent before), the consolidation of educational policies around the issues of access and distribution occurred during the Labour government of the 1960s.

Historically, the labour movement has been one of the most significant sources of the view that education should be universally available because it is an intrinsically valuable commodity. This view of education inspired, among other things, the development of the Workers' Educational Association (WEA). Albert Mansbridge, who was instrumental in the formation of the Association, wrote of it that 'education was recognised as a force enabling man to develop to the limit of his powers' [doc 37]. He regarded it as a serious matter that the 'ordinary working man had been disinherited through neglect from the right to education' – women's access to education presumably was of less concern to him. Mansbridge is drawing here upon that socialist tradition mostly closely associated with William Morris, whose thinking had a profound effect on socialists in the late nineteenth century and afterwards. Morris's interest was in creating an educative society, which would be a society of equals where labour was a creative rather than an oppressive experience, and where there would be ample opportunities for developing individual gifts.[8(pp. 52-8)]

This influential vision, whilst clearly concerned with the needs of the individual, also incorporates a belief in social progress. As Simon puts it, Morris believed that: 'the creative labour of men in a society of equals can give rise to new human characteristics and lead to further social and individual progress'.[8(p. 58)] Morris's view of education, and the initiatives it inspired, demonstrates that the focus on the 'individual's benefit' is seldom the whole story. Even those who argue that education is an intrinsically valuable commodity which should not be withheld from any citizen, often also see 'society' or 'the community' as another (perhaps the ultimate) beneficiary.

As far as English educational policy is concerned, the view that education should be provided because it is intrinsically valuable to the individual is perhaps most clearly reflected in the Newsom report on pupils of average and below-average ability, and in the Plowden report's emphasis on 'child centred' education in the primary school (cf. sect. 2.4). The extracts from Newsom in document 38 are an excellent statement of the translation of the 'education as a valuable commodity' view into educational policy. The report claims that pupils of average ability and below need to have their minds and imaginations fully engaged, to develop the capacity for curiosity and for forming judgements. The purpose of acquiring the basic skills of literacy and numeracy is also for the individual's benefit, to enable him or her to be able to share fully in human thought and experience. These are, par excellence, statements about education as a means to personal fulfilment and above all of 'doing something worthwhile for its own sake' as a principal aim. They contrast sharply with views about the 'needs of the economy' as the guiding principle for educational provision (cf. sect. 6.2.1).

An examination of the weight given to these kinds of issues in the Newsom report indicates that there have indeed been points in educational policy-making where the emphasis on 'society's needs' has not been paramount. However, the kind of education which 'makes sense to the society' which provides it has always to be balanced against cultivating the capacity to do something worthwhile and for its own sake [doc 38]. Moreoever, at the point where recommendations are translated into concrete policies, the fate of the Newsom report (cf. sect. 2.3) suggests a rather pessimistic conclusion about the likelihood that the individual needs of below-average pupils will be taken sufficiently seriously to commit significantly greater resources to them, as Newsom recommended. Even the minimal action of extending the school-leaving age from fifteen to sixteen, which had already been recommended four years earlier by Crowther and accepted in principle by the Conservative government, was not finally accomplished until 1972, and then after a two-year delay because of public expenditure cuts. In addition, there must be considerable doubt about

whether sufficient resources were committed to ROSLA programmes
(cf. sect. 2.3) to seriously test Newsom's view that the additional
year's schooling was likely to offer considerable benefits to those
young people who otherwise would not have had it.[9(pp. 73-4)]

The pessimistic conclusion suggested by this example is that educational policies designed primarily for the benefit of the individual –
especially for disadvantaged individuals – stand relatively little
change of competing for public resources. Although, as Marshall
argued [doc 35], the balance between individual and collective
concerns may have shifted somewhat in favour of the former after
1944, that Act certainly did not initiate an education service based
solely on the idea of education for the sake of the individual recipient.
As long as education must, in the words of Newsom, 'make sense to
society', considerations which derive from collective interests (of
various sorts) seem to exercise the more compelling pressures.

4.1.3 The case of adult education

The argument presented above suggests that the 'individual's benefit'
rationale for educational provision is seldom found in a pure form in
policy-making and implementation but more usually is mixed with
considerations which have a great deal more to do with issues of
'society's benefit'. This section will consider to what extent this
analysis can be applied to the field of adult education.

The example of adult education has been chosen in this context
because it does not form part of compulsory provision. The compulsory basis of schooling must lead one to question whether the benefit
of the individual is the major consideration in this sector. However,
where education is made available but is not compulsory, should we
expect to find that it is provided solely for the individual's benefit,
untainted by other considerations – or at least that considerations
about the individual benefits are much more prominent?

The development of adult education certainly reflects a strong
commitment to the idea of individual self-improvement, as reflected
in Mansbridge's writing on the foundation of the WEA [doc 37]. In
the most recent government report on adult education, the Russell
committee [doc 39] gave strong support to the view that education is
for the benefit of individuals, arguing that: 'education is concerned
with developing the ability of individuals to understand and articulate, to reason and to make judgements; and to develop sensitivity
and creativity.' Following from this, the committee (unlike Mansbridge, concerning themselves with women's education as well as

men's) took the view that the major purpose of adult education should be: 'opportunities for men and women to continue to develop their knowledge, skills, judgement and creativity throughout adult life.' [10(para. 8)] Room argues that the Russell report is a good example of promoting educational policies based on rights, since each citizen would be granted a life-long claim upon education without having to demonstrate that he or she merited access on some other criteria (such as the possession of certain credentials).[2(pp. 133-4)] In the context of this discussion, it is very interesting to note that these recommendations have not been translated into legislation.

The potential has also long been recognised, not only for adult education to foster *self*-improvement, but also to promote the advancement of the working classes as a whole. Within the trade union and labour movements: 'a number of motives underlay the development of adult education: a desire for self-improvement, a desire for self-advancement, a pursuit of civic and political enlightenment, and a hope of enhancing the efficiency of trade unionists.' [11(p. 123)] The oppositional, even revolutionary, potential of education is implied here. This certainly was the view of the Italian Marxist Gramsci, who saw the political education of workers as a crucial task of adult education, with the aim both of developing class consciousness and of fostering working-class intellectuals who would challenge the dominance of ruling class ideologies (cf. sect. 6.2.4 and Ch. 7).

There is therefore an important strand within adult education which sets it firmly within the 'recipients' benefits' rationale, both on an individual and a collective level: the education of adults can foster the personal development of individuals and advance the cause of the working classes. This may indeed be its promise, but the reality is often very different. Adult education can either be 'the practice of freedom' or an exercise in producing conformity. Building on this insight, Lovett notes that adult education has failed to make an impact in Britain except on the most elite sections of the working class. Far from being a vehicle for the advancement of the working classes as a whole, it seems to have been mostly successful in identifying a potential working-class elite, then educating them in such a way as to remove them from working-class culture.[12(pp. 140-41)] Although individual recipients may have derived considerable benefit thereby, the collective interests of the working classes may be ill served by the removal of potential leaders. Further, such a strategy may well be in the interests of more powerful groups, since the political and economic status quo remains intact.

Much of the writing on adult education (significantly, including government reports) reflects a profound tension between what Paterson calls 'personal development' and 'social purpose'. In a rather pompous way, he argues that adult education is: 'something which a wise society ought . . . to promote because of the unique contribution which it can make to the well-being of society itself.' [13(p.254)] The examples which he gives [doc 40] strongly suggest that what he sees as the benefits to the 'well-being of society' are principally the production of a compliant labour force and conformity to dominant norms of family life and of personal hygiene.

A similar tension between the individual and the social purposes of adult education is reflected in public policy. Although the Russell report rejects a narrow justification of adult education – that the purpose of adult education should be the vocational training and re-training of workers – none the less it takes seriously the potential in adult education for 'society's benefit' [doc 39]. The main emphasis here is upon improving the quality of life and the development of a free, democratic society:

> The value of adult education is not solely to be measured by direct increases in earning power or productive capacity or by any other materialistic yardstick, but by the quality of life it inspires in the individual and generates for the community at large . . . (the aim is) that those engaged in it develop a greater awareness of their own capacities and a more certain knowledge of the totality of their responsibilities as human beings. [10(para. 6)]

Set alongside the statements from Russell quoted earlier, these reflect an important tension between the individual's and society's benefit in the public policy rationales for providing adult education.

The same tensions were present in a specific and significant government initiative in adult education: the setting up of the Open University. [14] As is clear from Hall *et al.*'s careful account of this as a case study in social policy, it was an unusual piece of policy-making in that it was a personal initiative of the then Prime Minister, Harold Wilson, and was 'protected' despite being a contentious proposal which attracted diverse opposition. [15(Ch. 10)] Wilson promoted this policy on four grounds, which in a sense enabled it to appeal to all tastes [15(pp. 248–53)]:

1. technological (the need to use all advanced technology to best advantage, including broadcasting);
2. economic (the need to use hitherto untapped talent);
3. egalitarian (an opportunity for those who had not previously had the chance of higher education);
4. political (the need to maintain Britain's prestige abroad).

Education as social policy

Of these four, only one – the egalitarian – seems to be primarily to do with benefiting individuals: the others are all various forms of the 'society's benefit' argument. In contrast with the more obviously 'individual's benefit' recommendations of the Russell report, proposals for the Open University *were* implemented, making it a most significant development in the field of adult education.

The case of adult education therefore supports the general conclusion that 'individual's benefit' rationales for education seldom get translated into public policy unless they are linked with justification which relate to 'society's benefit'. This does not mean, of course, that individuals derive no personal benefits from adult education – on the contrary, the benefits may be very considerable. But as public policy, educational initiatives probably stand little chance of attracting public funds if they are justified on these grounds alone.

4.1.4 Securing access to compulsory education

The view of education which sees it as a valuable commodity, of benefit to the individual and properly available to all citizens as a matter of right, leads naturally to a concern with distributive justice. The focus therefore is upon who gets access to how much of this commodity.

Certain features of the educational system seem overtly designed as mechanisms whose main purpose is to ensure that all children have *effective* access to the education which is theoretically available to them, including many 'welfare' provisions (cf. Ch. 2).

The issue of financial support for young people who remain in full-time education after the statutory leaving age is one which raises questions of access to education, since those from poorer families may well feel obliged to leave school and contribute to the family budget at the earliest opportunity. In 1954, *Early Leaving* identified this issue as crucial (cf. sect. 2.2). Although local authorities have permissive powers to make grants on a means-tested basis to enable young people to remain in full-time education, many do not exercise this power except in very limited fashion. The provisions of such grants was the subject of review by the Weaver committee in 1957 and again by the House of Commons Expenditure Committee in 1974. In both cases, the 'individual's benefit' rationale was strongly promoted [doc 41]. The House of Commons committee endorsed the sentiments of the 1944 Act and argued that such allowances should be to enable pupils 'to take advantage without hardship to themselves or their parents of any educational facilities available to them'. Other issues considered by the committee concerned the independence of young people and the limits of parental responsibility. They recommend that all existing allowances should be combined into one Education Maintenance Allowance, that this award be made mandatory, and that the criteria of eligibility should be the same as for free school meals.

The report represents a good example of an attempt to secure access to education solely for the benefit of the recipients: in the light of the foregoing discussion, it will come as no surprise that its recommendations were not implemented. More recently, renewed interest in financial support for young people who do not pass straight from school to work at the age of sixteen is more a product of 'society's benefit' rationales, in that it is related to rising youth unemployment and to attempts to make education more explicitly a preparation for the labour market (cf. sect. 2.5 and 6.2.1). So the example of maintenance allowances illustrates how one item of provision can be appropriated for several different policy ends, although its form may get changed in the process. The same would be true of another interesting measure whose overt purpose is to facilitate access to schooling: the provision of school transport.

Local education authorities were first given the powers to provide transport to school in 1907. Under the 1944 Education Act, section 55, LEAs have the duty (not merely the permissive power) to either provide free transport or to pay the travelling costs of any pupil under compulsory school-leaving age whose home is not within walking distance of the school, except for pupils in private education [doc 4]. Walking distance is defined as two miles for children under the age of eight and three miles for older children, except in the case of children whose physical handicap makes it necessary to waive these regulations. In 1973, the report of the Hodges committee recommended a new basis for the provision of school transport.[16] This entailed abolishing the statutory walking distance and placing the onus on parents to decide whether transport was necessary for their child. This was a response to the many anomalies created by the statutory designation of a 'walking distance', which makes it entirely possible for one child to have free travel while another who catches the bus at the same bus stop has to pay fares, simply because they happen to live on marginally different sides of the two or three-mile limit. Under the Hodges proposals, all parents would be charged a flat-rate fare, with means-tested relief to be available, on criteria of eligibility linked to free school meals.[16(para. 100-03)] The proposals of this report were not implemented, but the original draft of the 1980 Education Act proposed changes which would have eliminated the idea of *free* transport, this time in the interests of public expenditure cuts (cf. sect. 2.5; doc 24).

School transport is an example of a policy measure which seems to be designed to secure the rights of the individual and make them effective: no child can claim his or her right to education if it is impossible to get to a suitable school. The continuing importance of this provision to individual children was highlighted in a report by the Child Poverty Action Group in 1976, compiled as a response to the Hodge's proposals.[17] On the basis of available evidence, collected mainly by CPAG members and a survey conducted by the Advisory Centre for Education, Tunnard argues that some children are absent from school because their parents cannot afford the bus fares; that others send their children to school late or tell them to leave early because cheap fares are available only at off-peak times; that parents' choice of schools is eroded by poverty, since a child can have free travel only if attending the school nearest to home; and that children can be exposed to physical dangers if they have to walk to school [doc 42]. All this amounts to a compelling case for continuing to view the right to free school transport as an important element in securing children's access to the education to which they are entitled, along with certain considerations about individual's welfare, primarily their physical safety. Because of the importance of facilitating access to education, especially for children from poorer families, Tunnard is opposed to the Hodges' recommendations, on the grounds that the costs of fares would still hit poorer families hard, and means tests do not usually help those families most in need.[17(pp. 15-18)]

There are, however, considerations other than individuals' benefit and children's welfare which enter into policy debates about school transport. The notion of the 'statutory walking distance' does not result simply from a benevolent concern that children should not get too tired. As a concept, it dates from the introduction of universal education in 1870, when school boards were given powers to frame regulations about compulsory attendance subject to certain exemptions, one of which was distance. In other words, the idea of the statutory walking distance essentially was an issue of who should be able to claim exemption from attending school: clearly a child could not be compelled to attend if no school was accessible. There was some considerable debate in the 1870s about what constituted a reasonable distance to walk, and the two and three-mile limits date from this time.[18 pp. 35-40] When powers to provide transport were introduced in 1907, this meant effectively that *no* child was to be exempt from attending school: transport is not simply a means of making *access* to education effective, it is also a necessary part of making *compulsion* effective.

Other major considerations in the provision of transport are economic, administrative and political. Again, these date from the 1870s when there was considerable concern about the under-utilisation of capital if school places were not filled: 'Unfilled school places represented under-utilised capital, and for some the remedy was in direct compulsory attendance and the largest possible catchment areas. Legal definitions of walking distance are, for reasons such as this, always suspect'.[18(p. 35)] A rather different kind of economic consideration was apparent in the 1970s, and led to the setting up of the Hodges committee: pressure from local authorities to alter transport regulations as a means of saving money.[19(pp. 51-8)] In 1979, transport – like school meals – was treated as a 'peripheral' area of education, where public funds could be saved (cf. sect. 2.5). It is ironical that transport should be treated as peripheral, since it is an essential quid pro quo of compulsion. What these changes in fact represent is an attempt to compel parents to send their children to school and then get them to pay for the privilege. Hutton argues that the kind of changes proposed by Hodges, especially the introduction of a flat-rate charge for transport, would have the effect simply of transferring this part of educational expenditure from ratepayers and taxpayers to parents, and that there seems no coherent reason for doing this. He concludes that 'from an economic standpoint there is no a priori argument for reducing school transport or introducing charges'. [19(p. 57)]

The political considerations have to do primarily with the position of rural schools and especially of church schools, which were a major consideration in the negotiations prior to the 1944 Act (cf. sect. 2.1). As Lord Butler put it in his contribution to the debate in 1979:

> It seems very peculiar, but this issue of transport was, if not an integral part – as I said in my Second Reading speech – at any rate a vital part of the concordat or settlement of 1944. Why was that? It simply was that the denominations and all those partners involved in that settlement were given the assurance that their children would be taken to school [doc 24].

The feeling that introduction of charges would break faith with the parties to that settlement was further reinforced by the belief that in some cases further changes in schooling, especially comprehensive reorganisation, had only been agreed because of existing transport arrangements: 'the right reverend Prelate, the Bishop of Lancaster, has written to me saying that he only agreed to the reorganisation in Lancashire, provided that the right of transport remained. That is only ten years ago, so there is no doubt that there is before your Lordships, and certainly before my own conscience, what really amounts to a double pledge.'[20] Transport arrangements, of course, are vital to the continued existence of denominational schools, because their catchment areas are usually much larger than state schools. Providing for their needs was a vital part of securing the basis of the 1944 Act, and those needs continue to receive sympathetic treatment. A letter from the Secretary of State to CEOs, dated December 1981, encouraged them to be flexible in their funding of transport arrangements, especially in helping to defray the costs of children who attend voluntary schools on religious grounds, even where they are not statutorily obliged to give such support – a very interesting move at a time when progressive cuts in the education budgets of local authorities were being implemented.

This example of school transport is an illustration of the extent to which concerns with issues of individuals' rights to education are embodied in policies which secure access. Although it is clearly the case that free transport *does* help to secure access, the 'citizenship rights' rationale in fact slots into a set of policy considerations which are to do with quite different issues about the basis upon which education is provided. When all of these considerations point in the same direction, it is clearly difficult to disentangle what should be regarded as the 'true' basis for the provision. When they conflict, however, it appears that the rights and benefits of the individual come a rather poor second to the considerations of political and economic policy. This happened in 1979, when attempts were made to introduce charges: the fact that charges were *not* implemented has comparatively little to do with the likely effects upon children and much more to do with political considerations about disrupting the basis of the 1944 settlement. Had the proposals *been* implemented, they would have resolved the conflict between securing access to education and cutting public expenditure by shifting the cost of transport to parents. This amounts to pressurizing parents from both ends by first compelling them to send their children to school and then compelling them to pay for doing so – hardly a policy in which the 'rights' of citizens are a significant consideration.

4.2 MEETING NEEDS AND SOLVING PROBLEMS: EDUCATION FOR THE RECIPIENTS' BENEFIT

One common definition of social policy is that it is a collective response – or, more narrowly, a response by the state – to meeting individual needs and solving social problems. A classic statement of this approach can be found in Titmuss' work, where he defines social policy as 'society's response as it identifies or fails to identify social needs and problems'.[21(p. 22)]

Although the solving of social problems often seems to imply wider *social* change – for example in the distribution of resources – the discussion in this chapter is concerned with the many attempts to solve social problems which focus upon individuals, and which seek to produce change either in individuals themselves or in their circumstances. The 'needs' and the 'problems' perspectives share a common focus on individual welfare as a central goal of social policy, and are characteristic of the view of social policy which George and Wilding call 'reluctant collectivist', where the role of the state in welfare is 'to abolish avoidable ills; the role is to be reactive rather than promotional; it is problem centred'.[1(p. 58)]

In so far as facets of educational provision can be seen as social policy, in this sense, the idea of using education to meet individual needs and to solve social problems is another version of providing education for the recipients' benefits. The focus, however, is somewhat different from citizens' rights. The needs-and-problems rationale seeks more explicitly to change and improve people's circumstances, not just to give them their rights. Perhaps more importantly, it also implies provision based on difference *between* individuals, rather than the 'rights' emphasis, which tends to suggest giving everyone the same. Such differences need not rest upon the assessment of the individual circumstances of every child: socially defined categories of children (for example, the handicapped) are seen as having particular educational and other needs. In this 'problem-oriented' sense, education can be seen as only one part of a broader social policy strategy for solving particular 'social problems'.

The remainder of this chapter will examine more closely the concepts of 'individual needs' and of 'social problems', and discuss some of the ways in which they have been applied in the context of education.

4.2.1 Education and the concept of need

The concept of need is one of the major categories within which discussions of social policy conventionally operate.[22a, b] It is, however, a notoriously slippery concept. On first sight it appears to refer to inherent features of the human condition and sometimes gets used as if 'human needs' could be unproblematically identified. It is essentially, however, a political concept: identification of need always implies some claim on resources, and claims pursued on behalf of certain 'needs' are more successful than others.[23(pp. 71-82)]

The most influential discussion of the meaning of 'need' in social policy is Bradshaw's taxonomy of social need,[24] in which he identifies four different meanings: normative needs (where a professional, administrator or social scientist defines who is in need with reference to some 'desirable' standard); felt need (need is equated with want); expressed need (felt need turned into a demand); and comparative need (a measure obtained by asking whether people in similar circumstances are in receipt of similar services). How far can any or all of these four meanings of 'need' be applied to education? As far as felt and expressed need are concerned, one could argue that the history of the labour movement's involvement in pressing for universal elementary education is an example of both, although the 'need' here is felt and expressed by parents, not by the potential consumer. However, once education becomes both universal and compulsory, need in this sense is less obviously applicable.

'Need' in the other two senses – normative and comparative – has been clearly present as a rationale in various important instances of educational policy-making. Although not expressed in this language, the idea of comparative need has been implicit in all educational policies concerned with territorial injustice in education. The recognition that there are considerable regional and geographical variations in the educational facilities to which a child has access leads quite naturally to proposals for eliminating such variations.[25] The application of the concept of educational priority areas (cf. sect. 5.3.1) is a prime example of such a policy. Further, the whole concern with the poor access of the working classes to grammar school education under a selective system (cf. Ch. 2 and sect. 5.2) can be seen as an application of the principle of comparative need, leading to attempts (albeit largely unsuccessful) to meet the unmet needs of the working classes through comprehensive reorganisation. The application of the concept of the need in a comparative sense implies that resources will be redistributed, or at least remedial action will be taken to make good the unmet needs of certain people.

'Need' in the normative sense has been a very important concept in educational policy thinking but again the language of need has seldom been used. The attempt in the 1944 Education Act to provide educational facilities appropriate to different 'ages, abilities and aptitudes' suggests a notion of different educational needs. As applied in the context of the tripartite system, the nature of different needs essentially was decided in individual cases by professionals, that is, by teachers and administrators, and through the use of apparently objective tests (cf. sect. 2.2). Access to many aspects of educational provision which lie outside the compulsory sector entails a professional or administrative assessment of 'need': as, for example, when educational welfare officers become involved in assessing a child's 'need' for nursery education.[26(p. 42)] Because the recipients of education are children, who are usually seen as being incapable of defining their own 'needs', there is wide scope for professionals, administrators and policy-makers to act as the definers.

It is interesting in this context to consider the case of special education, now called the education of children with 'special needs'. The concept of need was first used in relation to special education in 1946 [27(p. 72)] but it was the report of the Warnock committee which promoted the concept of 'special need' as the key one which should govern provision in this area. The Warnock committee was set up in 1973 to enquire into the education of handicapped children, and it reported in 1978.[28] Its recommendations included issues about the indentification of children in need of special education and a major theme was the integration of handicapped children into 'ordinary' schools. Some of the issues were taken up in a White Paper published in 1980.[29]

The discussion of special needs in paragraph 1.4 of the Warnock report is an excellent example of the use of the concept of need in education [doc 43]. Although the 'goals', of education are the same for every child, the 'needs' of each child in relation to these goals vary from one to another: different individuals need different kinds of help in progressing towards these goals of personal development and the capacity to operate as an independent adult. So needs appear to be defined on a very individualistic basis and education as solely for the benefit of the recipients. The White Paper explicitly accepted the Warnock definition of special needs.[29(para. 23)]

There is, however, more to it than that. When the Warnock report clarifies what special needs consist of, it identifies the following 'needs' (of which any individual child may have more than one): special means of access; special curriculum; special social and emotional climate.[28(para. 3.19)] This entails, as Tomlinson points out, a definition of need couched solely in terms of provision.[27(p. 75)] Although meeting special needs is presented as a benevolent good for individual children, Tomlinson argues that the concept of 'needs' acts often as little more than rhetoric which rationalises the shape and character of special educational provision [doc 44]. Since it was first used in 1946, she argues, the concept of 'need' was taken up by philosophers, who played down the question of who decides needs, and by psychologists, who are accustomed to thinking in individualistic terms.[27(pp. 72-3)] In fact, since 'needs' are always relative, there are crucial issues to be raised about who has the power to define them, and an unquestioning acceptance of the notion of 'need' masks this. In Tomlinson's view, the expansion of special education can be seen as being largely in the interests of the professionals who work within this system, and in the interests of controlling 'troublesome' children in such a way as to prevent their disrupting the operation of the 'normal' schooling system. Certainly, the way in which the concept of 'need' is applied here raises some fundamental questions about need in its normative sense. The very process of professionals' assessment and allocation to specific services should lead one to examine carefully the basis of such judgements, and whose interests they serve.

The example of special education highlights some of the issues which have to be addressed in a critical examination of the concept of need as it applies to education. The question of who defines need (applicable especially to 'need' in the comparative or the normative sense) is obviously an important question, since needs are always potentially subject to redefinition. Bradshaw suggests that need in the normative sense can be 'tainted with a charge of paternalism' [24(p. 72)] and this certainly would apply in education, where the charge of imposing middle-class norms upon working-class children can be made to stick fairly easily (see next section).

A further range of issues arise from asking what hides behind the rhetoric of need. Tomlinson suggests that, in the case of special education, it masks the interests of professionals but that also it may provide a basis for the development of a new tripartite system, in which special education forms the bottom rung.[27(Ch. 8)] In examples outside the field of special education the rhetoric of 'need' seems to place a fairly thin veneer over attempts to exert various types of control. An example of this is to be found in the study by Johnson *et al.*,[30] where a key concept is that education is an exercise in meeting pupils' needs. Their study of secondary school teachers produced the typology of pupil needs to be found in document 45. Although the authors do not elaborate the point, by asking teachers to identify needs implicitly they are using the concept in its normative sense. The 'needs' which teachers identify include items such as the 'need' for moral guidance, for motivation, and even for control. It seems unlikely that these are 'needs' which pupils themselves would feel or express. This example makes it very clear that the rhetoric of need in a normative sense can be simply a legitimation of some feature of education which is imposed in the interests of the school, of the teachers, or of 'society', but certainly not at the behest of the recipients.

4.2.2 Education and problem-solving

The problem-solving approach to social policy is one which appears in several guises, and perhaps has the most immediate popular appeal as an understandable definition of what social policy is meant to be about.[31] There is, however, an important distinction to be made between problem-solving which attributes the 'cause' of the alleged problem to specific attributes of the individuals concerned, and problem-solving which analyses the issues in relation to social, economic and political processes. The latter can lead to proposals for quite ambitious social engineering (cf. Ch. 5), but the former tends to produce proposals for changing those people who 'have' the problem in question, who are assumed to be 'in some way a special group, a group that is *different* from the population in general'.[32]

This 'social pathology' approach, which attributes the problems identified to peculiarities of the individuals concerned, has characterised much of British social policy in the nineteenth and twentieth centuries. As Marshall puts it: 'According to the old orthodoxy, the prime cause of social distress and destitution was to be found in the persons or individual circumstances of the victims, and it was usually identifiable as moral weakness'. [33(p. 23)] The key distinction to be made here is (in C. Wright Mills' terms) between 'personal troubles' and 'public issues'. 'Personal troubles' are private matters of individual biography, while 'public issues' are matters of social organisation and social structure. It is crucial, argues Mills, to be able to make the links between the two. Thus, if one person in a large city is unemployed, it might be proper to treat that entirely as a 'personal trouble' and look for its resolution in the character and skills of the individual; but if a significant proportion of the population is unemployed, then clearly it is a 'public issue' as well as personal trouble for the individuals concerned, and 'possible solutions require us to consider the economic and political institutions of the society, and not merely the personal situation and character of a scatter of individuals'. [34(p. 15)]

The same kinds of themes have been important in social policy as applied to education. One example of this would be the interest taken in the notion of the cycle of deprivation as an explanation of why certain children seem virtually destined to do badly at school. Major research was initiated into this topic by Sir Keith Joseph when he was Secretary of State for Social Services in the early 1970s and, as

Education as social policy

Robinson points out 'a thesis so close to the heart of government needs careful examination'.[35(p. 33)] The essence of the idea of the cycle of deprivation is that problems of poverty and associated 'maladjustments' persist because they are transmitted from one generation to the next. Robinson argues that Sir Keith Joseph's view of this confuses individualist and structuralist explanations. On the one hand, Joseph suggests that the circumstances which produce the 'cycle' are to be found in social and economic arrangements (e.g. low income, poor housing), but the logic of this position is not followed through into policy proposals. These derive instead from an essentially individualist view, in which the real causes are located in the social pathology of the poor, and solutions lie in changing their lifestyle:

> The logic of the structuralist position is not followed through . . . only passing attention being given to what would be an effective policy of income support, or of security in housing and employment, and no consideration to the necessary relationship between wealth and poverty. The prescription advocated has two ingredients: family planning and preparation for parenthood. Policy must be directed towards getting the deprived to curb their fecundity and to teaching them how to meet the social, emotional and intellectual needs of their children.[35(pp. 33-4)]

This mixture of individualist and structuralist approaches to problem-solving (with the emphasis tending to be on the individualist when specific proposals are formulated) is evident in a major example of the problem-solving approach to social policy as applied in the field of education: that is, the analysis of the reasons for working-class children's 'failure' in the school system, and proposals to overcome it. The 'cycle of deprivation' of course is one version of this. I shall not attempt to re-evaluate the very considerable body of evidence on the issue of working-class failure, but rather to look at it as illustration of the implications of promoting social policies based on the concept of problem-solving, in its various forms.

Although much evidence was already accumulating from academic research,[36] the Newsom and Plowden reports were primarily responsible for focusing public policy upon the educationally 'deprived' (cf. sect. 2.3 and 2.4; docs 11, 12, 16, 17). The discussion in Newsom (about children of average and below-average ability) includes both the highly individualistic notion of 'low ability' and the implied structuralist approach of attempting to relate school performance to other features of pupils' lives. When it comes to proposals, however, the report recommends measures which concentrate on how to educate individual children more effectively. It argues that the educational problems of less able pupils are no different in slum schools from other schools, but that schools in the slums do require 'special consideration if they are to have a fair chance of making the best of their pupils'. The measures recommended are better staffing ratios and incentives for the most able teachers to work in these schools.[37(paras 67,68)]

These proposals foreshadow the Plowden report's recommendations about educational priority areas [doc 17]. While Plowden did firmly locate the causes of educational failure in the social and economic circumstances of the children who fail, rather than in their inherent incapacities, its recommendations still concentrate on proposals for educating them more effectively, by giving the schools sufficient resources to provide a compensating environment.[38] The way to solve the 'problem' of educational failure, in other words, is to be more effective in changing the children themselves; but an alternative approach to this 'problem' would be to propose more thorough-going changes in those economic and social features of children's lives which seem to produce the 'failure'; or to examine closely why it is that we have an educational system whose major aim is to designate some people as 'successes' and others as 'failures'.

These are precisely the kinds of issues which have been taken up subsequently by writers on this topic.[39a-d] Most writers take up one or other of two broad positions, set out very clearly by Woodhead in the extract in document 46. The major difference is between explanations of working-class failure which locate the deficiences in the children themselves and their families, and those which locate them in the schools and the educational system. The former model leads to a policy of compensatory education (of the type recommended by Plowden) which attempts to overcome the disadvantages inherent in the children's background by additional education, specially tailored to these children's needs. The alternative view, less commonly argued, sees compensatory strategies really as an attempt to impose uniform middle-class standards and values. Instead, it is argued, the 'problem' of working-class failure lies in the schools, where middle-class values are rewarded and working-class culture is devalued. One outcome of the logic of this position is a radical, 'deschooling' critique, developed initially by Illich.[40a, b]

The less radical implications of this position are that schools and teachers must change so that the education which they offer builds upon the experiences of all children and does not favour those with a middle-class upbringing. This distinction between a view of working-class culture as 'deficient' and one which regards it as merely 'different' is reflected in Rutter and Madge's authoritative review of the evidence, funded under Keith Joseph's transmitted deprivation initiative. They conclude:

> . . . that social circumstances can and do influence children's intellectual development. What is much less clear is which aspects of the social environment are most important in this connection . . . In terms of the linguistic environment in working-class homes, it is not so much that it is deficient in comparison with the middle-class home, but rather that it is different in a way which puts a child at an educational disadvantage.[39c(p. 114)]

The 'deficit, and 'difference' explanations of working-class failure are implicit in the two different approaches to social policy as problem-solving identified at the beginning of this discussion. The deficit model implies an individualistic, social pathology explanation, and therefore leads naturally to proposals for solutions which depend upon making changes in the people who 'have' the problem. That approach has been importantly challenged by William Ryan in his influential discussion of poverty in the United States.[41] Ryan argues that the dominant perspective in US welfare programmes has been one which treated social problems as social pathology and that this 'problem' perspective embodies class interests and interest in maintaining the existing social order. In this perspective, deviation from dominant social norms becomes constituted as failed or incomplete socialisation, thus ignoring a range of highly relevant factors such as the distribution of incomes. This, argues Ryan, is tantamount to 'blaming the victim' for his or her own fate. When applied to education [doc 47], blaming the victim entails designating certain children as 'culturally deprived', and then producing policies designed to change, manipulate or treat the child. Although these may be 'cloaked in kindness and concern', and may arise from a quite genuine, liberal desire for social welfare, their effect is to leave entirely untouched the processes in the schools which produce this 'deprivation', and to preserve the status quo in education.

The idea of 'victim-blaming' is a powerful tool with which to approach a number of policy initiatives in the field of education. Consider, for example, the important DES report on the education of immigrants,[42] which proposed what is, in many ways, quite a liberal approach to this topic, arguing for example, that immigrant children should not be treated as inherently problematic just because of their immigrant or ethnic status. At the same time, however, it does constitute a fairly sophisticated version of victim-blaming [doc 19]. It is said that immigrant children 'find their way' into lower streams and remedial classes, and that their education ought to be characterised by the pupils making special adjustments to meet their particular situation. The focus therefore is on the pupils' inherent differences from the white 'norm' and upon the need for *them* – rather than the schools – to change.

The whole 'victim-blaming' thrust of the deficit model of failure overlooks the material underpinning of cultural deprivation. Many studies have demonstrated clear – although not necessarily straightforward – links between poor educational performance and material deprivation.[39a, d] Working-class children are not inevitably condemned to fail at school and there are many examples of working-class parents who have successfully mitigated the effects of their class background through 'a high level of involvement with their children in intellectually stimulating activities . . . and an effective interest in their education'.[39d(p. 354)] The recognition that it is possible, in individual instances, to modify the links between class and education performances does not undermine the overall strength of that link, which has remained almost as consistent since 1944 as it was before.[43] Equally, one cannot avoid the question: why does the school system favour children (whatever the occupations of their parents) whose upbringing has been handled in this way? That question leads right away from a focus upon education for the benefit of individuals and into discussions around the 'society's benefit' theme, most importantly to consideration of the arguments about education and social reproduction (cf. sect. 6.2).

An alternative approach, which shifts the 'blame' from the individual to educational institutions, is also supported by a considerable literature. This demonstrates the contribution which schools and teachers make to the 'failure' of certain children (see [39c(pp. 123–30)] for a summary of these studies). A recent example, which also serves to illustrate the limitations of this approach from the point of view of social policy, is the study conducted by Rutter and his colleagues of secondary schools and their effects on children.[44] On the basis of their research they argue that, even after taking account of different intakes, secondary schools vary markedly on measures of pupils' behaviour, attendance, examination success and delinquency. They conclude that schools themselves do seem to be able to make a difference to the outcome of the educational experience of their pupils. The researchers identified a number of features of the ways in which teachers manage both classrooms and individual pupils, and also point to the general 'ethos' of the school, as being significantly related to these outcomes. The implication of their findings is that 'schools constitute one major area of influence, and one which is susceptible to change.'[44(p. 182)]

This study has been much quoted and also criticised on a number of grounds, including failure to control for major aspects of family background or pupils' studies, and failure to develop the concept of 'school ethos' in such a way that its effects could actually be tested. [45(pp. 3–20)] None the less, one implication of being able to identify practices associated with 'success' and 'failure' is that schools characterised by the latter should be able to substitute more successful practices. As a matter of policy, however, the issue is not that simple. Certain schools and certain teachers may indeed be able to change, but it is impossible for *all* to do so, since a central feature of the educational system involves an exercise in ranking pupils so that some are more successful than others. The corollary of this is that some pupils – indeed quite a large number of pupils – must always (in comparative terms) be failures, and this is necessarily true in any such competitive system. Any policy which aimed to change educational outcomes by changing practices in schools could aim at best to ensure that success and failure was no longer linked to class background, but to some other criterion which appears morally more justifiable, such as a notion of inherent individual ability. That is, working-class pupils would be enabled to compete more effectively for the accolade of 'success'. An educational system in which *no* pupils were designated failures would be a very different type of system.

The argument that schools are at fault in the production of working-class 'failure' does not always lead to the conclusion that working-class pupils have to be enabled to compete better within the existing system. Indeed, much of the work which challenged the notion of cultural deprivation, and replaced it with cultural difference, suggested a quite different conclusion, not too far removed from the 'deschooling' critique. An important example of this is to be found in Keddie's work,[46] where it is argued that ideas about who is 'educable' themselves are socially constructed. A recognition that each child has experience of a distinctive culture, with its own structures of thought, should lead to a positive valuing of all cultures within the school and a 'willingness to recognise and value the life experience that every child brings to school'.[46(p. 19)] The implication of this position would be a radically altered educational system in which very different types of educational experience were offered to different groups of children, based upon the cultural and social experience which they bring to the school.

That is clearly a view of education in which considerations of the recipients' benefits are uppermost, but it is possible to argue that such changes would not necessarily serve the real interests of working-class children, if implemented. Robinson [doc 48] argues that Keddie's position depends upon a relativist approach which over-romanticises the lot of the deprived and 'attacks the irritants in the system when the basic structure is at fault'. In his view, one cannot just reform the curriculum for the disadvantaged if other structures remain unchanged, because that in the end puts them in an even worse position. His own solution is that one has to pursue broader strategies of social justice in the long term, whilst ensuring that the poor get into a better position to compete within the system as it exists now.

Robinson's argument is interesting, in that he demonstrates the problems in over-simplifying the distinction between the deficit and the difference models of failure, and of too crude a presentation of the deficit model, which leads to its immediate rejection. Rather, he argues, we should consider seriously whether some cultural forms *are* represented not only in schools but also in structures of employment and other social institutions. If pupils leave school lacking, for example, basic skills of literacy and numeracy, they are in a very real sense deprived of the possibility of full participation in social, economic and political life.[35(pp. 42-3)] Even if we recognise that no single type of cultural experience is inherently more valuable than any other, that need not lead us to reject all attempts to make good the relative disadvantages with which some children enter school. In the short term, at least, such changes may be an essential precondition of modifying the links between class and educational outcomes. In the long term, more radical changes may be possible, but Robinson is quite clear [doc 48] that this implies change well beyond the confines of the educational system.

Thus the kind of problem-centred approach to social policy discussed in this chapter – where solving problems is seen as an exercise in producing change in the lives of individuals but not necessarily in social structure – can only be taken to a certain point before it begins to raise issues which imply a much more thorough-going type of social engineering. The 'reluctant collectivist', who seeks to be reactive rather than promotional, to abolish avoidable ills but to maintain the status quo, in a sense almost inevitably finds that the exercise is a contradiction in terms. In the case of education at any rate, the 'ill' of working-class failure may only ultimately be avoidable if the status quo *does* change – and perhaps quite radically.

4.3 CONCLUSION

The arguments and evidence reviewed in this chapter have concerned those facets of education which appear to be oriented to the benefit of their recipients. Whilst it undoubtedly is true that some recipients *do* benefit from measures to secure their access to education (e.g. financial support or provision of transport), from the provision of adult education or of special schools, such measures seem seldom to be provided solely in their interests, nor do they necessarily serve those interests in more than a limited fashion.

A mixture of interests is represented in measures based overtly on the rationales of rights, needs and problems. Citizenship is clearly double-edged, because 'rights' are also taken to entail 'duties'. The rationale of 'needs' sometimes can be little more than a rhetoric which masks and legitimates the interests of professional groups, or the structures of control in schools. Moreoever, measures designed for the benefit of the recipients seem likely to attract significant support from state funding only if they are also promoting some other kind of interest which derives from a 'society's benefit' rather than an 'individual's benefit' rationale. Measures which are conceived initially – and may continue to be promoted by some parties – as solely for the benefit of individuals can be appropriated to serve other interests, and perhaps become subtly changed in the process. Maintenance allowances may facilitate access to education but, in a slightly different form, they can be the means of producing a labour force which serves the needs of capital; adult education may be able to offer the skills to enable the working classes to be better organised in securing their own interests, but it also can be the means of encouraging them to be 'responsible' and compliant citizens.

The interests of the recipients may be served quite well on an individual basis, but rather badly on a collective basis, by measures both based on the 'rights' and 'problems' rationales. The problem-solving approach leads to limited and possibly ineffective reform if the problems and their solutions are located in the individuals who 'have' the problem. Meanwhile, the status quo remains unchanged. Similarly, the notion of citizens' rights quite explicitly does not challenge underlying structural inequalities. Measures of this sort may well be the means which enable individuals to 'succeed' in the educational system, and thus change their own position in the structures of occupation, wealth and power with which the educational system is intimately linked; yet such measures make virtually no impact on those structures themselves.

NOTES AND REFERENCES

1. GEORGE, V. and WILDING, P. (1976), *Ideology and Social Welfare*. Routledge & Kegan Paul: London.
2. ROOM, G. (1979), *The Sociology of Welfare*. Blackwell: Oxford.
3. (a) PARKER, J. (1975), *Social Policy and Citizenship*. Macmillan: London; (b) MISHRA, R. (1977), *Society and Social Policy*. Macmillan: London.
4. MARSHALL. T. H. (1950), *Citizenship and Social Class and Other Essays*. CUP: Cambridge.
5. PINKER, R. (1971), *Social Theory and Social Policy*. Heinemann: London; pp. 210–11.
6. CENTRE FOR CONTEMPORARY CULTURAL STUDIES (1981), *Unpopular Education: Schooling and Social Democracy in England since 1944*. Hutchinson: London.
7. *Special Educational Needs* (1978), Cmnd. 7212. HMSO: London.
8. SIMON, B. (1965), *Education and the Labour Movement, 1870–1920*. Lawrence & Wishart: London.
9. ROGERS, R. (1980), *Crowther to Warnock*. Heinemann: London.
10. DEPARTMENT OF EDUCATION AND SCIENCE (1973), *Adult Education: a Plan for Development*, The Russell Report. HMSO: London.
11. BARKER, R. (1972), *Education and Politics 1900–1951: A Study of the Labour Party*. Clarendon: Oxford.
12. LOVETT, T. (1975), *Adult Education, Community Development and the Working Class*. Ward Lock: London.
13. PATTERSON, R. (1979), *Values, Education and the Adult*. Routledge & Kegan Paul: London.
14. TUNSTALL, J. (1974), *The Open University Opens*. Routledge & Kegan Paul: London.
15. HALL, R., LAND, H., PARKER, R. and WEBB, A. (1975), *Change, Choice and Conflict in Social Policy*. Heinemann: London.
16. DEPARTMENT OF EDUCATION AND SCIENCE (1973), *School Transport*, The Hodges Report. HMSO: London.
17. TUNNARD, J. (1976), *Taken for a Ride*, Welfare in Action: a Child Poverty Action Group Report. CPAG: London.
18. HOUGHTON-EVANS, W. and CATENBY, R. (1979), 'Walking distance to school and legislation in the U.K.: an historical investigation', *Journal of Educational Administration and History*, Vol. XI, No. 2.
19. HUTTON, J. (1976), 'The economics of school transport', *Social and Economic Administration*, Vol. 10, No. 1.
20. *Parliamentary Debates (Lords)*, Vol. 406, 1979–80, Col. 1221.

21. TITMUSS (1974), *Social Policy: an Introduction*. Allen & Unwin: London.

22. (a) FORDER, A. (1974), *Concepts in Social Administration: a Framework for Analysis*. Routledge & Kegan Paul: London, Ch. 3; (b) JONES, K., BROWN, J. and BRADSHAW, J. (1978), *Issues in Social Policy*. Routledge & Kegan Paul: London, Ch. 2.

23. DEMAIN, J. (1980), 'Compensatory education and social policy', in M. Craft, J. Raynor and L. Cohen (eds) *Linking Home and School*, 3rd edn. Harper & Row: London.

24. BRADSHAW, J. (1972), 'A taxonomy of social need', in G. McLachlan (ed.), *Problems and Progress in Medical Care*. OUP: Oxford.

25. TAYLOR, G. and AYRES, N. (1969), *Born and Bred Unequal*. Longman: London.

26. MACMILLAN, K. (1977), *Education Welfare*. Longman: London.

27. TOMLINSON, S. (1982), *A Sociology of Special Education*. Routledge & Kegan Paul: London.

28. *Special Educational Needs* (1978), The Warnock Report, HMSO: London.

29. DEPARTMENT OF EDUCATION AND SCIENCE (1980), *Special Needs in Education*. Cmnd. 7996. HMSO: London.

30. JOHNSON, D., RANSOM, E., PACKWOOD, T., BOWDEN, K. and KOGAN, M. (1980), *Secondary Schools and the Welfare Network*. Allen & Unwin: London.

31. FINCH, J. (1982), 'The sociology of welfare', in R. Burgess (ed.), *Exploring Society*. British Sociological Association: London.

32. RYAN, W. (1971), *Blaming the Victim*. Orbach & Chambers: London.

33. MARSHALL, T. H. (1965), *Social Policy*. Hutchinson: London.

34. MILLS, C. WRIGHT (1970), *The Sociological Imagination*. Penguin: Harmondsworth.

35. ROBINSON, P. (1976), *Education and Poverty*. Methuen: London.

36. SILVER, H. (1973), *Equal Opportunities in Education*. Methuen: London.

37. MINISTRY OF EDUCATION (1963), *Half our Future*, The Newsom Report. HMSO: London.

38. DEPARTMENT OF EDUCATION AND SCIENCE (1967), *Children and their Primary Schools*, The Plowden Report. HMSO: London, especially Ch. 5.

39. (a) CHAZAN, M. (ed) (1973), *Compensatory Education*. Butterworth: London; (b) WOODHEAD, M. (1976), *Intervening in Disadvantage*. NFER: Slough; (c) RUTTER, M. and MADGE, N.

(1977), *Cycles of Disadvantage*. Heinemann: London; (d) PILLING, D. and PRINGLE, M. KELLMER (1978), *Controversial Issues in Child Development*. Elek: London.

40. (a) ILLICH, I. (1973), *Deschooling Society*. Penguin: Harmondsworth; (b) LISTER, I. (1973), *Deschooling*. CUP: Cambridge.

41. RYAN, W. (1971), *Blaming the Victim*. Orbach & Chambers: London.

42. DEPARTMENT OF EDUCATION AND SCIENCE (1971), *The Education of Immigrants*. Education Survey No. 13. HMSO: London.

43. HALSEY, A., HEATH, A. and RIDGE, J. (1980), *Origins and Destinations: Family, Class and Education in Modern Britain*. Clarendon: Oxford.

44. RUTTER, M., MAUGHAN, B., MORTIMORE, P. and OUSTON, J. (1979), *Fifteen Thousand Hours: Secondary Schools and their Effects on Children*. Open Books: London.

45. HEATH, A. and CLIFFORD, P. (1980), 'The seventy thousand hours that Rutter left out', *Oxford Review of Education*, Vol. 6, No. 1.

46. KEDDIE, N. (ed.) (1973), *Tinker, Tailor . . . the Myth of Cultural Deprivation*. Penguin: Harmondsworth.

Chapter five
EDUCATION AND SOCIAL ENGINEERING

5.1 INTRODUCTION

In the last chapter it was suggested that a 'problem-solving' approach to social policy (focusing on the alleged needs and problems of individuals) cannot proceed very far without beginning to attempt to effect changes in wider social and economic structures, not merely in the individuals who 'have' the problem. Education has provided some major examples of social policies of this sort, referred to here as social engineering. The essential characteristics of these strategies are that the state assumes an active, interventionist stance in which it takes initiatives to bring about social change, rather than a more passive stance in which it simply responds to problems and needs; it is promotional rather than reactive. The aim is to change the shape of social, economic and political life, promoting reform through peaceful, democratic means.

There are three main types of social engineering which can be pursued in and through education. Although many actual policies contain elements of more than one, it is useful to keep them conceptually distinct.

1. *Change in education itself, designed to change educational outcomes*. An example of this would be one argument which was commonly used for abolishing the eleven-plus examination: to ensure that 'late developers' should not be excluded from a more academic form of education. In an indirect way, this kind of strategy may eventually produce changes beyond the educational system, but that is not its overt aim. Social engineering of this type tends to concentrate upon attempting to change the position of individuals within social and economic structures, rather than changing the structures themselves.

2. *Changes in other areas of social policy, designed to change educational*

outcomes. The ends of this type of social engineering are the same as in the first type, but the means are different. An example would be programmes for urban renewal in inner cities, based on the assumption that improved housing conditions and physical environment will enable children in such areas to perform better at school.

3. *Changes in education designed to produce social change outside the educational system*. An example of that would be the argument that girls need to be given the kind of education which will enable them ultimately to break out of the inferior social position to which women are assigned; or that working-class children need to be given, through education, the weapons with which to wage the class struggle more effectively. Clearly this is the most ambitious of the three types, because its horizons are widest and because usually it involves trying to change social structures themselves, rather than simply changing the position of individuals within them.

At the end of this chapter, the discussion returns to and evaluates these three types of social engineering in the context of education.

Any social engineering strategy contains assumptions both about the *ends* to which such policies are put and about the *means* of achieving them; and the two can be treated as conceptually separate. Typically in Britain, social engineering has meant action on the part of a benign state to create a more just society, in the interests of those social groups who hitherto have been the underprivileged, the disadvantaged, the dispossessed. In this classic social democratic view of welfare, education has been seen as an important means of producing greater social equality (cf. Chs 1 and 2). As Halsey has put it: 'To find a strategy for educational roads to equality! That has been the central theme of educational discussion from the beginning of the twentieth century . . . the underlying question is whether, and in what circumstances, education can change society.'[1(p. 3)]

Making this distinction between ends and means helps to clarify the issues raised by the major critics of social engineering through education: the authors of the Black Papers and associated works (cf. sect. 2.5), usually represented as a right-wing attack. One of the ten basic points of the Black Paper platform is that 'Schools are for schooling, not social engineering.'[2(p. 1)] More recently, Rhodes Boyson has set out his critique of social engineering in a ministerial speech in which he argues that too much has been expected of education which, he says, cannot be a social cure-all [doc 49]. But while such critics use 'social engineering' as a term of abuse, they are really attacking the ends to which it is usually put (i.e. to produce a more egalitarian society) rather than social engineering as a method, which indeed they themselves endorse, in so far as they wish to see an educational system which will reinforce and perpetuate the status quo.[3(pp. 148-9)]

The ends to which social engineering strategies are put clearly is a matter of political choices, and the ends sought need not necessarily be benign. For many years, the English education system has been organised so as to ensure that people who can afford to pay can more effectively secure the best form of education for their children, thus successfully excluding the children of the poor from the elite jobs. Heath has shown that boys who have attended the major public schools are still disproportionately likely to secure the most elite jobs and that the influence of school connections is still strong, especially where they work as self-employed professionals.[4(pp.472-4)] Similarly, former pupils of direct grant schools have been very successful in securing jobs, especially as higher grade officials and administrators. In so far as the state allows these forms of schooling to continue – indeed actively supports them with financial assistance (cf. sect. 2.4 and 2.5) – this constitutes a form of social engineering in which the ends are to produce a more *un*equal society.

The main sections of this chapter concentrate upon two of the most important social engineering strategies which have been applied in the English educational context: redistribution, and its important variant, positive discrimination. Finally, the discussion returns to the three types of social engineering and evaluates them in the light of the examples considered in this chapter.

5.2 REDISTRIBUTION OF REWARDS

5.2.1 Models of redistribution

Redistribution has been one of the notions central to the development of the British welfare state. It has meant action on the part of governments to redistribute valued goods to those sections of the population whose access to them had hitherto been more limited. Like the 'citizens' rights' approach (cf. sect. 4.1.2), redistribution derives from principles of equality and justice. But whereas 'rights' can be implemented without necessarily making any change at all in social and economic structures, or indeed to the individual's position within them [doc 36], redistribution explicitly sets out to make such changes. As far as education is concerned, the principles of redistribution has been important for two reasons: first, because education can itself be seen as a valued good; second, because education is a mechanism for controlling access to other valued goods (primarily through the occupational structure). The redistribution of educational opportunities therefore would mean indirectly the redistribution of other valued goods.

The concepts of distribution and redistribution are so central to much writing on social policy that some authors would count them as a key to defining what constitutes social policy.[5(p. 239)] These issues are particularly important in approaches to social policy which derive from the standpoint of social justice.[6(Ch. 4)] Certain kinds of measures concerned with distribution were discussed in the previous chapter: maintenance allowances and the provision of transport are measures designed to ensure that effective access to education is distributed equitably among the juvenile population. The emphasis in these measures is upon removing specific barriers to access. *Re*distributive strategies, however, imply a more active stance towards pursuing the principles of justice and equity.

Various types of redistributive strategy are possible in social policy.[7(Ch. 4)] The particular kind of redistribution characteristically pursued in the educational setting is usually redistribution between individuals, who are usually identified by specific *social* characteristics – most often class, but sometimes gender or race. Typically, redistribution of educational opportunity is meant to take place between middle-class children and working-class children, to the benefit of the latter.

In the context of education in Britain, there have been two predominant models for redistribution in favour of the working classes: the meritocratic and the egalitarian. Historically, the idea of working-class access to education on the model of meritocracy has been strong in the labour movement. This strand in their thinking contrasts with the other idea promoted within the labour movement, that education should be available to all working classes as a right from which they have been dispossessed (cf. sect. 4.1.3). Meritocracy accords much more closely with Marshall's view that the right to education means equal rights to be recognised as unequal [doc 35]. In the early part of this century, meritocratic views were promoted within the labour movement by Sidney Webb and certain other Fabians.[8(pp. 196-207)] In Webb's view, secondary education ought to be made available to the most able children of the working classes so that they could progress up the 'scholarship ladder' and be recruited to the ruling groups in society. As Barker puts it:

> His intention was to seek out the most able children in the interests of
> national efficiency – and his own phrase – and to give them an intensive
> training to fit them for the public tasks and services which they would be
> called on to perform. Webb's empire was to be run by its officers, and his
> objections to a society divided on lines of class were not that it lacked
> cohesion nor that it distributed rewards and services unfairly, but simply
> that it was inefficient.[9(p. 16)]

Essential to the meritocratic view is the belief that only a limited
pool of talent exists among the nation's children and that it is an
important function of the education system to develop and foster it, as
the means of identifying and training the next generation of leaders, in
all walks of life. Such views have been a recurring theme throughout
subsequent discussions of education as social policy. The report of the
Public Schools Commission, for example (cf. sect. 2.4), adopted a
rather similar position when it argued that the leadership qualities
which independent schools claim to foster should be available to all
those with the talent to utilise them, since 'nobody of character and
competence should be denied the chance of achieving professional
competence which is the prerequisite of leadership' [doc 50].

The principle of meritocracy was central to the education system
developed in Britain after 1944. Halsey and his colleagues have argued
that the British educational system was built on the notion of meritocracy, and the specific purpose of their important study is to assess
how far it has achieved this professed goal.[10] This principle receives its
justification, they argue, both from its presumed relation to national
efficiency and from a desire to ensure distributive justice according to
the criterion of desert. These twin themes are a consistent strand in
meritocratic arguments. Although the idea of fostering talent
wherever it is found clearly does involve some form of redistribution
of education in favour of the working classes and thus appears to
conform to notions of social justice, it can also be part of a strategy
whose primary purpose is to serve national interests. Certainly in
Webb's view, the former seems to be more important than the latter.
In the report of the Public Schools Commission [doc 50] the two seem
more evenly balanced: both 'justice and efficiency' demand that talent
should be fostered. These twin themes producing the strategy of
meritocracy have been, as Halsey has argued elsewhere, central to the
policies of education in Britain, although they do not always easily
co-exist:

The dominant slogans are efficiency and equality. Efficiency for modernity. Equality for efficiency and justice. But both the meaning of these combined ends and the means postulated as adequate to their attainment remain dubious and confused. Thus the combination of equality of educational opportunity with the goal of national efficiency has led to policies designed to create and maintain a meritocracy – a principle which by no means commands universal acceptance.[1(p. 6)]

It is certainly the case, as Halsey notes, that the principle of meritocracy does not command universal acceptance. It is, however, one which can be espoused by various shades of political opinion. Webb promoted it from within the labour movement, but equally a right-wing critic of egalitarianism can embrace it. Bantock makes the important distinction between meritocratic strategies (designed to provide some new recruits for higher social positions and thus implying equality at the *starting* point in the educational race) and egalitarian strategies (designed to produce a more desirable kind of society, and therefore implying equality at the *finishing* point). The former is clearly more palatable to him than the latter.[11(pp. 115-19)]

The distinction made by Bantock would be widely accepted. Egalitarian strategies for redistribution differ significantly from meritocratic ones, and are more likely to seek to use education as a means of change beyond the educational system. Meritocratic strategies, on the other hand, tend to leave the economic and social structures essentially intact, changing only the pattern of recruitment to different positions.

The difference between the two positions can be seen in Tawney's critique of the idea of the 'ladder' of opportunity. He argues that the fact that everyone is able to enter the competition is in itself no guarantee of equality, other than the equal opportunity to become unequal. The very existence of 'ladders' of opportunity within the educational system means that the quality of services for the majority are overlooked. Moreover, the capacity to make use of such ladders is very closely related to inequalities of other circumstances: 'What a view of human life such an attitude implies! As though opportunities for talent to rise could be equalised in a society where the circumstances surrounding it from birth themselves are unequal! . . . Only the presence of a high degree of practical equality can diffuse and generalise the opportunities to rise.'[12(pp. 105-6)] It is the creation of 'a high degree of practical equality' which is a crucial hallmark of egalitarian strategies, for example, the various programmes of pre-school intervention which aim to ensure that the children of the working classes enter formal schooling with the same capacity to use the opportunities that the middle classes automatically confer upon their own children.

Some of the most virulent attacks upon egalitarian strategies have concentrated upon these attempts to create practical equality. As Boyson argues: 'Most people . . . would subscribe to the need to give equality of opportunity to develop their hereditary intelligence and abilities. This is very different from supporting equality of rewards or accepting equality of abilties.'[13(pp. 155-6)] The consequences of such strategies, it is argued, are that quality and talent are not fostered and that personal freedom is eroded by an excessive emphasis on equality.

In more recent discussions, the philosophical basis of the egalitarian position has been importantly influenced by the writings of Rawls on the theory of justice.[14(pp. 228-30)] This is a version of social contract theory, and has an important application to education [doc 51]. Rawls begins with the idea that the principle of fairness and equal shares naturally governs human affairs; but where inequities arise (as they inevitably do), he proposes the 'difference' principle; that is, an *un*equal distribution can be made provided it works to the advantage of the less favoured. The social policy principle implied here is that action ought to be taken by governments to redress the inequalities suffered by disadvantaged individuals. In the case of education, this would mean that education ought to be distributed *unequally* in favour of the least advantaged, which may well mean that educational resources are concentrated upon the least 'intelligent' or 'able'. The Rawlsian theory of justice thus offers a clear alternative to the meritocratic model: meritocracy is rejected because it bases rewards on endowments which essentially are undeserved, in that they derive from social or economic inheritance or merely good fortune. It represents, as Daniel Bell puts it, 'the most comprehensive effort in modern philosophy to justify a socialist ethic'.[15]

In the egalitarian position, the idea of social justice is much more important than a consideration of national efficiency or the needs of the economy. It treats education as a valuable commodity in itself and recognises that equity demands that effective access to it should not be denied to any citizen. It differs significantly from the meritocratic position in its view of the relationship between education and the wider social and economic structures. On the one hand, it rejects the meritocratic concern that talent and leadership should be fostered to feed high positions in those structures in the next generation. This does not, however, imply that the purpose of education is purely for the benefit of the recipients: far from it. Egalitarian strategies – as critics like Bantock recognise – propose to use a changed educational system as a vehicle for changing the social and economic structures which they feed. In this sense the Public Schools Commission was being asked to propose egalitarian strategies when it was invited to look at ways of eliminating the 'socially divisive influence' which such schools exert (cf. sect. 2.4).

The concept of equality of opportunity has been the single most important way in which debates about redistribution have entered educational policy in Britain. The next two sections consider this principle and its application in some detail.

5.2.2 Equality of opportunity as redistribution

The concept of equality of opportunity, as applied to the English educational system in the 1944 Act and after, has in many ways been *the* educational issue par excellence. It lies, as Silver notes [doc 52], at the heart of any discussion of education as social policy. In the context of the foregoing discussion, it can be seen as an example of the debates about redistribution translated into practical strategies in an attempt to alter the rules which govern the distribution of education, and hence of other rewards.

The concept of equality of opportunity, as embodied in the 1944 Act, was set out in the preceding White Paper: 'to provide the means for all of developing the various talents with which they are endowed' [doc 2]. The major way in which this was to be translated into practical policy was in the principle of secondary education for all, a move which had long been a platform of the labour movement and had been promoted in a series of influential writings and government reports in the interwar years.[16(Part I), 9] The emphasis was upon the right of every child to have *access* to secondary education, regardless of means; but there was no suggestion that every child would have access to, or be able to benefit from, what had hitherto constituted secondary education – that is, in a grammar school. The basis of access was to be individual ' ability and aptitude' (cf. sect. 2.1). Thus the notion of equality of opportunity, as applied in 1944, essentially is a meritocratic version of equality. George and Wilding suggest that this is the version of equality most often incorporated into social policy in Britain. Its emphasis is upon equality of competition rather than equality of results, and thus it represents a compromise between laissez-faire individualism on the one hand and equality of results on the other. As far as education is concerned, this means that everyone has the opportunity to enter the race [doc 53].

Although in many ways the idea of equality of opportunity did (and still does) command widespread support, it increasingly became the object of critical scrutiny on a number of grounds in the 1950s and 1960s, especially on the grounds that the system of secondary education based on this concept in practice was failing to offer real equality in education to the working classes.[16(Part 2)] In the 1970s it became much more difficult to sustain confidence in its potential when the economy was in stagnation or decline. As Silver notes, by the end of the 1970s 'people either did not understand it, or had overestimated it, had been disillusioned by the research or the rhetoric, could not longer wait for it, or did not want it' [doc 52].

Part of this process involved shifts in understanding of what actually would constitute equality, as well as in policies designed to implement it. These link quite closely with different models of re-distribution. Halsey has identified three historical phases since the Second World War, each characterised by different thinking about how education can be used to produce equality: [1(pp. 6–11)]

1. From the beginning of the century to the late 1950s, the def-inition of equality was predominantly a liberal one, centring on the idea of equality of opportunity. Combined with a concern with efficiency, the logical outcome of this view is meritocracy. Such liberal policies were consistently demonstrated to be failing. The class composition of grammar school and student populations was not changing markedly, for example, despite expansion in both sectors.

2. The second phase is characterised by a change in the meaning assigned to the phrase 'equality of opportunity'. Instead of seeing equality of *access* as its major rationale, the efficacy of policies designed to produce equality was to be judged in terms of equality of *achievement*, that is, of outcome. This shift was taking place throughout the 1960s, but the Plowden report gave it significant impetus. One important implication of this shift was to emphasise the need to work upon those social conditions in the home and the community which helped to produce unequal educational outcomes.

3. In the third phase, in the 1970s, the debate was taken well beyond the concept of equal opportunities, to attempts to reappraise the function of education in contemporary societies.

Using Halsey's characterisation as the framework, it is possible to identify a number of themes within these shifts which link with the previous discussion about redistributive strategies in social policy.

First, the concept of equal opportunities may have many inherent attractions, but its translation into practical policies has been characterised by much confusion. Weale argues that the crucial question is whether to define it in input or in output terms.[6(pp. 91-2)] If defined in terms of input, that is, equal opportunities at the point of entry into the system, this is likely to prove unsatisfactory in relation to output. On the other hand, if equality of opportunity is defined in terms of output, there are problems about identifying when the requisite equality has been achieved. Equal outcomes does not have to mean *identical* outcomes, which would be a situation where all children achieved the same cognitive levels.[17(pp. 154-5)] But if we accept that children will achieve different cognitive levels, how do we know that each one has had equal opportunities to develop his or her own potential? The problem of translating equal opportunities into practical policies clearly are considerable.

Second, the shift from access to outcomes as a measure of equality of opportunity has been a highly significant one, with important implications for policy. As is clear from Tyler's discussion [doc 51], the injection of a Rawlsian concept of justice into discussions of equal opportunities shifts the debates firmly in the direction of looking at outcomes. That tends also to move the debate from meritocratic to egalitarian rationales, especially by introducing the concept of positive discrimination. Silver sees this shift as a 'third phase' in operationalising the concept of equal opportunities, where that is taken to mean equality of access *plus* positive discrimination in favour of the disadvantaged.[18(p. xxiii)] Clearly this fits much more easily into the egalitarian concept of justice than it does into meritocratic concerns. Meritocracy accords considerable importance to identifying and fostering talent; egalitarianism tends to imply that one concentrates resources upon those who are unlikely ever to show 'leadership' qualities.

Third, the eventual consequence of the attempt to implement equal opportunities was a rejection of the enterprise, especially by the left, who came to see the whole debate about opportunities, access and meritocracy as too narrow or irrelevant.[18(p. 39)] As Halsey notes, attention turned instead to questioning the purpose of educational systems in capitalist societies (cf. Ch. 6). The failure of redistributive strategies in education led eventually to a loss of confidence in the enterprise within that intellectual and political tradition which had once eagerly supported such strategies as a means of advancing the interests of the working classes.

5.2.3 *Comprehensive reorganisation: an exercise in equalising opportunities?*

No discussion of equality of opportunity as redistribution can ignore the issue of comprehensive secondary reorganisation, which is a major example of an attempt to translate the principle of equality of opportunity into effective practical policy.[19a-d]

The history of this reorganisation has been outlined in Chapter 2 and it is difficult to dissent from Caroline Benn's comment that: 'the case history of comprehensive reorganisation reads like a fever chart: plans in, plans cancelled: reorganisation begun, selection craftily reintroduced; refusal to budge, followed by a rush to catch up.[20(p. 199)] Nonetheless, in numerical terms, the commitment to comprehensive reorganisation seems to have achieved considerable success. By 1976, 75 per cent of secondary school children were in comprehensive schools.[21] Such figures need to be treated with caution, however: in some areas grammar schools still co-exist with comprehensives and, if the 'top' 10–20 per cent are being creamed off, the 'comprehensives' which cater for the rest can be left with both resources and expectations which do not make them easily distinguishable from secondary moderns.[19d(pp. 33-4)]

How does the history of comprehensive reorganisation advance our understanding of equality of opportunity as a redistributive strategy? On one level, the introduction of comprehensive reorganisation does not entail rejecting the concept of equal opportunities: rather, it is seen as a means of making equal opportunities more effective in practice. The tripartite system could be presented as having failed in its *own* terms: the meritocratic strategy of equal opportunities did not seem to be obviously identifying and fostering talent from the working classes, and this failure could be attributed to the principle of selection. Thus, it is quite possible to argue the case for comprehensive reorganisation on purely meritocratic grounds: that such a system improves *effective* access to the more elite forms of education for all working-class children.[22] On this level the aims of the 1944 Act are not being challenged, merely the means of achieving them; and the type of social engineering envisaged aims to change educational outcomes but not necessarily to make any significant impact on social and economic structures.

This, however, is a rather minimal account of comprehensive reform. Precisely because the case rests firmly on a recognition that ensuring equal access does not guarantee equality of outcome, the case for comprehensives helps significantly to shift the focus of the debate from access to achievement, and therefore at least moves it in the direction where the aims of the reorganisation can be cast in egalitarian rather than meritocratic terms. Most significantly, it challenges the 'efficiency' half of the efficiency-plus-justice equation which characterises meritocratic strategies, by proposing a form of educational organisation in which all children are given a broadly *similar* but not uniform educational experience.

So, although the case for comprehensives *can* be argued on grounds which hardly depart from the liberal version of meritocracy, it does also have a much more radical potential. The English educational system has always played a particularly important part in transmitting social and economic privilege,[20(p. 194)] and the structure of the educational system has mirrored the social structure – that is, it has been stratified along class lines. Parkinson argues that in the early part of this century, the public, grammar and secondary schools served the upper, middle and working classes respectively: a division which was confirmed by the major reports in the interwar years. Until 1938, the state sector had merely maintained the secondary/elementary distinction, but the Spens recommendations 'laid the foundations of stratification within the secondary sector itself'.[23(pp. 55–6)] To the extent that the tripartite system after 1944 could be seen as mirroring class stratification, any proposal to eliminate this from the system altogether has to be seen as a significant break with the pattern of previous educational provision. Indeed, the resiliance of the pattern may well re-emerge in the 1980s. As was noted in section 4.2.1, Sally Tomlinson has suggested that the combined effects of the proposed expansion of 'special' education (largely recruiting the children of the working classes) and of the independent sector, encouraged by increased state financial support, may recreate a tripartite system, in which 'ordinary' state education constitutes the middle tier.[24(Ch. 8)]

Comprehensive reform can be seen as a means of changing society, not just changing educational outcomes. Although many 'technical' educational arguments were produced in its favour, the main motive force was always ideological and egalitarian.[23(pp. 56-7)] One right-wing critic claimed that the real aims of comprehensive reform were to produce a 'socialist society in miniature',[25(p. 20)] a prospect of which he clearly disapproved. Such an idea was by no means new within the labour movement: one of the grounds on which Tawney had advocated secondary education for all was his strong commitment to the idea that it is possible to teach the next generation to *want* socialism.[26(p. 410)]

In terms of its more modest, meritocratic aims, comprehensive reform can be judged to have achieved some success. There is evidence, for example, that such schools do 'permit "late developers" to find courses to fit their abilities at whatever stage'.[19c(p. 115)] Moreover the claims of right-wing critics, that the education of the least able would be promoted at the expense of the most talented, whose interest would be badly served in comprehensives, seem to be unfounded.[27]

On the other hand, advocates for comprehensives on grounds of improved access for working-class children have sustained considerable disappointment. Julienne Ford's study offered early evidence,[28] indicating that social class background is as closely related to placement in streams within a comprehensive school as it is with selection for different schools under a tripartite system. Moreover, even those working-class children who did get into the 'A' stream were four times more likely to leave school at the statutory leaving age than their middle-class counterparts. These findings are confirmed by Stephen Ball's much more recent study.[29] He found that the operation of streaming and selection within Beachside comprehensive school meant that – on meritocratic criteria – the school was failing to provide greater equality of opportunity than the bipartite, selective system which it replaced.

In the face of such evidence, there seems little ground for optimism that comprehensive education is likely significantly to modify the link between social class and educational attainment, if it merely means that patterns of class stratification are replicated *within* schools. One response to this has been to look at the way comprehensive reorganisation is implemented; that is, seeking more effective methods of social engineering within comprehensive schools, rather than abandoning the enterprise altogether. This position has been taken by Hargreaves, who argues that we need both to recognise that the potential of comprehensives has not been realised, and to go back to the 'old' questions: what kind of society do we want, and how is education going to help us to achieve it?[30]

The more radical potential for social engineering which comprehensives seemed to promise certainly has not been realised. If their capacity to modify the class structure *within* education has been limited, their potential impact upon structures outside the educational system must at best be considered unproven. Partly this can be seen as a result of the ambivalence within the Labour party itself about whether the real interests of the working classes are actually served by this measure. Although the Labour government took some important steps in the direction of comprehensive reorganisation, its progress is described by Benn and Simon as 'slow and indecisive, rather than hurried and doctrinaire, as is sometimes asserted'.[19a(p. 15)]

There is, however, an alternative account of comprehensive reform which suggests that it was never seriously intended to serve the collective interests of the working classes, nor to radically alter prevailing social and economic structures. Interestingly, a version of this is offered by critics from both right and left. Rhodes Boyson argues that the reorganisation was directly against the interests of those working-class children who would have otherwise obtained grammar school places, and points to the reluctance of some Labour authorities to implement the reorganisation as an indication that they recognised this.[13(pp. 171-2)] The reorganisation was really, he argues, the product of an alliance of the professional interests of teachers and the interests of middle-class intellectuals, who did not want any system of selection which might exclude their own children. A very similar account is offered by Bellaby, who argues that the expanding 'new' middle classes in the postwar period wanted to secure for their children maximum access to the type of education upon which (in most cases) their own success had rested: and that secondary school teachers wanted an organisation of schooling which would enable all of them to take part in 'O' and 'A' level work. For both, comprehensive reform offered an ideal solution.[19c(pp. 46-8)] This alternative account suggests that (whilst one does not necessarily have to question the motives of those who advocated the reforms on egalitarian grounds) to produce a situation in which these reforms become politically possible may involve the formation of alliances with groups whose own interests effectively subvert egalitarian aims.

The case of comprehensive reorganisation also highlights the problems of devising practical strategies which will be effective and not counterproductive, in the pursuit of attempting to engineer the redistribution of educational resources. Most importantly, it suggests that such strategies achieve only modest success (even in their more limited goals) if they concentrate simply upon redistributing the means of access to education. It is natural, therefore, that egalitarian advocates of social engineering, in the face of these failures, should turn to strategies which appear to offer the means of ensuring that disadvantaged groups are given the effective means to make use of a resource like education, which in formal terms is universally available. Such a strategy is positive discrimination, to which we now turn.

5.3 POSITIVE DISCRIMINATION

5.3.1 Positive discrimination and the EPA experiments

The principle of positive discrimination derives from a concern with distributive justice understood in a Rawlsian sense, where justice is produced by concentrating resources upon particular groups and individuals hitherto disadvantaged. It represents a highly interventionalist strategy of social engineering, for which education has provided a major testing ground.

Pinker provides a very useful framework which serves to clarify some of the social policy issues around the principle of positive discrimination.[31(pp. 227-41)] It is a concept which can be traced, he argues, to some interwar approaches to housing programmes; but it made its most significant impact in social policy in the field of education, through the ideas developed in the Newsom and Plowden reports. Logically, there are three ways in which 'discrimination' can be practised: negative discrimination against the underprivileged; positive discrimination against the privileged on their own behalf; and positive discrimination on behalf of the underprivileged, in a framework of universalism (that is, with basic minimum services available to all). This latter strategy, he suggests, is a device for intervening directly at key points in the social structure. As he suggests:[31(p. 190)] '(Positive discrimination) is the only form of discrimination compatible with the idea of a welfare society because its ultimate goal is the achievement of optimal rather than minimal standards. Discrimination becomes a process of inclusion rather than exclusion.'

As is clear in the extract from Tyler's book [doc 51], when applied to education, the Rawlsian concept of justice implies that *more* resources should be concentrated on the least advantaged, both in social and educational terms. The Newsom report's discussion of 'education in the slums' advocates this when it argues that, in order to receive an adequate education, boys and girls from such areas need to be given priority for attendance on courses, overseas visits and other school journeys, because their education will be inadequate if confined to the slums where they live. Action is also necessary in other fields of social policy, such as housing and public health, if their educational experiences are to be genuinely improved [doc 12]. The same broad concern for the total life situation of pupils was apparent within the Plowden report which advocated the principle of positive discrimination some four years later. In a much quoted section they argue that a 'new cutting edge' is needed to tackle the educational needs of deprived areas. This is the principle of positive discrimination, which goes well beyond an attempt to equalise resources[doc 17]: 'Schools in deprived areas should be given priority in many respects. The first step must be to raise the schools with low standards to the national average; the second, quite deliberately, to make them better.' The exercise of deliberately making such schools better than the average is justified, in the committee's view, because most of the children who attend them come from homes where there is little support for learning, and the schools should supply a compensating environment. As a later paragraph makes clear, they see the principle of positive discrimination as entailing both an overall increase in resources and some element of redistribution: more advantaged children must, by implication, have some resources taken away from them, or at least their share must remain static while others' share is increased. The committee recommended that these ideas should be implemented by designating educational priority areas (EPAs), through which various kinds of additional resources would be channelled. These areas would be identified by features such as a high proportion of unskilled manual workers, large families, single-parent families, children who play truant from school, and overcrowded housing.[32(para.153)]

A limited amount of money was set aside and a number of projects started (cf. sect. 2.5). From the point of view of evaluating the principle of positive discrimination as an exercise in social engineering, a great advantage of the EPA example is that it was carefully monitored and researched in the series of action research projects directed by A. H. Halsey.[1] The principle of positive discrimination emerges from these reports, if not entirely unscathed, at least with qualified approval; although clearly one important aspect of such strategies is that their real success can only be judged in the longer term. Despite its many drawbacks, the research teams concluded [doc 18] that the EPA was a socially and administratively viable unit, and that educational policies concentrated upon it could be a success if part of a much wider strategy for community development. Conversely, the idea of community schooling (as developed in the EPA projects) (cf. sect. 2.5) could make a powerful contribution to community regeneration. Preschooling emerges from the reports as *the* positive discrimination strategy par excellence, and an effective means of raising educational standards. So positive discrimination appeared to offer a promising strategy through which changes could be effected both in educational outcomes and in social life.

There are, however, some significant weaknesses in the principle of positive discrimination as applied in the EPA example. First, there are problems with the use of a geographical area as the unit through which to channel positive discrimination policies. Despite the fact that the Halsey report found it to be broadly a viable unit, it remains the case that, on criteria of individuals' needs, more people 'in need' live outside these areas than within them[33](pp. 269-82) and, as Pinker notes, the 'area' definition makes the problems look geographical rather than political.[34]

Secondly, there are different ways in which the term 'positive discimination', has been used and applied. Some of these do not necessarily entail any very significant redistribution of resources. It is possible for 'positive discrimination' simply to be a form of compensatory education in which the *child* is seen as 'the problem', and therefore it becomes another version of victim-blaming (cf. sect. 4.2.2): examples of this usage can be found in documents 44 and 46. Alternatively, positive discrimination strategies can throw the onus on to the educational system, and advocate that schools themselves must change [doc 48]: if defined in this way, it can look much more like a strategy for the pursuit of social justice in the long term. The likelihood of its being implemented as a radical redistributional strategy is questioned by Glennerster and Hatch, when they argue that it has become a fashionable concept which lacks rigorous analysis [doc 54]. The experience following Plowden suggests that it cannot be an efficient device for tackling deprivation in general. Any strategy which makes the deprived its target without also looking at the wealthy, they argue, may simply end up redistributing resources between the poor: unless part of a general redistributive strategy, such policies may well be only tokenism.

Finally, a more radical critique of the whole EPA idea suggests that not only may it contain no really significant gains for the poor but it may be positively to their disadvantage. The authors of *Unpopular Education* see the EPA schemes as an early example of the tightening of state planning and management of citizens, for purposes which are more to do with surveillance and control than with any benefit which citizens might derive.[35] This echoes Cynthia Cockburn's discussion of the idea of community schooling as developed in EPAs:[36](pp. 122-3)

> We face a contradiction. We *need* more sensitive, caring education over which we have more say. Yet it is important to make the *effort* to remember that education described in this way is nonetheless a *reproductive function* performed for capital . . . The fact that children, once educated, free from alienation, full of civic sense and eagerly seizing every opportunity to vote and participate, are nonetheless still waged workers (perhaps unemployed), still tenants in a capitalist system, is nowhere pointed out.

Cockburn's argument is a reminder that, while looking at social engineering strategies which are explicit and overt actions on the part of governments to modify the distribution of resources in favour of the poor, we must not overlook the fact that these strategies are inevitably grafted onto an educational system whose relation to social political and economic structures is complex (cf. Ch. 6) and often the product of processes which are never made explicit, rather than of overt social policies.

5.3.2 Positive discrimination in favour of girls

The principle of positive discrimination holds considerable attractions for anyone concerned with improving the position of any disadvantaged groups. Of the range of possible alternative targets – ethnic minorities, girls, the mentally handicapped – I shall consider here the particular case of girls (cf. sect. 6.2.3), looking at some of the suggested positive discrimination strategies within education, evaluating their likely strengths and weaknesses and how they link with the EPA experiments.

The case for some action to change girls' educational experiences rests on the recognition that their rates of 'success', as measured by educational outputs, are somewhat lower than boys', especially in certain fields like mathematics and science.[37a, b] This had been recognised as a feature of secondary education as early as 1954, in the report *Early Leaving* (cf. sect. 2.2). In part, it is an inevitable product of the fact that many girls have been traditionally offered a somewhat different curriculum from boys, emphasising preparation for the domestic work for which it was assumed they were destined.[38] Since the passing of the Sex Discrimination Act such practices are unlawful but, as in other examples, simply removing the barriers which previously prevented girls' access to the 'boys' curriculum (and vice versa) does not of itself inevitably produce radical change. The case for following this up with strategies of positive discrimination (just like the arguments about equal opportunities for the working classes) is based on the need to make equal treatment for girls more effective. This case is set out in a book produced by the National Council for Civil Liberties NCCL:[39] '[Positive action] is action which recognises that women are, and have been, discriminated against in education, training and employment, and that only positive commitments will provide for equal treatment, regardless of sex.'

The principle of positive discrimination specifically is allowed in the Sex Discrimination Act. The NCCL have set out a programme for making this effective, which, as far as education is concerned, concentrates upon three areas: the organisation and administration of the school; equal opportunities for women in academic study; careers advice and counselling. The kind of positive action which they envisage includes: phasing out teaching and careers material based on conventional views of the role of men and women in society; seeking to incorporate in the school curriculum material which promotes the fact of women's equality with men; developing a continuous and innovative careers counselling service which encourages and supports men and women who want to move into areas of employment previously associated with the other sex. It is clear from these examples that such proposals go well beyond a desire to equalise access to education, or even to alter specifically educational outcomes: they are also designed to produce significant social and economic changes in the lives of women and men. Education is in fact seen as a crucial means through which such changes can be effected, partly (as in the case of arguments about the working classes) because it is the means of channelling people to positions in the occupational structure. In the case of girls, however, there is an additional reason why education is an important mechanism for producing social change: it offers potential for altering what young people *think* about themselves and each other as men and women, and for changing girls' self-image and increasing their self-confidence. It is therefore an ambitious strategy of social engineering which seeks not only to change educational outcome but also social structures, culture and beliefs.

Can such a strategy be successfully implemented? This question will be considered in relation to the specific example of science. The idea that positive action is necessary for girls in relation to science was promoted in an HMI report in 1980,[40] which included the following specific proposals: primary schools should give girls more experience of the physical sciences; there should be particular help with practical work in secondary schools; there should be a structured guidance programme when option subjects are chosen; teachers should take active steps to overcome girls' reluctance to give 'wrong answers' in front of boys; girls need a calm, orderly and disciplined atmosphere in science lessons. These proposals clearly draw upon the experience of research on girls and science and, on the basis of her own and other people's attempts to introduce such programmes, Alison Kelly suggests proposals which might contribute to redressing the balance, including: the elimination of sexism in text books; not allowing girls to 'drop' science; using teaching styles to which girls respond; actively promoting contact with women scientists and science teachers; ultimately changing the law to reinforce the provisions of the Sex Discrimination Act. [37a(Ch. 20)] Rather similar proposals are set out by the NCCL [see doc 55].

A number of questions can be raised about this kind of approach.

First, of course, there are questions about whether it 'works'. In a sense this needs to be answered in the longer term, but there is some indication from experience in the United States that positive action programmes have to be treated carefully if they are to achieve any success. There are many ways in which the spirit of the law can be ignored even if the letter is fulfilled, and this can (if anything) be counterproductive to the interests of women. Quota systems, for example – in which a number of places on 'desired' courses, or a number of senior jobs, *have* to be filled by women – seem to attract particular hostility. Women who fill these positions may be treated as not really competent, and the whole exercise can amount to little more than tokenism, in which case the gains, although real for some people, are limited in scope.[41] American experience suggests that programmes which set goals and targets to be reached at some stage in the future are likely to be more effective, although programmes have to be planned in considerable detail to have any impact and possible avoidance strategies must be anticipated.[39(pp. 22-42)]

Second, there are ambiguities in some cases about what actually *counts* as a positive discrimination strategy for girls. The case of single-sex education is important here. The proposals of the NCCL clearly imply that continuing instances of segregation by sex are bad and should be eliminated.[39(pp. 75-6)] This argument would suggest that a positive discrimination strategy requires that boys and girls should be taught in co-educational groups. There is, however, considerable evidence that this is not necessarily to girls' advantage. Especially in the case of science (as the NCCL in fact acknowleges), it seems that girls perform better if taught in single-sex groups. There is therefore a case to be made that 'support for contemporary all-girls schools can, in a sexist society, be viewed as a mode of affirmative action'.[42]

This example demonstrates the difficulties of devising strategies of social engineering which will not in the end be counterproductive to the interests they were meant to serve. It also underlines the implication that positive discrimination strategies, if taken seriously (and not merely as the tokenism which Glennerster and Hatch see as more likely – see Doc 54), do imply that hitherto advantaged groups must suffer by comparison. Summarising the evidence of single-sex education, Delamont concludes that it looks as if boys benefit academically and socially from being in co-educational schools, while girls are better off in single sex establishments. 'If this is so', she asks 'who is going to be sacrificed, and at what cost?'[43(pp. 105-8)] Discriminating positively in favour of girls by developing single-sex education brings their interests directly into conflict with those of boys. As Roberts has argued,[41] the principle of positive discrimination (unlike the principle of equal access) does involve taking away from people some privileges which hitherto had seemed an inalienable right.

Third, there are issues about how various types of positive discrimination relate to each other. Again, these raise questions about who are the main beneficiaries and losers. Delamont raises the important issues of the relationship of sex and class inequalities in programmes of positive discrimination. She argues that there is some evidence that the outcome of programmes aimed at girls may be little more than to ensure that middle-class girls replace working-class boys in, for example, entrance to higher education.[43(pp. 108-9)] This argument is rather similar to Glennerster and Hatch's view [doc 54] that positive discrimination may in fact end up simply redistributing resources between ths poor without touching the rich. Issues are raised here about the need to co-ordinate programmes; about the need for re-distribution to be real, not token; and not least about programmes aimed at working-class girls, who are clearly doubly disadvantaged.

Finally, there are important questions about the limits of positive discrimination within the educational system: can real social change in the position of women be achieved just by working within education? In relation to girls and science, for example, Saraga and Griffiths argue that the 'underachievement' of women in science is accounted for by their structural position in society, and therefore is not easily amenable to change simply by altering what happens in schools. While they do not deny that short-term gains may be possible in the educational system, they do not see that fundamental change can be produced in that way.[44] An alternative, more optimistic view (rather similar to the Halsey report's conclusion on EPA), is that while education *alone* cannot change the position of women action must be taken in that area as well as in others.[45(pp. 275-94)]

Clearly there are limits upon what can be achieved *through* education in changing broader social outcomes. There are probably also limits even in changing *educational* outcomes. These limits can be seen by asking the question: what is education for? As far as girls are concerned, the fact that they are offered different educational experiences from boys, and that the measured outcomes of their education are different, is not a coincidental, random phenomenon but part of the process of channelling women into certain sections of the labour market and preparing them for domestic work (cf. sect. 6.2.3). This brings us back to the point raised at the end of the discussion of EPAs: positive discrimination strategies are grafted onto an existing educational system in which different categories of pupils (in this case boys and girls) are actually being prepared for different outcomes in the 'adult' world.

5.4 SOCIAL ENGINEERING IN AND THROUGH EDUCATION

Since social engineering is an approach to social policy which entails explicit intent to produce social change, it naturally invites the question: did it work? This final section draws together some of the answers to that question suggested by evidence reviewed in this chapter, before moving to an evaluation of the use of social engineering in and through education as a social policy strategy.

5.4.1 The failure of redistributive policies?

Halsey argued quite explicitly in 1972 that 'the essential fact of twentieth century educational history is that egalitarian policies have failed'.[1(p. 6)] If their failure is measured in relation to the actual distribution of educational resources, more recent evidence seems to offer little reason to dispute that judgement. LeGrand has calculated that while people in the top socio-economic group received slightly less than average state expenditure on the education of their children (largely because of their use of private schools), for post-sixteen education they received substantially more than other groups: in universities, for example, they received 2.75 times the mean amount of state expenditure, and 5 times that received by the lowest socio-economic group.[46] This evidence certainly bears out Titmuss' claim, in his classic discussion of redistribution, that the major beneficiaries of the high-cost sectors of the educational system since the establishment of the 'welfare state' have been the higher income groups.[47a, b] The state's involvement in redistribution does not always entail a transfer of resources from rich to poor, even if it is intended to [doc 36].

The evidence of the more recent study by Halsey and his colleagues[10] both supports this view and suggests why it has happened. This study is based on a sample of about 8.5 thousand men (women were not included) aged between twenty and sixty-four in 1972, and thus offers the opportunity to compare educational experience and outcomes for cohorts passing through the educational system both before and after the 1944 Act. The researchers set out specifically to examine whether the Act had succeeded in its own meritocratic aims of creating equal opportunities. Broadly the answer is that it has not. The chances, for example, of a working-class boy receiving a selective education in the mid-1950s and 1960s was no higher than it had been for his parents' generation thirty years earlier. This is partly a result, argue the authors, of a paradox of universalist social policy: if one creates good, free services so that the poor can have access to them, they also become more attractive to the rich. It is fair to assume that, in the postwar period, middle-class parents who might otherwise have paid for private education opted for the *free* grammar schools instead, thus introducing more competition for places for the sons of the working classes. The consequences basically were horizontal, not vertical, redistribution: elite education resources were redistributed *within* the middle class, rather than *between* classes.

The evidence reviewed in the previous section, on the more radical redistributive strategy of positive discrimination, is somewhat more optimistic; although again it is possible that this may in the end also redistribute horizontally, if projects are under-resourced, applied in token fashion, and fail to take seriously the implication that the advantaged must lose some of their privileges.

The fact that redistribution appears so far to have been a relative failure does not necessarily mean that it can never succeed. There is a case for arguing that it has not seriously been tried. One important issue here is the continuation of independent schools. Discussions of equality of opportunity have been confined almost exclusively to the state sector, [18(p. 39)] and: 'Equality of opportunity is seldom taken to imply that the better off should be prevented from purchasing un- usually generous educational opportunities in the private sector'. [48] The capacity to purchase such opportunities is (in terms of Pinker's distinction between different types of discrimination) one of the ways in which the advantaged exercise positive discrimination on their own behalf. The independent schools emerged from the Halsey cohort study as significant in maintaining a cycle of privilege: they represent 'a bastion of class privilege compared with the relatively egalitarian state sector'. [10(p. 203)] With very few exceptions, such schools have remained closed to working-class children.

One might imagine, therefore, that the abolition of the independent sector would be an essential prerequisite of any serious attempt to implement equal opportunities. Governments however, including Labour governments overtly committed to expanding educational opportunities for the working-classes, have been reluctant to consider this as a serious possibility. Despite the fact that a Labour government set up the Public Schools Commission in order to devise ways of reducing these schools' 'socially divisive influence', little action was taken on the recommendations (cf. sect. 2.4). Indeed, this sector continued to flourish, in practice with support from the state: by the mid-1970s, taxpayers were subsidising this sector in excess of £100 million per year.[20(p. 192)] Whatever the reason for Labour's failure to take decisive action after the report of the Public Schools Commission, the fact that these schools continue to flourish (cf. Ch. 2) means that all redistributive strategies so far attempted have inevitably been limited in their scope.

5.4.2 Social engineering as a social policy strategy

At the beginning of this chapter, three different types of social engineering in and through education were identified. Each of these will be evaluated in turn, in the light of the specific examples discussed in this chapter.

Can changes in education alter educational outcomes? The material reviewed in this chapter tends rather to suggest the answer: 'it depends on what kind of changes'. It is certainly the case that changes designed merely to secure access to education are a considerable disappointment to those who hoped they would produce equal outcomes. As George and Wilding note, [48(Ch. 6)] one of the most striking features of social policy in the postwar period is the failure of services to meet the aspirations of those who planned them in the late 1940s. On the other hand, policies designed to promote the effective *use* of education, as well as access to it, may well have more promising outcomes, and some of these can be implemented within the educational system itself. The expansion of nursery schooling, for example, emerges from the EPA projects as having considerable potential; as perhaps do some of the proposals for making changes within school curriculum and organisation to encourage more girls to study science.

Moreover, there is the important issue of what basic standard of educational facilities is being offered to disadvantaged groups. Bernstein's influential article entitled 'Education cannot compensate for society' points out that one cannot be talking about additional 'compensatory' education for children who are currently being offered materially inadequate schools and a high staff turnover. The idea of compensatory education diverts attention from the very real issues of the basic distribution of resources within the educational system.[49(pp. 344-7)] This position again suggests that action within the educational system is itself capable of producing certain educational changes.

At the same time, both theory and practice suggest that any strategy which considers simply the individual attributes of children to be 'the problem' can meet with only limited success. As Halsey has argued, certain versions of egalitarianism in education have assumed that equality was to be attained by changing the culture and the character of the disadvantaged, thus missing the whole point that the unequal allocation of resources is an integral part of a class society.[50(pp. 19-26)] He suggests that any policy which seeks seriously to erode the relationship between social class and educational attainment has to encompass such matters as standards of housing, employment prospects, and the allocation of educational resources.

Can other types of change alter educational outcomes? Halsey's argument suggests that effective action to alter educational outcomes may need to be taken in other areas of social policy. This is consistent with the position taken by both Newsom and Plowden [docs 12 and 17]. Indeed, it is possible to argue that action of this sort is more effective than action within education itself. Reviewing the literature on preschool intervention, Smith and James note that the changing view of deprivation has increasingly pushed education itself from the centre of the stage; and have suggested that, if poor housing is a really significant barrier to educational performance, then it is better to develop housing policies rather than educational policies as a means of altering educational outcomes.[51(pp. 223-40)]

To some extent, the EPA projects attempted to implement this view. They did see poor educational performance as part of broader social, economic and environmental deprivation. However, they tended to look for solutions within schools and the educational system, characteristically developing preschool programmes and 'community' schools, rather than campaigning to bring jobs back into inner cities or to invest in new building programmes. While a programme of co-ordinated strategies clearly might, as Halsey suggests, prove more effective, the implications for the scale and scope of government interventions in people's lives is daunting, and one is reminded of Cockburn's warning about the extension of state surveillance and management of communities.

Moreover, one is still left with the problem of how far limits are set upon possible changes in educational outcomes by the relationship of the educational system to other social and economic structures, especially the occupational structure [doc 35]. A successful programme of co-ordinated social engineering in inner cities could not possibly result in all children in such areas obtaining university places, given that such places are intended (in the British system) to be available to a minority only, and to provide access to the elite forms of employment. The most which one could hope for would be on the meritocratic model: that talent would be fostered wherever it was found, and that *some* children from such areas would rise. Supposing this more limited aim were achieved, the implication would then be that some children of the middle classes (who might otherwise have expected to secure their places in the more elite positions in the social and economic hierarchy) would be displaced. This prospect (more likely at a time of economic stagnation perhaps) raises what is, in many ways, the crucial but often unspoken issue of any redistributive strategy designed to alter educational outcomes. If actual redistribution takes place, some people gain and others by comparison must lose. This is not merely an unfortunate by-product: in a very real sense it is the whole purpose of the exercise. Thus the likely effectiveness of any redistributive strategy can be judged by the extent to which it reduces the capacity of the privileged to exercise positive discrimination on their own behalf. Action of *that* sort outside the educational system of course might well radically alter educational outcomes.

Can changes in education bring about changes in other areas of social life? This is the most ambitious version of social engineering in relation to education: changes in education are introduced with the specific intent of eventually producing change in social, economic and political structures. This issue (as Halsey puts it in the well-known passage quoted at the beginning of this chapter) of whether education can change society has preoccupied many writers who propose social engineering strategies through education. Undoubtedly there have been unrealistic expectations of what education can achieve, not least from those who do not wish to engage with the more fundamental problems. As Halsey puts it: 'There has been a tendency to treat education as the waste paper basket of social policy – a repository for dealing with social problems where solutions are uncertain, or where there is a disinclination to wrestle with them seriously.'[1(p. 8)]

Are there any circumstances in which education can be a means of producing social change? On the evidence of the instances reviewed in this chapter, two kinds of answer, neither of which is entirely pessimistic, can be offered. The first answer is that, while education alone may not be especially effective in *producing* social change, it may be important both in preparing the ground for it and in sustaining the change once it has occurred. In their discussion of preschool intervention programmes, Smith and James, having noted that education has been pushed somewhat from the centre of the stage, argue that it should be reinstated; first because it provides an important means whereby disadvantaged groups become aware of their inequalities; and second because (if opportunities are genuinely made more equal) disadvantaged groups need access to the skills necessary to take advantage of, and to maintain, these gains. The latter point accords with Halsey's view that: 'the society of equals has to be created by economic and political reform . . . the role of education must largely be to maintain such a society once it has been attained.'[50(p. 10)] This argument, when applied to positive action programmes for girls, for example, would suggest that their key role is to raise the consciousness of girls about their own position, to give them the confidence to challenge their assumed inferiority and to give them the skills (such as scientific skills) necessary to operate in a changed social world where women are more visible and more powerful. What it may *not* be able to do by itself is to bring about those substantive changes.

Secondly, it can be argued that education can only produce social change if this is recognised for the political activity which essentially it is, and if there really is the political will to make the changes.[1(p. 5)] One can point to the very small amount of money committed to the EPA programmes, or to the failure to acknowledge that independent schools undermine equality of opportunity in the state sector, as examples of policies of social engineering in which the political commitment appears to have been less than total. As suggested earlier, one can hardly argue that such policies have failed if they have never seriously been tried.

Thus it is possible to maintain a relatively optimistic interpretation of the prospects for social engineering in the production of a more egalitarian society, provided that changes are genuinely sought. That is the conclusion of Halsey *et al.*'s study: 'Education has changed society [in certain ways] and it can do more. It does so slowly and against the stubborn resistance of class and class-related culture. But it remains the friend of those who seek a more efficient, more open, and more just society.'[10(p. 219)] On the other hand there is every reason to suppose that producing the political commitment to such changes is no easy matter. The potential for education to foster even those changes which it *can* produce is limited if they conflict with other powerful interests. As George and Wilding argue, the values of freedom and individualism, so deeply embedded in social and economic structures, are directly challenged by policies which are overtly egalitarian:[48(p. 128)] 'Freedom and individualism fit well with a belief in equality of opportunity, less well with policies such as positive discrimination, which might make a reality of such beliefs.'

At this point the real problem begins to look like the *ends* to which social engineering strategies are put, rather than the inadequacies of such strategies as a *means* to those ends. Strategies such as positive discrimination may well provide quite successful means of producing certain egalitarian social changes, if applied wholeheartedly. The question is: who wants them to be?

This brings the argument back full circle to the point raised at the beginning of this chapter: that it is quite possible for social engineering strategies to be employed in pursuit of ends which are anything but benign from the viewpoint of disadvantaged groups in society. If one accepts the argument that welfare was being restructured from the late 1970s onwards (cf. sect. 2.5) and the previous gains of the working classes began to be eroded, it may well be that the 1980s will produce examples of social engineering in and through education, where the ends pursued are far removed from the themes of equity and social justice which have characterised the major instances since the 1940s.

NOTES AND REFERENCES

1. HALSEY, A. H. (1972) *Educational Priority*, Vol. 1. HMSO: London.
2. COX. C. B. and BOYSON, R. (eds) (1979), *Fight for Education: Black Papers 1975*. J. M. Dent & Sons; London.
3. WRIGHT, N. (1977), *Progress in Education*, Croom Helm: London.
4. HEATH, A. (1981), 'What difference does the old school tie make now?' *New Society*, 18 June.
5. See for example, Alan Walker's discussion: WALKER, A. (1981), 'Social policy, social administration and the social construction of welfare', *Sociology*, Vol. 15, No. 2.
6. WEALE, A. (1978), *Equality and Social Policy*. RKP: London.
7. FORDER, A. (1974), *Concepts in Social Administration: a Framework for Analysis*. Routledge & Kegan Paul: London.
8. SIMON, B. (1965), *Education and the Labour Movement* 1870–1920. Lawrence & Wishart: London.
9. BARKER, R. (1972), *Education and Politics 1900–1951: A Study of the Labour Party*. Clarendon: Oxford.
10. HALSEY, A. H., HEATH, A. F. and RIDGE, J. M. (1980), *Origins and Destinations: Family, Class and Education in Modern Britain*. Clarendon: Oxford.
11. BANTOCK, G. H. (1975), 'Equality and education', in, B. Wilson (ed.) *Education, Equality and Society*. Allen & Unwin: London.

12. TAWNEY, R. H. (1964), *Equality*, revised edn. Allen & Unwin: London.

13. BOYSON, R. (1975), 'The school, equality and society', in B. Wilson (ed.), *Education, Equality and Society*. Allen & Unwin: London. See also Cox and Boyson, *op. cit.*

14. RYAN, A. (1981), 'John Rawls and his theory of justice', *New Society*, Vol. 55, No. 251.

15. BELL, D. (1977), 'On meritocracy and equality', in J. Karabel and A. Halsey (eds), *Power and Ideology in Education*, OUP: New York.

16. SILVER, H. (1973), *Equal Opportunities in Education*. Methuen: London.

17. ROBINSON, P. (1981), *Perspectives on the Sociology of Education: an Introduction*. Routledge & Kegan Paul: London.

18. SILVER, H. (1980), *Education and the Social Condition*. Methuen: London.

19. No attempt is made here to summarise the vast literature that has developed on this topic. For useful summaries and discussions, see: (a) BENN, C. and SIMON, B. (1970), *Half Way There*. McGraw Hill: London; (b) SILVER, H. (1973), *op. cit.*; (c) BELLABY, P. (1977), *The Sociology of Comprehensive Schooling*. Methuen: London; (d) JAMES, P. (1980), *The Reorganisation of Secondary Education*. NFER: Slough.

20. BENN, C. (1979), 'Elites versus equals: the political background to comprehensive reform', in D. Rubenstein (ed.), *Education and Equality*. Penguin: Harmondsworth.

21. DEPARTMENT OF EDUCATION AND SCIENCE (1977), *The Growth of Comprehensive Education*, Report on Education No. 87. DES: London.

22. MARSDEN, D. (1971), *Politicians, Equality and Comprehensives*, Fabian Tract 411. Fabian Society: London.

23. PARKINSON, M. (1970), *The Labour Party and the Organisation of Secondary Education 1918–65*. Routledge & Kegan Paul: London.

24. TOMLINSON, S. (1982), *A Sociology of Special Education*. Routledge & Kegan Paul: London.

25. NAYLOR, F. (1975), in C. Cox and A. Dyson (eds) *Fight for Education; Black Paper 1975*. J. M. Dent & Sons: London.

26. RYAN, A. (1980), 'R. H. Tawney: a socialist saint', *New Society*, Vol. 54, No. 941.

27. STEEDMAN, J. (1980), *Progress in Secondary Schools – Findings from the National Child Development Study*. National Children's Bureau: London.

28. FORD, J. (1969), *Social Class and the Comprehensive School*. Routledge & Kegan Paul: London.
29. BALL, S. (1981), *Beachside Comprehensive*. CUP: Cambridge.
30. HARGREAVES, D. (1982), *The Challenge for the Comprehensive School*. Routledge & Kegan Paul: London.
31. PINKER, R. (1968), 'The contribution of the social scientist in positive discrimination programmes', *Social and Economic Administration*, Vol. 2, No. 4.
32. DEPARTMENT OF EDUCATION AND SCIENCE (1967) *Children and Their Primary Schools*, The Plowden Report. HMSO: London.
33. SMITH, G. (1977), 'Positive discrimination by area in education: the EPA idea re-examined,' *Oxford Review of Education*, Vol. 3, No. 3.
34. PINKER, R. (1971), *Social Theory and Social Policy*. Heinemann: London.
35. CENTRE FOR CONTEMPORARY CULTURAL STUDIES (1981), *Unpopular Education: Schooling and Social Democracy in England since 1944*. Hutchinson: London.
36. COCKBURN, C. (1977), *The Local State*. Pluto: London.
37. (a) KELLY, A. (ed.), (1981), *The Missing Half: Girls and Science Education*. Manchester University Press: Manchester. (b) SPENDER, D. and SARAH, E. (1980), *Learning to Lose: Sexism and Education*. The Women's Press: London.
38. DEPARTMENT OF EDUCATION AND SCIENCE (1975), *Curricular Differences for Boys and Girls*, HMI Education Survey No. 21. HMSO: London.
39. ROBARTS, S. (1981), *Positive Action for Women: the Next Step*. National Council for Civil Liberties: London.
40. DEPARTMENT OF EDUCATION AND SCIENCE (1980), *Girls and Science*, HMI Series, Matters for Discussion No. 13. HMSO: London.
41. ROBERTS, H. (1980), 'Affirmative action: the US experience', Paper given to the EOC/SRHE conference on Equal Opportunities in Higher Education, March.
42. SHAW, J. (1980), 'Education and the individual: schooling for girls or mixed schooling – a mixed blessing?', in R. Deem (ed.), *Schooling for Women's Work*. Routledge & Kegan Paul: London.
43. DELAMONT, S. (1980), *Sex Roles and the School*. Methuen: London.
44. SARAGA, E. and GRIFFITHS, D. (1981), 'Biological inevitabilities or political choices? The future for girls in science', in A. Kelly (ed.), *op. cit.*

45. KELLY, A. and WEINREICH-HASTE, H. (1979), 'Science is for girls?', *Women's Studies International Quarterly*, Vol. 2, No. 3.
46. LEGRAND, J. (1982), *The Strategy of Equality: Redistribution and the Social Services*. Allen & Unwin: London.
47. (a) TITMUSS, R. M. (1968), *Commitment to Welfare*. Allen & Unwin: London, p. 194. See also: (b) FORDER, A., *op. cit.*, p. 68
48. GEORGE, V. and WILDING, P. (1976) *Ideology and Social Policy*. Routledge & Kegan Paul: London.
49. BERNSTEIN, B. (1970), 'Education cannot compensate for society', *New Society*. Vol. 15, No. 387.
50. HALSEY, A. H. (1975), 'Sociology and the equality debate', *Oxford Review of Education*, Vol. 1, No. 1.
51. SMITH, G. and JAMES, T. (1975), 'The effects of preschool education: some American and British evidence', *Oxford Review of Education*, Vol. 1, No. 3, pp. 223–40.

Chapter six
MEETING 'SOCIETY'S NEEDS'

6.1 INTRODUCTION

This chapter focuses on some features and interpretations of educational provision in which the interests of individuals (and potential benefits to them) are a fairly low priority. Instead, education is provided because it serves the needs of 'society', the economy or the 'national interest' – either explicitly or implicitly. At the most general level, the whole of education can be regarded, as William Beveridge argued in 1944, as a communal investment, likely to bring a variety of benefits to the whole society.[1(p. 60)]

There are different versions of what constitutes these wider interests. Some writers conceptualise them as primarily the country's economic 'needs'. Certainly there is evidence that, in recent years, government ministers have been placing top priority on economic concerns in their attempts to encourage schools to take more account of national needs (cf. sect. 2.5). A good illustration of this is to be found in a speech made by Baroness Young in 1980 [doc 56], in which she argues that 'economic and industrial concerns are of the highest importance' when planning the curricula of schools. However, she claims the government will not confine themselves to this 'narrow view', promoting other policies such as equal opportunities for girls as well.

This speech illustrates two further points which need to be taken account of before beginning a discussion of how the 'society's needs' rationale actually applies to education. First, there is no clear and obvious consensus either about what constitutes the 'needs' of the economy or the 'national interest', or about what significance they should be accorded within the educational system. Just as when the concept of 'need' is used to apply to individuals (cf. sect. 4.2.1), its apparently unproblematic use actually obscures vital questions like: who defines what those 'needs' are? How and for what purpose? Do all 'needs' count equally? Moreover, even if one takes a fairly narrow definition – such as, education should serve the immediate employment requirements of industry – clarity is not assured. This is evidenced in a report by the Central Policy Review Staff, which reviewed education, training and industrial performance and argued that there are 'quite serious difficulties about interpreting what the needs of industry are'.[2(paras 6, 7)]

Different versions of the 'society's needs' argument have different policy implications. Policies which focus on the needs of 'society' rather than the individual are not necessarily repressive, directive and constraining. In certain circumstances the needs of the economy, for example, may be defined as requiring educational policies which are highly expansionist. An illustration of this can be found in the Robbins report on higher education. In its discussion of the aims and objectives of higher education, the committee offers as its first rationale 'instruction in skills suitable to play a part in the general division of labour'. The traditional 'good general education' is, they argue, no longer sufficient to assist in solving the country's problems [doc 13]. This is a very explicit espousal of an 'economy's needs' rationale, yet the report recommended an expansion of places in higher education almost three-fold within twenty years.

Any discussion of the 'society's needs' rationale in education looks very different in the 1980s than it would have done in the 1960s, because of the restructuring of welfare which took place from the mid-1970s onwards to accommodate, it can be argued, changes in the capitalist economy (cf. sect. 2.5). In such circumstances, as Gough notes, policies in the educational sphere are likely to be adjusted to adapt the labour force and the potential labour force more effectively to the needs of the labour market, and discussions about the need to produce a more 'relevant', 'basic' and 'disciplined' educational system fit well with this.[3(pp. 138-9)]

Changes in the educational climate and the direction of educational policies themselves were paralleled in the 1970s by changes in the dominant modes of analysis of education, especially by some writers on the left who adopted an explicitly Marxist framework. A growing body of knowledge had the effect of 'unmasking' statements about education and 'society's needs'. The move to conceptualise the relationship between school and society in new ways, is according to Hall, a consequence of the acknowledged failure of liberal policies like equal opportunities and compensatory education; that is, reforms based on redistributive and efficiency criteria.[4(pp. 16-17)] The essential point of departure was, as Young and Whitty put it, that the left began to question whether schooling was unequivocally a 'good thing' for the working classes. They began to realise what the political right certainly also realised: that schooling has a great potential for control rather than liberation, for 'gentling the masses'.[5(p. 1)]

The exercise of 'unmasking' the education-society relationship has taken many different forms. It is variously argued that: no-one should be fooled into thinking that education is a service designed largely for the benefit of those who receive it; labour recruitment, industrial discipline and political pacification of the working classes are all importantly accomplished through education; education acts as an agent of social control even when often it does not appear to; its indirect support for the social order is more powerful and important than any direct indoctrination; it plays an important part in adapting, training and sorting the future labour force. [6(pp. 194-5)] In this chapter, the analysis of the relationship between education and 'society's needs' in the contemporary English context focuses upon three key concepts in recent Marxist accounts: reproduction, regulation and control.

6.2 REPRODUCTION

The concept of reproduction has been central to many neo-Marxist analyses of the welfare state. For example, Gough defines the welfare state as: 'the use of state power to modify the reproduction of labour power and to maintain the non-working population in capitalist societies.'[3(pp. 44-5)] When used in this context, 'reproduction' does not refer primarily to biological reproduction but to the continuation of specific patterns of social and economic life over time, and between one generation and the next. Most importantly, labour power needs to be reproduced if a capitalist industrial economy is to be sustained. This means, first that the current work force must be cared for to enable them to go on working; and second, that the next generation must be physically nurtured and prepared in appropriate ways to take its place in the capitalist productive process. The preparation of the next generation entails adapting its productive capacities to enable it to fill different positions in the labour force; and also socialising people into appropriate habits, ways of behaving, and so on, so that they will fit easily into the social relationships required in capitalist production.[3(pp. 46-7)]

Clearly education has a major potential contribution to make to this process of 'reproduction'. The material considered in this chapter will be grouped under five interlocking headings, each focusing on a slightly different account of *what* is being reproduced: the social division of labour; the class structure; the sexual division of labour; the dominant culture; the political order. There are, of course, other features of social life which could be considered in this way: racial divisions, or relationships between generations.

6.2.1 Reproducing the labour force

The idea that the education system supplies the labour force needed by industry is by no means confined to Marxist analyses. For example, other writers on social policy employ the concept of 'social capital' to refer to those elements in the social services which are in the interests of industry and contribute to economic development. Education, it is argued, has made a very significant contribution to social capital by expanding to cater for a whole range of technical and white-collar skills within higher and further education.[7(pp. 98-106)] What distinguishes many Marxist accounts is that they see the education-economy relationship as intimately linked with other features of social and political life. Because the mode of production in a given society is seen also as the basis of *social* structure, economic relationships give rise to political and social relationships, and an ideology which justifies these arrangements.[8(pp. 34-9)] This directs our attention to the reproduction both of skills and of the social relations of production.

The authors of *Unpopular Education* see the concept of 'skills' as central to the social democratic consensus which dominated educational policy in the 1960s. Postwar society, it was argued, demanded a wider diffusion of skills and an expanded educational system which could supply them.[9(pp. 145-9)] This sounds a relatively straightforward matter but in fact it is not, as Gleeson and Mardle's study of technical training in further education makes clear.[10] The overt purpose of apprentice education is direct instruction in skills relevant to work. Yet in practice, competing groups (unions, employers, teachers themselves, and so on) make varying demands upon the syllabus, and a simple 'fit' between training and the workplace is rarely achieved, certainly from the students' perspective, as they are often unclear about the relevance of what they are being taught: even in this situation, where training for the workplace seems clearest, it is problematic in practice. However, although students may not be acquiring job skills often they *are* acquiring something just as central to the reproduction of the labour force: they are being initiated into patterns of social relationships and into associated habits and attitudes which are appropriate for the workplace.[11(p. 261)] The same, it can be argued, also applies to schools: they have an important role in reproducing the *relations* of production, through their emphasis on hierarchy, authority and discipline.

The most well-known account from a Marxist perspective of how schools reproduce the social relations of production is to be found in the work of Bowles and Gintis in the United States.[12] Their argument [doc 57] concentrates on the *form* rather than the content of the educational encounter. Drawing explicitly on Marx, they argue that the relations developed variously between teachers, administrators and students correspond to, or mirror, the relationships of the workplace. The fragmentation of the learning process, the students' lack of control over their own work and the attitudes required of them all reflect the capitalist productive process. Thus schools prepare young people for the social relations of production by imposing equivalent relations upon them from an early age.

Looking at the processes of reproducing the social division of labour in an empirical study, Willis has illuminated the process by which 'working-class kids get working-class jobs'.[13] Although the official ideology of the educational system emphasises equal opportunities (or at least equal access) it is, he argues, an 'absolute requirement' that the same ideologies and aspirations are *not* passed on to everyone, since the outcome would be chaotic if they were. As Willis expresses it: 'Either a gigantic propaganda exercise of wartime proportions or direct physical coercion would be needed to get the kids into the factories.' The educational experiences of working-class boys in fact ensure that mostly they accept the kind of working-class jobs to which they are consigned.

Accounts of the educational system which emphasise its 'servicing' function for the economy seem particularly attractive in respect of changes which have occurred from the mid-1970s onwards, when political rationales for educational provision have more explicitly emphasised the 'needs of the economy'. Most obviously in the Great Debate (cf. sect. 2.5) the twin themes of training young people in specific skills and of preparing them for the social relationships of the productive process were very apparent [docs 21 and 22].

Such accounts, however, have to be treated with some caution. At a theoretical level they can be criticised for employing an oversimplified, functionalist model of social life (see section 5 of this chapter). Specifically, any assumption that there is a straightforward relationship between the 'needs' of the economy and the form and character of educational provision leaves out of account the many other processes (e.g. the struggles of the Labour movement, the activities of parental pressure groups or the power of the churches) which undoubtedly have shaped educational provision in England. Further, such accounts imply a one-way determinism (i.e. the economy determines education) which overlooks the ways in which the economy itself depends upon the knowledge and skills accumulated in and transmitted by educational institutions.[14(Ch. 1)] Finally, historical and comparative studies reveal that the relationship between education and the economy can vary significantly in different societies.[15a, b]

At an empirical level, it is clear, that the 'fit' between the 'needs' of the economy and the experience of schooling is less than perfect in the short – and often in the longer – term. Evidence of this in relation to apprentice training has already been mentioned. Reviewing a wide range of literature on schools and socialisation into work, Ryrie shows that schools commonly attempt other kinds of preparation for adult life than simply managing the school-work transition.[16(pp. 65-76)] Some teachers attempt, for example, to produce mature young adults, personally autonomous and capable of developing good relationships with others (cf. sect. 6.4.4). In so far as they succeed, they may be producing young adults rather *un*suited to fragmented and alienating work situations. Moreover, argues Ryrie, it is not clear that all teachers will give preparation for work increasing priority in the classroom, at a time when many of their pupils cannot realistically expect a lifetime of continuous paid employment.

So the idea that educational systems reproduce the labour force has to be treated with some caution if presented in a rather straightforward fashion. However, the use of schooling for this kind of 'reproduction' is clearly one significant – and increasingly explicit – feature of the contemporary English educational system. At the same time, the translation of that particular aim into practice within classrooms and schools leaves room for it to be reshaped by other considerations and material interests – and perhaps, on occasion, subverted.

6.2.2 Reproducing the class structure

The concept of reproduction raises again the issue of class links within the educational system, but in a rather different form. If 'class' is taken to mean a hierarchy of social positions based on occupations (or, for women, their husband's occupations), then in reproducing the social division of labour – and preparing individuals for slots within it

– education is also reproducing the class structure. On the other hand, 'class' can be defined in a sense which derives more directly from Marx, and locates an individual's class according to his or her relationship to the means of production – the most fundamental distinction being between capital on the one hand and labour on the other. Again, education is important in reproducing these divisions, especially by preparing the next generation to be wage-labourers.

There are two distinctive senses in which the class system can be said to be reproduced through education: through intergenerational class *placing* and through reproducing structure itself. In the first case, increased social mobility of the children of the working classes up the occupational hierarchy has been a major (but largely unachieved) aim of educational reformers in the twentieth century. Indeed, there is evidence that, since the Second World War, education has become increasingly important in keeping one generation in a similar class position to their parents. Processes such as middle-class parents' very effective use of grammar school education (cf. sect. 5.4.1) have ensured that, as Halsey has put it, 'education is increasingly the mediator of the transmission of status between generations.'[17(p. 184)]

The second sense on which reproduction of the class structure takes place is that the structure itself is reproduced through education. Since education prepares people for different positions in the social division of labour, it recreates the class structure based on that division for each succeeding generation. That structure can remain intact even if people get recruited to middle-class jobs from working-class backgrounds, and vice versa. In a sense, the structure itself is almost independent of how individuals get slotted into it.

Recognising that reproducing the class structure is an integral part of the educational system helps to make sense of certain features which, despite the rhetoric of free and universally available schooling, seem to actively discriminate against the poor. Although state schooling is free in the sense that no fees are charged, 'free' schooling has many attendant costs which fall to parents, as David Bull has shown.[18] He lists these as: costs of getting to school (transport, essential clothing); surviving the rigours of the school day (meals, uniform); pursuing the curriculum (sports kit, materials for domestic science, textbooks). Although the statutory basis of 'free' schooling is that no fees shall be charged (Education Act 1944, section 61), a ministerial circular in 1945 interpreted this as applying to the 'ordinary school curriculum', and it is quite in order to make charges outside that. Clearly *any* costs fall proportionately more heavily upon poorer families. What this means in cash terms is not known with accuracy. Although the costs of school meals can be documented accurately, very little is known about items such as music lessons, examination fees, or contributions to the school fund.[18(p. 10)] As far as uniform is concerned, the Child Poverty Action Group calculated that the cost of school uniform in north London was about £80 at 1979 prices, and had evidence that children do still miss school because they do not have appropriate clothing, especially footwear; that they sometimes get excluded from certain lessons because they do not have the right equipment (eg. for PE); and that they can be humiliated in front of other children because they do not have the right uniform.[19(p.3)]

The hidden costs of schooling are a very clear instance of how the educational system actively discriminates against the poor. There is good reason to suppose that this situation has worsened in recent years. Although LEAs do have the power to make grants for uniform and clothing, they are not obliged to do so. There is evidence that this provision has been cut back in recent years.[19(p. 3)] Meanwhile, other measures are combining to ensure that effectively the gap between the educational experiences available to wealthier and poorer children is widening. As a result of successive cuts in educational spending since the mid-1970s, items such as textbooks and other equipment have increasingly become a cost on parents [doc 25]. The annual report of HMI on educational provision in local authorities in 1981 found that this trend was leading to 'marked disparities of provision between schools serving affluent and poor areas'.[20(para. 73)]

All of this fits well with the argument that the welfare state is being restructured and former gains for working-class people being eroded. The effect seems likely to reinforce the processes by which the class structure is reproduced through education.

6.2.3 Reproducing sexual divisions

The fact that the educational system reproduces the social division of labour has been recognised for a long time, even if interpreted in terms other than the concept of 'reproduction'. It is only much more recently that feminists have been responsible for demonstrating that it also reproduces the sexual division of labour between men and women. This applies in two senses: education reproduces the conventional division of labour in the family, whereby men are in paid employment and women do unpaid work in the home; and it reproduces sexual divisions within the labour market itself, so that when women do take paid work, they tend to be concentrated in particular types of jobs and at the lower level of organisational hierarchies. The contribution of the educational system to sustaining both of these processes is significant and helps to account for difficulties experienced in some positive action programmes (cf. sect. 5.3.2.).

It seems that the inclusion of girls in compulsory schooling was always seen in somewhat different terms from the schooling of boys [doc 7]. The traditional concentration upon teaching domestic subjects to girls (especially working-class girls) demonstrates that the main benefits of their education were meant to accrue to homes and families, rather than to the girls themselves. It can be argued that it is in the interest of the capitalist mode of production aim to prepare girls for a future of work, in the home where they will care for male wage-workers and raise the next generation. [21(19–20)]

Just as with the social division of labour, the argument that girls are being prepared for a specific future can be pursued at two levels: in terms of skills (in the broadest sense) and in terms of relationships relevant to the productive process. First, following Deem's argument, schooling can be seen as essentially a preparation for domesticity, either instead of or as well as for waged work. [22(p. 32)] This process operates even when girls are obtaining similar formal educational qualifications to boys, because girls are seen as a group who can always, if circumstances in the economy make it valuable, be 'returned' to non-waged work in the home, and therefore they provide a very useful flexible source of labour for capitalist employers. [9(p. 155)]

This rather calls into question, as Wolpe has convincingly argued, strategies which seek to encourage girls to do either or both of these: the structural relation of women *in general* to the labour market seems to preclude change on a large scale. The 1977 Green Paper, one of whose stated aims is to encourage girls in precisely these ways, sees girls' aspirations and motivations as the problem, and aims to change them. This is mistaken, argues Wolpe, because it ignores the ideologies and social processes which designate most women as home-makers and therefore peripheral to the labour market. [23(pp. 150-62)]

The second sense in which girls are being prepared for different futures is that they are being prepared for different social relations within the economy and in the home. Just as it is argued that the reproduction of the social division of labour entails preparing a workforce with appropriate work habits and attitudes, so too the sexual division of labour involves a parallel process. This is, as McDonald puts it, [22(p. 32)] that the social relations of schooling not only prepare the working classes for class obedience, but they also prepare women to be subordinate to men (cf. doc 7). Clearly these are not two entirely separate processes, but their relationship is complex. In another article, McDonald has argued that people are prepared for a division of labour which is 'structured by the dual, yet often contradictory, forces of class and gender'. Girls' contradictory relation to the labour market is often accentuated by their schooling, she argues. If they are being prepared for waged work it is usually indirectly.[24]

Another aspect of this is that girls' experience of schooling may often be different according to their own class location. As Deem has argued, middle-class girls may well have benefited from the comprehensive reorganisation in secondary schools, but working-class girls certainly did not. Indeed, the curriculum which most of them were offered remained if anything more firmly tied to their presumed future in the home.[25(p. 137)] At the other end of the social hierarchy, it is interesting to note that the Public Schools Commission regarded girls' public schools as less 'socially divisive' than boys' schools – a point in their favour from the Commission's point of view.[26(paras. 110-15)] This brings out very neatly the cross-cutting effects of the social and sexual division of labour: public schools are clearly in the business of reproducing both the social division of labour and the class structure which is tied to it, but girls' schools presumably have fewer benefits which they can confer upon their pupils in the economic and public domains since, as girls, they are being prepared for a future in the home rather than in paid work.

How far can these processes of reproducing the sexual division of labour be seen in the British educational system as it has developed since 1944? Whilst Newsom's views in 1948 about the education of girls [doc 7] cannot necessarily be regarded as typical, less explicit and slightly less extreme versions of the idea that girls have to be educated to be women can be found in official reports and in educational practice. Wolpe has produced a careful study of the Norwood, Crowther and Newsom reports,[27] and concludes that all three accepted the popular belief that women's main role was in the home, and that work outside the home was a peripheral activity. Thus, she argues, they failed to consider seriously the preparation of girls for waged work and justified this omission by concentrating upon marriage and their likely future. In so doing, the reports provided an ideological basis for perpetuating an educational system which fails to open up new horizons for most girls.

In her consideration of the period between 1944 and 1980, Deem argues that there have been changes in policies towards the education of girls and that these have usually been accompanied by changes in general social policies, linked to the needs of the economy and prevailing ideologies about the role of women.[25] She detects a shift in the

1950s and 1960s to a greater recognition of women's participation in wage labour, but argues that any notion of preparing girls for a dual role (in waged work and in the family) was confined to middle-class girls. For working-class girls the emphasis remained largely on preparation for marriage and childrearing. Such advances as have been made, she argues, have occurred in periods of full employment, so the prospects for the 1980s are not good. Attempts made in the latter part of the 1970s to deal with youth unemployment gave no recognition to the fact that the often inferior education of girls rendered them as much in need of help in entering the labour market as boys, as is shown by Helen Roberts' interesting study of girl school-leavers in Bradford.[28] However, instead of further advancing the position of women in and through education, the social policy emphasis by 1980 was stressing issues like the need to strengthen family life (cf. sect. 6.4.4).

So there seems to be a good case for viewing the educational system since 1944 as important in reproducing the sexual division of labour, despite the fact that instances can be found – such as *Early Leaving* (cf. sect. 2.2) or the 1977 Green Paper – where there is an explicit awareness of the need to expand educational opportunities for girls. Limits appear to be set on such an expansion by the relationship of women in general to the labour market.

6.2.4 Cultural reproduction

The fourth type of reproduction which, it is argued, takes place through the educational system is cultural reproduction: that is, reproduction of ideas, beliefs, values and meanings. In the sense in which 'reproduction' has been used in recent literature, this does not imply that there is an infinitive variety of types of ideas and values, any of which *could* be passed on through schooling, depending upon the personal preference of teachers or the way that textbooks are written. Rather, cultural features are seen as tied quite firmly to structural features of a capitalist society. Thus a particular type of 'culture' is reproduced through schooling which serves the interests of dominant groups (seen variously as capitalists, the ruling classes, men, or indeed whites as against other ethnic groups) and maintains the status quo to their advantage. Thus the act of cultural reproduction is closely linked to the other types of reproduction considered here: it facilitates the reproduction of the social and sexual division of labour, of the class structure and of the political status quo.

Two rather different versions of what is meant by cultural reproduction will be considered briefly here, each of them associated with writers who have had a major influence upon research and writing about education in the 1970s. The first focuses on the transmission of cultural capital and is derived initially from the work of Pierre Bourdieu, whose work puts emphasis upon how 'cultural capital' is distributed and transmitted between generations.[29(p. 387)]

Bourdieu's account of these processes runs broadly as follows: the education system itself embodies the beliefs, practices, norms of the dominant culture. It therefore demands of children a certain competence in the appropriate cultural practices. It does not, however, *give* that competence to those who do not already have it. Therefore, it is only the children from what he calls 'cultured families' who have the necessary competence to receive the message of education and to make use of it. This means that such children are the most successful within the terms set by the education system. Those terms, however, operate in such a way that it does not appear that children are merely being rewarded for coming from the 'right' kinds of families: the educational system accords places in academic, not social hierarchies, and those places are apparently awarded on the basis of individual 'gifts', merits, and so on. This means that the 'cultured' families can use the educational system to ensure that their own children achieve the same advantaged position in adult life, but without its appearing overtly that the rules of the game have been fixed in their favour. Just as the ruling classes have devised various strategies for transmitting economic capital to their own children, so too they have successfully devised the means of transmitting their cultural capital. Bourdieu recognises that the system does not always work perfectly in their favour, nor can it, since it must give the appearance of being open and fair in order to work successfully. However, he argues that it remains overwhelmingly the case that those who possess economic capital still also have a much greater chance of possessing cultural capital. The final twist is that, even if the economically privileged do not possess cultural capital as well, they can probably manage quite successfully without it; whereas cultural capital on its own is rather weak currency, since its value is confined to the academic market.

How far can Bourdieu's analysis be applied to education in Britain since 1944? Clearly it makes sense of a good deal of the research on class and education conducted during this period. However, Halsey *et al.*, in their longitudinal study of boys passing through education before and after 1944, recommended caution about the utility of the idea of the transmission of cultural capital. Their data, they argue, show that state selective schools during this period contained a large number of boys who were first generation in this sector. They see the concept of cultural capital as a 'useful umbrella term for a set of mechanisms through which families influence the formal educational experience of their children'. It should not, however, be pressed too far: cultural capital; they argue, can be disseminated more widely than before, as well as concentrated and preserved.[30(p. 88)]

Bourdieu's account of the transmission of cultural capital suggests the importance of concealment in the process of cultural reproductions. Mechanisms for transmission are accepted as legitimate because they seem to be based on democratic notions of fairness: if the actual processes of reproduction were more apparent, they might be resisted. This idea that education produces the means by which many people consent to and endorse their own subordinate position is explicit and central to the second version of cultural reproduction, the idea of hegemony, which derives from the work of the Italian Marxist, Antonio Gramsci. Hegemony refers to the domination of one class over another, but not by force or by economic means. It is rule by moral and cultural domination, in which power is founded upon producing consent and acquiescence among the ruled class.[31(p. 12)]

Education is clearly important in the process of producing acquiescence to ruling ideas. Gramsci believed that schooling provided the means of transmitting a particular consciousness necessary to maintain a particular class rule.[31(p. 16)] The way in which this is achieved is not a straightforward indoctrination of children; it is rather, as Apple puts it,[32(pp. 3-6)] a saturation of consciousness by the meanings, values and practices which are already deeply embedded in the social structure in which we live. Partly because these are already part of the life lived around us, accepting them makes sense of social reality and therefore is easy. At the same time, however, these 'ruling ideas' are being reinforced and reproduced in the next generation. Further, these processes of cultural reproduction facilitate and reinforce other aspects of reproduction through education, enabling them to operate more smoothly by producing a consciousness in which they seem legitimate.

The idea of cultural reproduction through education is powerful, provided again that it is not presented as an over-simple way. The reproduction of beliefs and values is by no means always successful, as can be seen in relation to political beliefs, which are discussed in the next section.

6.2.5 Reproducing the political order

When R. A. Butler was given oversight of education in the wartime Cabinet he had an interview with Winston Churchill, who expressed himself sceptical about the possibilities that education could change people's natures, but added that: 'I should not object if you could introduce a note of patriotism into our schools.'[33(p. 1)] It seems unlikely that such a 'note' was entirely absent from wartime schools. Indeed, the wartime evacuation of children and the re-establishment of their education in country districts itself was seen as part of the patriotic effort.[34(Ch. 1)] The use of education to reproduce the political status quo has been a common theme from the introduction of compulsory schooling, when there was some concern to offer at least minimal education to all those who had been granted the vote (see following section for further discussion).

The structures of power and domination in the economic and the political spheres overlap considerably. Nevertheless it is important, Hall has argued, that the school's function in reproducing the relations of productive life in captialist societies must be clearly demarcated from its political function in cementing particular forms of class domination.[4(pp. 22-3)] Tapper and Salter see a crucial role for education in maintaining the power of the ruling classes through cultural hegemony, especially by *legitimating* their control.[35(p. 48)]

In what ways is the political order reproduced in schools? Firstly, it is reproduced by the ways in which children are taught about the society in which they live. This may not involve any 'indoctrination' of an overt and crude kind, but within the hidden curriculum of the school, tacit messages are given about how issues like conflict, authority and hierarchy in social life are to be understood. Writing of the way that conflict is dealt with in schools (principally in the United States), Apple says that most teachers neglect to look at the creative potential of conflict or its possibilities for producing desirable change; nor is it presented as a systematic product of the changing structure of society. Rather, it is treated as an abnormal and undesirable state. The hidden message is that society is to be understood in terms of consensus, the maintenance of order, and that 'happy co-operation is the normal way of life'.[32(pp. 92-9)]

Apart from the tacit messages of the hidden curriculum, many schools express the aim of preparing their children to play a full part in the adult world, in terms like education for citizenship in a democracy. This sounds innocuous enough, but the way in which it is accomplished almost always depends upon one particular version of political life, which prepares young people to accept and accommodate themselves to the structures of political power as they currently exist, and certainly does not give them a basis upon which to challenge those structures. Morecover, it is not simply a matter of ideas. Through their dealings with hierarchies and processes of authority which exist within the school itself, young people are learning to relate to and deal with structures of authority in the wider world.[32(pp. 84-5)]

From time to time, various groups have attempted to introduce political education more directly into the schools. These have tended to follow the education-for-citizenship line. In the 1930s, the Association for Education in Citizenship aimed: 'to advance the study of training and citizenship, by which is meant training in the moral qualities necessary for citizens of a democracy, the encouragement of clear thinking in everyday affairs'.[9(p. 53)] More recently, there has been pressure again for some formal political education in schools, consequent partly upon the lowering of the voting age as well as the expansion of the secondary curriculum.[35(pp. 70-71)] Advance reports of a national study indicate that more than half the secondary schools in England and Wales were engaging in some direct form of political education in 1982.[36] The Hansard Society, in conjunction with the Politics Association, produced a detailed report in 1978 advocating that political education should be included in a common curriculum at all levels of schooling; all teacher training should include an element of politics and there should be a growth in curriculum development for political education.[37]

The idea that young people should be given political education in schools raises in the minds of some people the spectre that they might be taught the 'wrong' ideas. This appears to be Rhodes Boyson's response to recent experiments introducing peace studies into secondary schools. He was reported in the press as attacking the unilateral disarmament movement for trying to introduce peace studies, claiming that: 'These are the people whose 1930 equivalents would have left us unprotected against the Nazis and would leave us undefended against colonial Soviet aggression.'[38] Clearly, political education in schools is potentially contested territory, although it may not always appear so.

The kind of political education envisaged in the Hansard report is very far from direct explicit indoctrination, from whatever viewpoint. Its central aim is to enhance what they call 'political literacy', which means: 'the knowledge, skills and attitudes needed to make a man or woman informed about politics; able to participate in public life and groups of all kinds, both occupational and voluntary; and to recognise and tolerate diversities of political and social values.'[37(p. 1)] This approach concentrates upon concepts of authority, order, individuality and pressure (rather than, for example, conflict, solidarity and change). Thus education for political literacy will, if successful, help to maintain the structure of the existing political order rather than to undermine it. This may indeed be its aim, but the apparently neutral terms in which such discussions are often conducted does rather obscure that fact. As Tapper and Salter say, the advocates of education for political literacy tend to emphasise its value to the individuals who receive it, but this plays down the part that such a political education plays in cementing the established order.[35(p. 73)]

So education can be important in reproducing the existing political order and thus leaving the power of the politically dominant groups unchallenged. Such an outcome is not, however, always and invariably successful. As Entwistle has pointed out, many political radicals are the product of conventional educational systems; and in some ways, paradoxically, educational systems seem to foster oppositional potential, say in periods of student radicalism. [31(pp. 87-9), 35(p. xii)] This essentially contradictory relationship between politics and schooling again calls into question any explanations based upon a simple notion of 'correspondence' between the two spheres. As Tapper and Salter comment, 'education is not the automatic servicing agency of the ruling class that some Marxists believe it to be; it is an instrument of class control, but not one that operates in a blanket fashion to the permanent and inevitable advantage of that alleged ruling class.' [35(p. xii)] This point can be applied equally to other aspects of reproduction through education. It leads on to important questions about how far one can push the notion that processes like reproduction, regulation and control constitute the 'real purpose' of education; and whether the state straightforwardly represents the interests of dominant or powerful groups when it acts in the sphere of education, and indeed other social policy. These questions form the central theme of the final section of this chapter.

6.3 REGULATION AND CONTAINMENT

6.3.1 Introduction

The focus in this section is upon the use of social policy as a mechanism for reducing and containing social conflict, essentially an exercise in the political regulation of the population, especially the working classes. The idea of 'regulating the poor' has been demonstrated influentially by Piven and Cloward in relation to public welfare in the United States.[39] They argue that social policies (and in their case, the granting of financial relief to the poor in particular) have to be understood in terms of the functions they perform for the social and political order. Historically, they argue, relief has been initiated and expanded during periods of mass unemployment when civil disorder was seen as an actual or potential threat, and then contracted when order was restored. Expansive relief policies, therefore, can be seen as attempts to mute civil disorder, and restrictive ones as attempts to reinforce work norms.

More recent neo-Marxist analyses of the British welfare state have developed rather similar arguments. The welfare state has been shaped, it is argued, in the process of struggle between capital and labour, whose material interests ultimately are fundamentally opposed. In certain cases, however, those interests appear to coincide and produce expansions in welfare. One circumstance in which this can happen is, as Ginsburg argues, when welfare is used as a bribe, a way of buying-off the working classes by mitigating the worst aspects of their lives in order to secure political quiescence. The effect is that welfare 'cushions' working-class experience, obscuring the real structures of inequality and the appropriation of their labour.[40(p. 12)]

In what way can these general arguments about social policy be applied to education in the context of the welfare state? Clearly, it cannot be quite so direct a bribe as financial payments, but there is a long history of education of the masses being seen as an important part of securing political peace. The introduction of compulsory education in the nineteenth century was intimately bound up with issues about political control, especially of the 'dangerous' classes. It is well known that the extension of the franchise to give many working-class men the vote was seen by some as making a minimal level of universal literacy essential. Hurt, in his review of the period, warns that this is only part of the picture. There was also 'a much more primitive emotion, the fear of the mob, a fear which extended back through the memory of the propertied classes to the sturdy beggar of Tudor England and earlier. Industrialisation and urbanisation had created a new mob in the 'residuum' of the slums and rookeries of England's towns and cities.'[41(p. 68)] It was the fear of political unrest from these classes which, in Hurt's view, was an important trigger for attempts to include the whole of the working classes in schooling. Educators were to be sent in to reclaim the people from the errors of their ways and to secure political pacification in the longer term.[42] Contemporary examples of the use of education in ways which apparently either reduce or avert potential social conflict can be found in the use of education as a palliative, and its use as the means of legitimating inequality.

6.3.2 Education as a palliative

Education can be used as a palliative in circumstances where it is offered to people in lieu of some other commodity or opportunity which is what they really need. Since they are receiving *something* which may be of benefit (albeit limited), this reduces the likelihood that social conflict will ensue because they are not receiving the desired commodity.

The contemporary example par excellence of education being offered as a substitute for something else concerns the young unemployed. As has already been noted, the 1977 Green Paper commented on the mismatch between young people leaving school and the willingness of employers to offer them work, and saw the problems as lying rather more with education than with employers [doc 22]. This was quite characteristic of the approach being taken in the late 1970s to the growing number of young unemployed: the cause of this particular problem was said to lie with the school-leavers themselves, rather than with the structure of employment. As the authors of *Unpopular Education* argue in their discussion of the rise of the Manpower Services Commission, the mismatch between school-leavers and employers' needs was interpreted as a consequence of the 'poor quality' of school-leavers. The 'blame' was laid on young people, who allegedly lacked motivation and willingness to persevere. These kinds of complaints are, as Rees and Gregory argue, a 'traditional gripe' on the part of the employer, to which the Great Debate made little contribution other than to fudge the issue. What recent governments have completely failed to acknowledge, they argue, is that whole sectors of the youth labour market have actually collapsed.[43(pp. 7-24)]

From its inception, the Manpower Services Commission began to initiate programmes which can be seen as cultural interventions in the reproduction of labour power, with the purpose of enabling the trainees to 'adjust' to the conditions, disciplines and relationships of the workplace.[9(pp. 34-5)] The idea of providing this kind of programme is by no means new: in the 1930s, Juvenile Instruction (or Unemployment) Centres were set up in some parts of the country as a form of educational provision which would maintain the morale and employability of unemployed young people. They quickly came to be known as 'dole schools' and proved unpopular and – even in their own terms – unsuccessful.[44(pp. 26-33)]

However, the purpose of the temporary employment and training schemes which flourished from the mid-1970s onwards continued to be presented very much in terms of their benefits to the young people concerned. The initial piecemeal efforts were reviewed in the Holland report of 1977, which set the tone for subsequent initiatives.[45] It proposed a range of special measures 'designed to bring young people the kind of help they most need in the form they want it'. These courses fell into two main types: those designed to prepare young people for work, and those designed to offer some type of work experience (with a recommendation that further education and training should form a part of these latter schemes also). The Holland report explicitly did not intend to provide an opportunity for every young school-leaver, but by 1982 the government was making precisely that commitment.

This is not the place to attempt a full evaluation of such schemes; but from the viewpoint of political regulation they bear some scrutiny. On one level, they can be seen as an exercise in redefining the problem of youth unemployment, to be a problem of and for education. This involves a sleight of hand which says that if young people cannot get jobs, it is because they must be unemployable, not because there are insufficient jobs to go round. The implication is that better education can somehow solve the problem of unemployment. On that level, the development of such schemes is a diversionary tactic which may help to stifle more direct challenges to the structure of the labour market and its operation. On another level, the special educational and training schemes for the young unemployed can be seen as part of the process of ensuring that unemployed school-leavers do not spend their time generating political unrest. This is not to say that every unemployed school-leaver is likely to become a revolutionary if not rapidly diverted into an MSC scheme but, as part of the regulation and control of the working classes, adolescents have always been seen as a particularly important group. As Corrigan puts it: 'Adolescence was always seen as the period of greatest moral peril, for it was during adolescence that the first signs of the combination of moral decadence and political instability showed itself'.[46(p. 38)]

The links between youth unemployment and political unrest were being made very forcefully by many commentators on the summer riots in 1981. Whether or not unemployment can in any sense be said to have 'caused' these riots, the point remains that it is still a link to which many people easily have recourse. In these circumstances, education appears to offer a very neat option. It acts both as a palliative (in the sense of offering *something* potentially of benefit) while at the same time perhaps being able to postively counteract seditious and unruly tendencies in young people.

6.3.3 *Legitimating inequality: credentials and education*

The English educational system has increasingly provided a publicly available 'explanation' for social and economic inequalities which accounts for and legitimates the basis of inequality in individual, meritocratic terms.[35(pp. 38-40)] Those who occupy more privileged positions are defined as people who *deserve* to be there, and the occupants of less advantaged social and economic positions by implication 'deserve' their own status and material circumstances. The effect of this publicly available legitimation, pressed home to each individual through their own experience of schooling, is to obscure the other processes at work in the distribution of rewards and resources (e.g. the capacity of the privileged to pass on economic and cultural capital to their own children) which have nothing whatsoever to do with individual merits, however defined. Obscuring those processes presumably (among other things) defuses potential political dissent, which might be based on recognising that processes favouring the collective interest of certain social groups are at work in the distribution of social and economic resources.

Increasingly since the end of the Second World War, an important part of this process of legitimation of inequality through education has been accomplished through the qualifications or 'credentials' which education formally confers. As T. H. Marshall noted [doc 35], although the 1944 Act strongly expressed concern for the individual right to be educated to the limit of one's own capacity, there was never any pretence that this right was absolute, because educational plans are always likely to be adjusted to occupational demands.

That process begins to make sense of the paradox that, despite the great increase in the number of people gaining formal educational qualifications, the class-related basis of educational 'achievement' has not been seriously undermined. Partly this is a consequence of the 'inflation' of credentials, a process which Randall Collins has documented very effectively for the United States.[47] Basically, credential inflation refers to the process whereby, as more and more people gain educational qualifications, employers begin to ask for *higher* qualifications as an entrance requirement to given occupations. By the 1960s in the United States, Collins argues, this process had reached crisis proportions; the 'credential price of jobs' had risen so much that credentials which formerly had been quite highly valued no longer guaranteed an elite job – or even, in some cases, a respectable one.[47(p. 191)]

There is a sense in which this process of credential inflation is itself part of the process of maintaining class inequalities from one generation to the next. Halsey and his co-authors have argued that credentials in effect 'sabotage egalitarian reform' because 'as the working class clear one hurdle, so another is set up in their path, leaving the service class always one flight ahead'.[30(p. 218)] The ways in which employers both perceive and use qualifications are by no means straightforward. Macguire and Ashton have demonstrated that some employers adopt selection strategies which place comparatively little emphasis on qualifications and a good deal on 'background' and 'personality' factors which implicitly favour middle-class applicants. This calls into question any very straightforward account of credential inflation – a factor which they believe principally to be applicable to the more prestigious sectors of the labour market in recent British experience.[48(pp. 25-36)] Seen in this light, credentials are part of the means by which the middle-classes maintain and perpetuate their own position. Credentials are – as Parkin puts it – a 'handy device' for ensuring that those who possess cultural capital are able to transmit it to their own children.[49(p. 55)]

Another way of looking at credentials is that they give access to certain jobs but offer no guarantee of securing them.[50(pp. 413-34)] They give individuals a licence to *compete* in a specific sector of the labour market, but the rules of that competition are not necessarily the same for every individual. In Bourdieu's terms, young people from the working classes may not have the requisite cultural capital to match their educational credentials. Further, girls do not compete on the same terms as boys, nor in most cases do black and Asian children compete on the same terms as whites,[43] so that the distribution of jobs by individuals in these different social categories does not always match the distribution of educational credentials gained.

So the mechanism of credentials is one powerful tool developed through the educational system which has the effect *inter alia* of defusing potential social conflict by making social and economic inequalities appear 'fair'. It also has the important consequence of legitimating the activities *of* schools, and can act as a mechanism of control *within* their walls. Collins notes that teachers are presented with much greater problems of control of students or pupils in the wake of the credential crisis, where the capacity of schools to claim that compliance with their procedures and hard work should lead to a good job has become much less credible.[47(p. 192)] This argument also makes sense in relation to Britain: in his study of working-class boys at school in Sunderland, Corrigan shows that these boys did not see education as in any sense useful for its own sake. Where they found it rewarding, this was expressed in terms of the relationship between school and a job. Corrigan characterises this view as: 'If you behave yourself, you are more likely to work hard; if you do well, you will get good qualifications and a good reference; if you get a good reference you will get a good job; if you get a good job, you are likely to get lots of money.'[46(p. 50)] The opportunities for credentials to provide a means of control *within* the school setting clearly are reduced in time of high youth unemployment.

6.4 CONTROL OF LIFESTYLE

6.4.1 Introduction

There is a sense in which schools' attempts to mould the lifestyle of their pupils is part of a fundamental struggle for the control of the young. This is not to imply that 'control' is straightforwardly imposed upon immature human beings who are infinitely malleable: far from it. In the matter of control of lifestyle, it is quite clear that young people themselves put up various kinds of resistance. Nevertheless, adults do make attempts to control young people, and at times the battle lines are drawn very obviously between them. As Jenny Shaw says:

> It is all too easy to ignore the internal divisions within the adult world and assume that in the matter of the subordination and care of children that agreement as to what is best obtains. This obscures the stresses and strains of the process euphemistically known as 'socialisation', and which includes a conflict for the control of the young. In the course of such conflict appeals to legitimating ideologies are made and various agencies developed. [51.(p. 267)]

Of course the control of children is only one part of the process: their subordination and their care are intimately linked (cf. sect. 3.5; doc 33).

Historically, one theme in the struggle for the control of the young was that the state needed to take over from certain unsatisfactory parents, with teachers acting as substitutes. The idea that teachers should act in this capacity has been very well documented by Grace,[52] who shows how the development of popular education in nineteenth-century Britain was very much built on the idea that teachers were to act in the role of 'social and cultural missionaries – a kind of secular priesthood, dedicated to the idea of "civilisation".'[52(p. 11)] In this capacity, teachers were what Grace calls 'the agents of symbolic control' of the urban working classes. But although part of a massive apparatus of control, they were never entirely puppets of it. Indeed, Grace's work demonstrates that, in order to accomplish this outcome, teachers themselves had to be regulated and controlled, to ensure that they were passing on the correct messages.

Attempts to develop ways of morally regulating the young through education have to be set in the context of a whole range of welfare activities of the state which accomplish the same purpose. One of these is the separation of children from productive employment, which marks off childhood as a clearly defined 'phase', during which the child is economically dependent upon adults (cf. sect. 3.1). The mechanisms for the moral regulation of the young are seen most clearly in those activities of the welfare state where the law and/or the social services specifically intervene in a child's life because he or she is 'at risk', or because some delinquent or deviant activity has been committed and identified. In such circumstances it becomes very clear, as Fitz argues, that the state imposes definitions of which activities are to be sanctioned in children although permitted in adults (e.g. gambling, drinking, sexual activity), and that these rules of moral regulation operate somewhat differently for boys and for girls.[53]

Forms of regulation can vary from the crude to the subtle, the explicit to the indirect. Jenny Shaw, also looking historically at education in Britain, suggests that gradually the consent and co-operation of parents in the process of schooling became more reliable, and schools then shifted to milder and gentler forms of control than were possible when the assent of families could not be relied upon.[54] Thus achieving the consent and co-operation of parents to some extent has replaced earlier attempts to take over from the family. This is reminiscent of what Donzelot (writing of France) has called the 'colonisation' of the family by various professionals through whom the state acts, in partnership with the mother, as the child's social guardian. He regards teachers as colonisers of the family, especially in relation to delinquent youth.[55(p. 103)] So, in the struggle for the control of the young, the family may be either substituted or colonised.

This preliminary discussion has introduced a number of themes concerning the control of the lifestyle of the young through education. The following sections explore these themes in relation to several different aspects of education; both where the controls are direct and immediate, and where they are more indirect and long-term.

6.4.2 Compulsion, attendance and truancy

The most fundamental way in which the lifestyle of the young is controlled through education is the compulsion upon them to be educated, thus creating a publicly defined phase of childhood and youth which has been progressively extended as the school-leaving age has been raised. Compulsory education does not actually mean that everyone must attend school, since the law makes provision for parents to educate their children 'otherwise' [doc 4], if they can satisfy the local education authority that what they are being offered is satisfactory.[56(p. 133)] In practice this usually means education at home. This formal legal duty to see that their children are educated was first laid upon parents in 1880, when education became compulsory. It was principally a means of ensuring that working-class parents sent their children to school, which they seemed singularly reluctant to do when given the choice, in many cases.[57] The placing of legal duties upon the parents rather than the child has remained. The ultimate sanction is a court appearance for the parents, but this is seldom used.[58(p. 72)] Once legal compulsion has been introduced, the problem becomes, as Shaw puts it: what level of non-attendance can be tolerated while keeping the general principle intact?[54(para. 7.1)] In practice, levels of attendance are quite high: average attendance figures of around 90 per cent of the school population are usually estimated.[59(p. 119)]

Despite the common image that the school absentee is a wilful truant, missing school without the knowledge of his or her parents, many school absences are not of this type. Illness and holidays are two obvious examples. Various other kinds of absence are 'condoned' by parents for particular reasons, such as the child undertaking household duties or looking after younger children. The education welfare service – whose major work involves the enforcement of school attendance – (cf. sect. 3.3) normally only takes action if absence is both 'unjustified' and persistent. Even in these cases, however, as Galloway's study shows, straightforward truancy accounts for less than 15 per cent of absences, the other absences being a product of parental encouragement (or at least consent) and socio-medical reasons (such as exclusion from school because of infestation).[60]

So education welfare officers have the task of discriminating between different types of absence and deciding when direct control over a young person's life – an attempt to force him or her back into school – shall be exercised. In practice, these controls are still class-specific, in the sense that poor attenders are most likely to come from large families where the father is a manual worker. Absences increase as school-leaving age approaches.[61] The operation of sanctions against truants is also gender-specific. Jenny Shaw argues that is not surprising, given that education welfare officers have little to guide them but the traditions of their occupation and their own commonsense ideas about how children should be raised. Boys in fact are likely to be designated as truants much more frequently than girls, whose absences often are treated as some other form of non-attendance, usually related to household duties of one sort or another. The consequence (presumably unintended) of that particular operation of commonsense ideas is, as Shaw notes, that less action is taken on girls' absence. This means that they receive less schooling than they otherwise might; while boys, in being designated truants and treated accordingly, may be subject to the kind of labelling process which makes it more likely that they will fall foul of the law in other respects.[54(paras. 8,9-8.13)] Thus the operation of direct sanctions in respect of school attendance not only controls the lifestyle of the young by forcing them into school, but does so in such a way that other life patterns are reinforced. In this case, the pattern of traditional gender divisions, which treats it as legitimate for girls and women to be engaged in domestic work, is confirmed; and the fact that some girls are not actually at school very much makes it even more likely that their alternatives to domestic work in adult life will be limited.

Where truancy *per se* is discussed, various accounts are offered which for the purposes of this analysis will be considered separately. In the first account, truancy is wilful resistance which needs to be controlled directly. This is the approach taken by the Pack report on truancy and indiscipline in schools in Scotland. The report takes a rather bracing attitude to truants and their parents, recommending that: 'Truancy should be deal with at the first sign: action should be taken to establish the cause and then to apply whatever remedies are possible. Methods of dealing with truancy must be both speedy and effective.' As far as parents are concerned, measures should suit the particular circumstances, but: 'The parents should . . . firmly and quickly be made aware of their responsibilities as regards school attendance.' [62] This is very much a top-downwards view of the educational system, in which the authority of schools and teachers is paramount and children and their parents must be brought into line with them; although the report does also suggest that some changes in school curriculum and organisation might improve the situation.

The arguments about speedy response, direct and effective action, are often reinforced by the assumption that truancy is the first step on a slippery slope towards a criminal career. It is interesting therefore that 'truancy' and 'indiscipline' are often linked, as they were in the Pack report, and also in the more recent (but briefer) HMI pamphlet on the same topic.[63] Truancy in fact has long been seen as causing delinquency and a whole range of other forms of individual and collective pathology. [54(para. 8.11)] Thus the response to truancy becomes part of a wider attempt at the control of those sectors of the young population who are seen as prone to crime.

The second account of truancy, which appears initially to contrast sharply with the implied direct control of the first, sees it as merely a sign or symptom of (as the Seebohm report puts it) 'personal behavioural difficulties or family disturbance, misfortune or distress as well as possible signs of the child's unhappiness in school' [doc 58]. The implication of this approach is that one has to deal with causes rather than symptoms, and Seebohm firmly designates social workers as the appropriate persons to investigate and handle all 'serious' cases of truancy. Assigning social workers to truancy cases presumably would be one consequence of the merger of social services and the education welfare services, as envisaged by Seebohm [doc 31]. The social work perpsective is also reflected in the publication by the Association of Directors of Social Services, who argue also that social workers might well be concerned about absences of other kinds than truancy, many of which, it is argued, would be 'amenable to prevention, given appropriate social intervention.'[64(para. 47)]

Approaches to truancy on a 'treatment' model have been developed experimentally in various LEAs. Macmillan, for example, describes one such initiative in Salford, where EWOs were developing group work with truants and other children 'with associated problems'. Other initiatives based on therapeutic lines have been undertaken outside the confines of the education welfare service, often based in 'truancy centres' funded by education departments, social services departments and voluntary agencies.[58(pp. 75-8)] Accounts of the work of such centres suggest that where successful, what they do effectively is to offer *educational* experiences to young people which they can genuinely make use of, because these are of a very different type from the experiences offered in school settings.[65a, b]

The therapeutic response to truancy seems far removed from issues of control of the young. On the other hand, it can be seen to some extent as a form of control by different *methods*. The use of group work as a response to truancy is still usually oriented towards producing some behaviour change, albeit in a more human and perhaps a more useful way.[58(p. 76)] Moreoever, the type of therapeutic response which locates the child's problem within the family setting and attempts to deal with it there, effectively uses non-attendance at school as the trigger for various kinds of intervention within the family, to produce modes of childrearing which are more 'satisfactory'. Of course, in the process, adults and children may be provided with forms of assistance which they both need and want. But there is a long history of inter-ventions in the families of the disorderly poor in order to control the way in which the young are reared (cf. section 3 of this chapter). It is at least plausible to argue that some cases of therapeutic work with the families of truants represent that kind of intervention. This also aligns closely with the way in which the recalcitrant young are handled in other sectors of the welfare state. The way in which the juvenile justice system handles young offenders displays the apparently opposed alternatives of 'punishment' and 'treatment'; but, as Thorpe and his co-authors have argued, both these principles seek to control, to socialise and essentially to transform the individual in anticipation of future actions.[66(pp. 97-103)]

The third account of truancy – reflected very little in any 'official' literature on the topic – is that truancy is an entirely rational response to schools which offer very little indeed which seems of any value, say to adolescents who have already been designated as 'failures' within the system. They are, as Harris puts it, 'rebels with a cause', the product of an under-financed education system, incapable of fostering the potential in every child.[67]

The idea that truancy is a rational response is also suggested by Corrigan's study in Sunderland, where the boys whom he studied appear to see it as a means of protecting themselves from things which they did not like in school (often specific lessons). Their concern essentially, argues Corrigan, was with the *power* of the school over them, that is, the power of the law to compel them to attend school generally and specific lessons in particular.[46(pp. 28-9)] It is the principle of compulsion which creates the possibility of truancy, and it was precisely that compulsion which was being resisted. Truancy there-fore *can* be resistance to schooling, and provides an example of how the control of the young cannot be treated as a simple and unproble-matic process. Whether one interprets that resistance as a sign of deviance to be stamped out or as a rational response depends rather upon one's view of what schooling actually offers to young people, especially to those who have been 'sorted' to the bottom of the pile.

6.4.3 Discipline, rules and sanctions

The most obvious instances of the exercise of control in schools concern the disciplinary procedures which all schools develop in some form, sometimes in the guise of 'pastoral care' (cf. sect. 3.5; doc 34). This is a point at which attempts to control the lifestyle of the young in the broader sense overlap with issues of day-to-day management and control of the school population. Again, very explicit links may be made between control of the young within the school and the stifling of nascent criminal careers. The Pack report says that the purpose of disciplinary sanctions is 'both to deter those who are tempted to step out of line and to make those who transgress realise that *crime does not pay*'.[62(para. 3.24)] (my italics)

Because instances of what is usually referred to as 'indiscipline' in schools entails a rejection of control, the way in which it is handled reveals some interesting facets of the underlying processes. The legal basis of teachers' capacity to sanction and punish disapproved actions is their status as 'in loco parentis' (cf. sect. 3.5). What that means in the case of teachers was established by a legal judgment in 1860, when a judge ruled that it meant that a teacher must act as a reasonable parent would do. This is not necessarily the same thing as doing what the child's *own* parents themselves would do, but if parents believe a teacher's actions to be *un*reasonable, they may be able to initiate either civil or criminal proceedings.[68(pp. 200-03)] As Jenny Shaw has noted, the circumstances in which 'in loco parentis' is usually invoked are more frequently to do with the punishment of children than their care,[51(p. 253)] and as a concept it encapsulates notions both of the welfare of children and of the exercise of authority over them (cf. sect. 3.5). It is of course not always straightforward to teachers to decide how to exercise this function [doc 32].

The exercise of discipline in schools for the most part is a routine matter of school organisation, rather than a constant application of sanctions and punishments. School populations are broken down into homogeneous groups (through streaming, banding and so on), and the school day is broken up into 'lessons' or 'periods', all of which greatly assist the routine exercise of control.[54(paras. 10.9-10.11)] Further, within each lesson, a structure is imposed which facilitates the management of what Hargreaves *et al.* call 'routine deviance'.[69(p. 23)] This they define as 'the rapid "processing" by the teacher of common and minor breaches of the rules'. The major issues facing the teacher in these routine tasks of the management of deviance are when to intervene, and if so how. Often a pragmatic response prevails, since the immediate control of the classroom is the most pressing issue.[69(pp. 222-36)]

Control of the young is most visible when punishments are administered. The rationales offered for this usually emphasise that punishment acts as a deterrent to future offending, or that it is an educative exercise in itself. In both cases, the emphasis is upon the alleged good achieved through administering punishments. Punishment should be seen as 'bringing home to pupils the seriousness of action in a morally irresponsible way without thoughts for the consequences of one's actions on others'.[68(p. 236)] In order to have these positive effects, argues Docking, punishment must be administered in an atmosphere where the child feels basically accepted; must be based on legitimate authority; must encourage pupils to explore the reasons for the punishment so that they become less dependent upon extrinsic sanctions; must be administered consistently, and requires adults themselves to provide appropriate models for pupils to follow.[68(p. 236)]

Rather similar rationales prevail in the 'special case' of the administration of corporal punishment – special not least because Britain is alone among western countries in retaining it in schools.[54(para. 10.3)] This example of licensed brutality on the part of adults is most frequently justified as the ultimate sanction, important for its deterrent value rather than for its application. Available evidence, however, suggests that it does not act as a deterrent,[68(p. 230)] and against this must be set the ethical argument that it is humiliating and degrading for both teacher and pupil.[68(p. 232)] Its alleged 'educative' value has a long history, coloured with Victorian notions of original sin and the consequent need to correct what is inherently evil in the child. This rationale was quite apparent in the famous legal case in 1860 (*Regina* v. *Hopley*), which was brought against a schoolmaster whose pupil had died following a beating. It was this case which established that the schoolteacher's right to punish was based upon delegated parental authority, but that this was not unlimited and must be exercised in a reasonable manner.[70(pp. 1-5)]

The average rate of caning in English secondary schools has been estimated by the Society of Teachers Opposed to Physical Punishment as about five beatings per year per 100 pupils. Far from being the ultimate sanction reserved for exceptionally heinous crimes, it often seems to be administered for almost trivial offences. The analysis of punishments administered in one Bristol comprehensive school over several years in the late 1970s [doc 59] indicates that corporal punishment is most likely to be administered for fighting and bullying and for missing detentions. 'Horseplay-type offences' come quite high on the list, and these include incidents such as throwing fruit at the staffroom window; dancing about on the roof; squirting washing-up liquid; letting off stink bombs; and snowballing. Burgess reports similar incidents in his study of a different comprehensive school, and also shows that at least one teacher routinely caned for truancy.[71] As STOPP comments, many 'horseplay-type' acts, when committed in other contexts such as by undergraduates at the ancient universities, would be defined as merely youthful high spirits.[72] So it appears that in some contemporary secondary schools caning is part of the repertoire of actions available in the course of managing the school population and attempting to mould the lifestyle specifically of boys, since girls are less often subject to corporal punishment. Corporal punishment is thus gender but not class-specific, having a long history in our public schools.[73(Ch. 1)] Recently several British parents have successfully challenged in the European Court of Human Rights the right of teachers to administer it to their children.[74]

The various 'explanations' for indiscipline run along very similar lines as those for truancy. In some cases it is regarded as wilful and evil, as has already been indicated. In others, it is viewed as a product of unsatisfactory homes or the deterioration of social and cultural standards.[75(pp. 10-11)]

As with truancy, the 'personal pathology' explanation may also attract therapeutic response. This is predominantly the terms in which HMI see the 'behavioural units' which they surveyed in 1978. These had mostly been set up since 1974, to provide for pupils who need to be removed from the classroom on a short-term basis. The report sees this very much in terms of the characteristics of individuals who 'for a variety of reasons find it difficult to accept the normal framework of life and work in schools'.[76] The Pack report strongly recommended the use of such units as a short-term rehabilitative measure,[62(Ch. 3)] buh some pupils can spend up to four or five years in this type of provision, so that it effectively becomes alternative education, according to the HMI report.

As with truancy, some writers see disruptive behaviour as an understandable response to what the educational system offers: Davies, for example, suggests that pupils may be disruptive if they fail to see the point of their education, or do not wish to accept the fate to which it has assigned them.[77(pp. 30-33)] Corrigan, on the basis of his study, argues that the dislike for and rejection of teachers cannot be dismissed as a childish reaction but 'it must be seen as a rejection of the right of someone from a great social distance to try and change the boys' lifestyle'.[46(p. 55)]

Given the arguments developed above, it is also not surprising to find some advocates of the idea that parents should be involved in the disciplinary process. The Pack report suggests that one very effective response may be to invite parents to school to report to them the bad behaviour of their children. Unfortunately this may not always meet with the desired response in parents, in which case they too may have to be disciplined: 'where . . . parents are uninterested and refuse to co-operate, obviously more positive steps must be taken and these would include the use of statutory powers to enforce co-operation'.[62(para. 3.28)] There could scarcely be a clearer expression of the state's activity to colonise the family and ultimately to substitute for it, in the cause of controlling the lifestyle of the young.

6.4.4 Education for 'personal relationships' and family life

The final example in this section is the exercise of controls over the young which specifically are long-term in their aims and often indirect in their methods. The whole area of preparation for parenthood, family life and 'personal relationships' has become a growth area in education. The Newsom and Crowther reports (cf. sect. 2.3; doc 10) regarded it as an important feature of the education of adolescents, as did the 1977 Green Paper. There is evidence of a growing number of examination and non-examination courses in 'personal development' and 'preparation for life'.[78(p. 17)] These obviously shade into the more specific activity of sex education, itself often constituted as part of a 'health education' programme. These activities are very clearly concerned with the moral regulation of the young, both as adolescents and in their adult lives.

While there seems to be something of a consensus that this is an important area for schools, there is much less agreement upon *what* should be taught and learned. Certain writers treat education for 'family life' unproblematically as if it meant the assertion of traditional values. An example of this is to be found in the article by Brayshaw [doc 60] who, writing in the context of public policy and family life, believes that there is a consensus that the younger generation should be pointed in the direction of 'a happy and enduring marriage, bringing up a small family in a home of their own'. The particular contribution of education is, he argues, to train young people in the virtues which they will need to accomplish this, and to ensure that they resist sexual experiences which do not lead in that direction. This apparently can be accomplished by instructing them that 'a pre-marital pregnancy is a serious matter which is best avoided by refraining from intercourse'. Other writers are less certain. The report by the National Council for One Parent Families takes the view that conflicting morality within society makes it difficult for parents and teachers to give adequate advice and guidance on sexual matters, although both have a responsibility to do so.[79(p. 16)] Whitfield sees the whole field of family policy as essentially a contested area.[80(p.106)] Moreover, attempts at moral regulation may sometimes conflict with other features of the educational process, as was clear in the discussion of the dilemmas which schools face when deciding how to deal with pregnant schoolgirls (cf. sect. 3.5; doc 33): the educational needs of the girls suggest keeping them at school, but in doing so they run the risk of 'contaminating' other pupils.

In the whole area of 'personal relationships' and 'family life' education it is clear that girls in particular are being controlled, especially their sexuality. In an appendix to the Newsom report, the author (a headmaster) claims that girls in his school are taught that sex is 'a healthy and natural interest'. But when girls actually have their first sexual encounters, the deputy head advocates 'many and diverse interests to keep the body active and the mind alert so that sex takes no inordinate place'.[81(paras. 5, 6)] It is also clear that girls are being controlled as future mothers. Kellmer Pringle, for example, wants to raise the 'status and level of parenting in the whole population' by teaching girls to resist the pressures to engage in paid work if they are also mothers.[82] Brayshaw [doc 60] thinks that working-class girls especially must be persuaded not to marry too early; to select a partner wisely; to have a baby at the 'proper' time; and to make sure that the family owns its own home. This is a singularly clear case of an attempt to impose a bourgeois lifestyle upon working-class girls.

These of course are by no means the only views of education for family life. Some other writers are rather more liberal. Nevertheless, views similar to those of Brayshaw are given a certain legitimacy by various pronouncements of government ministers on the topic. For example, criticism was levelled in 1981 at a sex education pack produced for schools by the Brook Advisory Centre. Its handling of contraception was especially condemned for being too explicit and mechanical. Lady Young, in her capacity as a DES minister called it 'absolutely appalling' and added, 'What I don't like is that the whole thing is taken outside a concept of love and the responsiblity that we have as human beings to one another. I think a lot of young people are confused by this and the implication that as long as you don't get pregnant it's all right.'[83]

Sex education, it appears, is to be firmly placed in the context of marriage and family life, whose preservation and strengthening is an important task for schools, according to the Crowther report [doc 10]. Even the more liberal approaches tend not to question the desirability of preserving and promoting the nuclear family as the norm for the next generation. Whitfield, for example, is quite clear that the purpose of education for family life has to be set in the wider context of family policy, which aims to correct the significant 'under-functioning' of many children and those who care for them. The education service must develop a range of policies aimed at removing existing deficiencies in child-care practice and family membership, involving systematic preparation for parenthood for both boys and girls.[80(pp. 3-4)]

It is clear that education for family life, whether in a liberal or more reactionary form, constitutes one particular kind of intervention through schooling which aims to ensure that the *next* generation of parents bring up their children in a suitable manner: a kind of anticipatory colonisation which if successful would make substitution unnecessary.

6.5 CONCLUSION. WELFARE, CAPITALISM AND THE STATE: PROBLEMS AND POSSIBLITIES OF EXPLANATION

The material covered in this chapter raises some important issues of explanation in social policy. Although the accounts presented here are derived mostly from some version of Marxism, the problems which they raise are not confined to Marxist accounts. Putting it at its crudest, much of the material considered in this chapter could suggest an explanation of social policy which runs like this: social policies in general (and education in particular) take a specific form at a specific time because they serve the needs of a capitalist economy. If those needs change, the form of provision changes. Although people may be duped into believing that the provision is for their own good, actually capital is always the beneficiary.

It is easy to see that such an account could be derived from much of the evidence about education in Britain. However, in its crude form it is entirely unsatisfactory as the basis for explanation of the development of the welfare state, or of particular social policies. In order to bring out the problems with this kind of account, and to indicate where advances can be made, I will concentrate on two issues: first, the problem of functionalist explanations; second, the relationship between capitalism, welfare and the state.

In social science, explanations are called 'functionalist' if they imply a coherent, integrated social system in which what happens in one part is explained straightforwardly by its 'functions' for the rest of the system. Hence the crude explanation outlined above is functionalist, in the sense that the 'function' of welfare is said to be serving the needs of a capitalist economy. Functionalist explanations in social policy (and indeed generally in social science) are by no means confined to accounts which derive from a Marxist perspective. Indeed, they usually have implied a much more conservative political framework, in which a 'healthy' society is a smoothly functioning whole, based upon consensus and social harmony. The problems with these versions of functionalism, as they apply to social policy in particular, are well summarised by Mishra.[84(pp. 51-8)] Briefly, some problems include: these explanations are too mechanical; they often describe rather than explain; they overlook the unintended consequences of policies; they fail to incorporate the dimension of class; they do not coherently relate social policy to social structure.

Functionalist explanations which derive from a Marxist perspective share some (but not all) of the same problems. They do have a very clear notion of class; they attempt systematically to relate social policy to social structure; and they do offer an explanatory (rather than merely a descriptive) account, based mainly upon the imperatives of capitalism. But they still imply a very mechanical view of social life which does not take seriously the unintended consequences of actions, which has little to say about conflicts and struggles in the arena of social policy, and which leaves out any real account of human processes, in the sense that the great majority of people are seen simply as manipulated, duped and controlled.

Mishra (using a language which actually derives from a non-Marxist form of functionalism) divides the functionalist aspects of Marxist explanations into two types: system integration and social integration. By system integration he means 'the various measures necessary for the continuation, stability and efficient working of the capitalist system.[84(p. 70)] Much of the material considered under the 'reproduction' section of this chapter could in principle fall into that category. By social integration he means 'the other main function of the bourgeois welfare state [which] has to do with the maintenance of order and the reduction of social conflict and tension'.[84(p. 71)] The 'regulation' section of this chapter, and part of the 'control' section, could fall into this category. Any explanation, he argues, which holds that the needs of the economy determine everything else, do not fully match the evidence of the development of the British welfare state. The reality is much more complex. At the same time, there is evidence, especially in more recent years, that the 'core' institutions of capitalist society can reassert themselves, and welfare reforms be eroded. So the guiding principle of these Marxist explanations (namely that the institutions of welfare must be seen in relation to the capitalist system as a whole) cannot be faulted, but the *degree* to which welfare systems are determined by the needs of a capitalist economy can be overstated.[84(pp. 79-80)]

It is, then, a question of building into these explanations of welfare some space for accounts of conflict over policies, outcomes which do not exactly match intentions, victories for groups other than capitalists, and successful examples of resistance to unwelcome features of social policies. This is necessary even in somewhat more sophisticated 'functionalist' accounts which emphasise notions of ideology and culture. These accounts are functionalist if they imply that individuals can straightforwardly be controlled by the imposition of a dominant ideology, as if human beings were puppets who move obediently for whoever pulls the strings. Although explanations which see control based upon ideology may be less crude than some others, they do not necessarily avoid the problems of functionalism. They may merely suggest that control occurs by different *methods*, which are more subtle and less obviously coercive (for example, the colonisation of the family, rather than its straightforward substitution). Examples considered in this chapter demonstrate that in practice it is not that simple: political radicals may be fostered precisely by those educational systems which are meant to be securing the political status quo; and the attempts to control the lifestyle of the working classes by 'winning hearts and minds'[46(p. 66)] is conspicuously unsuccessful in many cases.

One of the problems with the crude 'serving the needs of the economy' account of social policy is that welfare services are not, for the most part, provided directly by capital. They are provided variously by charitable bodies, on an unpaid basis by women in the home setting, and by government. As far as education is concerned, state provision is the norm, apart from some provision in the private sector (over which government also exercises some control). Thus any account of the relationship between welfare and the economy (in the case of Britain, a capitalist economy) has to incorporate a satisfactory account of the state's relationship to these processes.

The crudest versions of a Marxist account would imply that governments are simply a tool in the hands of capitalists, acting on their behalf. However, discussions about the state in Marxist literature (especially over the past decade) suggests versions which are much more subtle and complex. These debates, as they apply specifically to state activity in the field of welfare, are well summarised by Gough.[3(Ch. 3)] He argues that the state cannot be seen as simply the instrument of the dominant class. It should be seen as having necessarily a degree of separation and autonomy from the interests of capital, although ultimately being constrained by the imperatives of the capital accumulation process. Within those constraints, there is room for competing strategies and for reforms to be won which are not straightforwardly in the interests of capital.[3(pp. 43-4)]

Certainly in the field of education, that kind of account of the activity of the state makes much more sense than a crude deterministic one. The history of the development of this aspect of social policy in Britain would not support the view that it has been simply imposed from above, because sometimes it has been demanded from below. Gains can be made in welfare through struggle on the part of the working classes, although these may also have the effect of buying off potential political opposition. The pattern implied is a complex one of struggles, bribes and concessions, which shape the form of welfare at any particular time. At the same time, policies which are implemented (whether imposed 'from above' or won 'from below') may have unintended and unanticipated consequences. Also, the policies themselves may contain inherent contradictions. Gough suggests that one example would be that an education system geared to the productive requirements of the economy may not serve the purpose of integrating and socialising the young: an example of contradictions between policies which reproduce labour power and those which produce social harmony.

We are left, therefore, with an account of social policy which is much more complex than the one at the beginning of this section. The idea that the welfare state in general (or education in particular) services the needs of the economy is certainly an important consideration in formulating explanations in social policy. But such explanations cannot be neat and tidy: they need to be substantially modified in the ways indicated if they are to make sense of social reality.

NOTES AND REFERENCES

1. GEORGE, V. and WILDING, P. (1976), *Ideology and Social Welfare*. Routledge & Kegan Paul: London.
2. CENTRAL POLICY REVIEW STAFF (1980), *Education, Training and Industrial Performance*. HMSO: London.
3. GOUGH, I. (1979), *The Political Economy of the Welfare State*. Macmillan: London.
4. HALL, S. (1981), 'Schooling, state and society', in R. Dale, G. Esland, R. Fergusson and M. McDonald (eds), *Education and the State*. Falmer Press: Lewes.
5. YOUNG, M. and WHITTY, G. (1977) (eds), *Society, State and Schooling*. Falmer Press: London.
6. WESTERGAARD, J. and RESLER, H. (1976), *Class in a Capitalist*

Society. Penguin: Harmondsworth.

7. FRASER, N. (1977), 'Social capital', in H. Heisler (ed.), *Foundations of Social Administration*. Macmillan: London.

8. LEVITAS, M. (1974), *Marxist Perspectives in the Sociology of Education*. Routledge & Kegan Paul: London.

9. CENTRE FOR CONTEMPORARY CULTURAL STUDIES (1981), *Unpopular Education*. Hutchinson: London.

10. GLEESON, D. and MARDLE, G. (1980), *Further Education or Training? A Case Study in the Theory and Practice of Day Release Education*. Routledge & Kegan Paul: London.

11. FRITH, S. and CORRIGAN, P. (1977), 'The politics of education', in M. Young and G. Whitty, *op. cit.*

12. BOWLES, S. and GINTIS, H. (1976), *Schooling in Capitalist America*. Routledge & Kegan Paul: London.

13. WILLIS, P. (1977), *Learning to Labour*. Saxon House: London.

14. VAUGHAN, M. and ARCHER, M. S. (1971), *Social Conflict and Educational Change in England and France 1789–1848*. CUP: Cambridge.

15. (a) VAUGHAN and ARCHER (1971), *op. cit.*; (b) ARCHER, M. S. (1979), *Social Origins of Educational Systems*. Sage: London.

16. RYRIE, A. (1981), 'Schools and socialisation into work', *Educational Analysis*, Vol. 3, No. 2.

17. HALSEY, A. H. (1977), 'Towards meritocracy? The case of Britain', in A. Halsey and J. Karabel (eds). *Power and Ideology in Education*. OUP: New York.

18. BULL, D. (1980), *What Price 'Free' Education?* Child Poverty Action Group: London.

19. TUNNARD, J. (1979), *Uniform Blues*. Child Poverty Action Group: London.

20. HER MAJESTY'S INSPECTORATE (1982), *The Effects of Local Authority Expenditure Policies on the Education Service in England, 1981*. DES: London.

21. DEEM, R. (1978), *Women and Schooling*. RKP: London.

22. MCDONALD, M. (1980), 'Schooling and the reproduction of class and gender relations', in L. Barton, R. Meighan and S. Walker (eds), *Schooling, Ideology and the Curriculum*. Falmer Press: Lewes.

23. WOLPE, A. M. (1978), 'Girls and economic survival', *British Journal of Educational Studies*, Vol. XXVI, No. 2.

24. MCDONALD, M. (1980), 'Socio-cultural reproduction and women's education', in R. Deem (ed.), *Schooling for Women's Work*. Routledge & Kegan Paul: London.

25. DEEM, R. (1981), 'State policy and ideology in the education of women 1944–81', *British Journal of the Sociology of Education*, Vol. 2, No. 2.

26. *Public Schools Commission* (1968), First Report. HMSO: London.

27. WOLPE, A M. (1974), 'The official ideology of education for girls', in M. Flude and J. Ahier (eds), *Educability, Schools and Ideology*. Croom Helm: London.

28. ROBERTS, H. (1982), 'After sixteen: what choice?' in R. Burgess (ed.), *Exploring Society*. British Sociological Association: London.

29. BOURDIEU, P. (1977), 'Cultural reproduction and social reproduction', in A. Halsey and J. Karabel, *op. cit.*

30. HALSEY, A., HEATH, A. and RIDGE, J. (1980), *Origins and Destinations*. Clarendon: Oxford.

31. ENTWISTLE, H. (1979), *Antonio Gramsci: Conservative Schooling for Radical Politics*. RKP: London.

32. APPLE, M. (1979), *Ideology and Curriculum*. RKP: London.

33. BUTLER, R. A. (1973), 'The politics of the 1944 Education Act', in G. Fowler, V. Morris and J. Ozga (eds), *Decision-Making in British Education*. Heinemann: London.

34. DENT, H. C. (1944), *Education in Transition*. Kegan Paul: London.

35. TAPPER, T. and SALTER, B. (1978), *Education and the Political Order*. Macmillan: London.

36. *Times Educational Supplement*, 28 May 1982.

37. CRICK, B. and PORTER, A. (eds) (1978), *Political Education and Political Literacy*. Longman: London.

38. *Guardian*, 4 May 1982.

39. PIVEN, F. and CLOWARD, R. (1972), *Regulating the Poor*. Tavistock: London.

40. GINSBURG, N. (1979), *Class, Capital and Social Policy*. Macmillan: London.

41. HURT, J. (1979), *Elementary Schooling and the Working Classes 1860–1918*. Routledge & Kegan Paul: London.

42. JOHNSON, R. (1976), 'Notes on the schooling of the English working class 1780–1850', in R. Dale, G. Esland and M. McDonald (eds), *Schooling and Capitalism*. RKP: London.

43. REES, T. and GREGORY, D. (1981), 'Youth employment and unemployment: a decade of decline', *Educational Analysis*, Vol. 3, No. 3.

44. POPE, R. (1977), 'Dole schools: the north-east Lancashire

experience 1930–39', *Journal of Educational Administration and History*, Vol. IX, No. 2.

45. MANPOWER SERVICES COMMISSION (1977), *Young People and Work*. The Holland Report. MSC: London.

46. CORRIGAN, P. (1979), *Schooling the Smash Street Kids*. Macmillan: London.

47. COLLINS, R. (1979), *The Credential Society*, Academic Press: New York.

48. MACGUIRE, M. and ASHTON, D. (1980), 'Employers' perceptions and use of educational qualifications', *Educational Analysis*, Vol. 3, No. 2.

49. PARKIN, F. (1979), *Marxism and Class Theory*. Tavistock: London.

50. HUSSAIN, A. (1976), 'The economy and the education system in capitalistic societies', *Economy and Society*, Vol. 5, No. 4.

51. SHAW, J. (1981), 'In loco parentis: a relationship between parent, state and child', in R. Dale, G. Esland, R. Fergusson and M. McDonald (eds), *Education and the State*, Vol. 2. Falmer Press: Lewes.

52. GRACE, C. (1978), *Teachers, Ideology and Control*. Routledge & Kegan Paul: London.

53. FITZ, J. (1981), 'Welfare, the family and the child', in *Education, Welfare and Social Order*, Open University Course E353, Block 5, Unit 12. OU Press: Milton Keynes.

54. SHAW, J. (1981), 'Family, state and compulsory education', in Open University, *ibid*, Unit 13.

55. DONZELOT, J. (1979), *The Policing of Families*. Hutchinson: London.

56. MEIGHAN, R. and BROWN, D. (1980), 'Locations of learning and ideologies of education: some issues raised by a study of "education otherwise"', in L. Barton, R. Meighan and S. Walker (eds), *op. cit.*

57. BALL, N. (1973), 'Elementary school attendance and voluntary effort before 1870', *History of Education*, Vol. 2, No. 1.

58. MACMILLAN, K. (1977), *Education Welfare*. Longman: London.

59. WRIGHT, N. (1977), *Progress in Education*. Croom Helm: London.

60. GALLOWAY, D. (1976), 'Persistent and unjustified absence from school', *Trends in Education*, Vol. 4.

61. TYERMAN, M. (1974), 'Who are the truants?', in B. Turner (ed.), *Truancy*. Ward Lock: London.

62. SCOTTISH EDUCATION DEPARTMENT (1977), *Truancy and*

Indiscipline in Schools in Scotland, The Pack Report. HMSO: London.

63. HER MAJESTY'S INSPECTORATE (1978), *Truancy and Behavioural Problems in Some Urban Schools*. HMSO: London.

64. ASSOCIATION OF DIRECTORS OF SOCIAL SERVICES (1978), *Social Work Services for Children in School*. ADSS: London.

65. (a) WHITE, R. and BROCKINGTON, D. (1978), *In and Out of School: The ROSLA Community Education Project*. Routledge & Kegan Paul: London; (b) WHITE, R. (1980), *Absent with Cause*. Routledge & Kegan Paul: London.

66. THORPE, D., SMITH, D., PALEY, J. and GREEN, C. (1980), *Out of Care: the Community Support of Juvenile Offenders*. Allen & Unwin: London.

67. HARRIS, F. (1974), 'Rebels with a cause', in B. Turner (ed.), *Truancy*. Ward Lock: London.

68. DOCKING, J. (1980), *Control and Discipline in Schools*. Harper & Row: London.

69. HARGREAVES, D., HESTOR, S. and MELLOR, F. (1975), *Deviance in Classrooms*. Routledge & Kegan Paul: London.

70. LEINSTER-MACKAY (1977), '*Regina* v. *Hopley*: some historical reflections on corporal punishment', *Journal of Educational Administration and History*, Vol. IX, No. 1.

71. BURGESS, R. (1982), 'The practice of sociological research: some issues in school ethnography', in R. Burgess (ed.), *Exploring Society*. British Sociological Association: London.

72. SOCIETY OF TEACHERS OPPOSED TO PHYSICAL PUNISHMENT (1981), *A Quarter of a Million Beatings*. STOPP: Croydon.

73. NEWELL, P. (1972), *A Last Resort? Corporal Punishment in Schools*. Penguin: Harmondsworth.

74. At time of going to press, it was unclear what response, if any, would officially be made to this ruling. *Times Educational Supplement*, 16 July 1982.

75. JONES-DAVIES, C. and CAVE, G. (1976) (eds), *The Disruptive Pupil in the Secondary School*. Ward Lock: London.

76. HER MAJESTY'S INSPECTORATE (1978), *Behavioural Units*. HMSO: London.

77. DAVIES, B. (1976), 'Piggies in the middle – or "Who sir? No, not me sir" ', in Jones-Davies and Cave, *op. cit.*

78. PUGH, G. (ed.), (1980), *Preparation for Parenthood*. National Children's Bureau: London.

79. NATIONAL COUNCIL FOR ONE PARENT FAMILIES (1979), *Pregnant at School*.

80. WHITFIELD, R. (1980), *Education for Family Life*. Hodder & Stoughton: London.
81. MINISTRY OF EDUCATION (1963), *Half Our Future*. HMSO: London, Appendix II.
82. KELLMER PRINGLE, M. (1980), 'Aims and future directions', in G. Pugh (ed.), *op. cit.*
83. *Times Educational Supplement*, 31 July 1981.
84. MISHRA, R. (1977), *Society and Social Policy*. Macmillan: London.

Chapter seven

CONCLUSION: EVALUATING EDUCATION AS SOCIAL POLICY

In this brief concluding chapter, I shall try to draw out some key themes which have emerged in this book, as they relate to the operation of social policy in and through education, and especially to the central tension between 'individual's benefit' and 'society's benefit' rationales.

The picture of education which has emerged contains many paradoxes. These accord very much with Silver's assessment that '[Education] has been seen both as a means of selecting and perpetuating elites and as a means of promoting social justice and undermining elites. It is discussed in terms of class domination and social control, but also of social liberation and progress'. [1(p. 19)] To these might be added: education is a universal 'service' but it has to be compulsorily administered; every citizen has a right to be educated according to his or her ability but the occupational structure, which the educational system feeds, requires individuals to be sorted and categorised for the purposes of employers; the 'welfare' offered through education is often double-edged and contains important elements of surveillance and control; and the principle of meritocracy, so fundamental to the development of education in Britain, pursues the twin (and often incompatible) aims of efficiency and justice.

These paradoxes arise in many cases from the individual/society tension. While they are complex in both their origins and their effects, they should not be regarded as the inexplicable products of historical accident. They need to be seen rather as the product of contradictions which arise from the nature of the welfare state itself, as was indicated at the end of the previous chapter. State activity in the provision of welfare often entails pursuing diverse and sometimes contradictory ends. In the context of a capitalist society this means that, while it may be true in most cases that welfare policies at least are consistent with (and may actively promote) the demands of the economy, the state also has to act to some extent in the interests of the community as a whole: as Mishra puts it, the state is necessarily Janus-faced as regards welfare.[2(p. 67)] One must develop an understanding of how these features operate within what Gough calls the 'contradictory unity' of the welfare state.[3(p. 11)]

The pattern of contradictions, and the paradoxes to which they give rise, is not entirely random or unpredictable. Their character can be seen as a product of identifiable features of social, economic and political life, say, the dominant form of politics being pursued by central government, or the prevailing conditions in the labour market. The relationship between these and the particular kind of policy being pursued in and through education is by no means simple or consistent. But one can see, for example, that the breakdown of the social democratic political consensus has had clear consequences for social policy in education; and that the 'radical right' restructuring of welfare, to align it more closely with the changing needs of a developing capitalist economy, is reflected in a more explicit linking of education to the economy and in certain changes of emphasis within the curriculum.

Further, there seems to be a fairly general pattern in many of the instances discussed in this book which suggests that there is a consistent tendency for policies to be 'pulled' in the direction of 'society's benefit' rather than the individual's. This pull has been stronger and more explicit from the mid-1970s onwards. It may become apparent either when policies are being formulated or when they are being applied. For instance in 'welfare' aspects of education, where there is a continuing tension between surveillance and treatment, and between benevolence and control, there is a tendency both in policy and in practice for surveillance and control to be treated as the primary activity, for example in relation to the health of schoolchildren, or to systems of pastoral 'care' in schools. In situations where the 'individual's benefit' rationale is prominent, it is usually the case that some version of 'society's benefit' is produced as support for the proposals. This was seen to be the case in the discussion of adult education, for example, and in the Newsom report. In fact, where (as in Newsom) proposals are based primarily upon the individual's benefit, it seems that they have little chance of being implemented. The contrast is marked here between the speedy application of the Robbins proposals for expanding higher education (explicitly linked with the labour market), and the fate of the other 1960s reports. If proposals which will benefit recipients *are* implemented, they may get appropriated for other purposes. Egalitarian strategies for comprehensive reform, for example, can be said to have failed partly because their implementation depended upon an alliance with groups of middle-class parents and teachers whose interests in the reform were not primarily egalitarian.

The single most significant lesson to be learned from the material reviewed in this book is probably the importance of developing accounts of education as a social policy which take account of the benefits both to the recipients and to 'society', and of the consequences of the tension between those two. Explanations which imply *either* that it is all a matter of benevolent state acting for the good of its citizens, *or* that everything can be explained by state activity on behalf of capital, are to be avoided – however seductively tidy and powerful they appear. Space needs to be found for understanding how some features are in fact concessions won from the dominant class as a product of struggle, or are the product of un-intended (or even subverted) consequences of policies, or how individuals can make real gains from policies which are designed primarily to serve national needs. In creating that space, interesting questions arise, both about what has happened and what *can* happen. I shall indicate what these questions are, and suggest some possible answers on the basis of the material reviewed in this book.

First: do the recipients of education ever derive any real benefits which are neither an illusion nor a palliative? If so, in what circumstances? If education is in any sense a valuable commodity, it must be possible for individuals to derive benefits from it. Indeed, the children of the privileged routinely seem to do so: for them, access to education is both desired and desirable. The fact that education *can* have illusory or negative consequences – and for the children of the working classes this often seems to be the case – does not mean that they can never experience more positive effects. As was noted in an earlier chapter, the Labour movement traditionally has pressed for an extension of educational opportunities for working-class children, and it seems absurd to suggest that there have been no gains as a consequence. Unless we are to say that education *never* has anything to offer to working-class children, the postwar reconstruction – which accorded the right to a full secondary education irrespective of parental income – is clearly an advance on a situation where privilege and wealth are the sole determinants of access. Similarly, comprehensive reorganisation, although in many ways disappointing, can be seen as a real gain: 'Comprehensive schools make possible higher general standards of education. In the old days, few cared much about the standard of education in secondary modern schools, to which most of the population went. Now at least standards of education for the ordinary child are on the political agenda.' [4(p. 54)]

In what circumstances are real benefits derived, especially by the hitherto disadvantaged? Several answers are suggested by the material reviewed in this book. Deem's discussion of the advances made in the education of women since the end of the Second World War suggests that they are made in periods when the political and economic climate is particularly auspicious. [5(pp. 131-44)] The lesson to be learned from this, presumably, is that opportunities to advance the cause of disadvantaged groups must be seized when the climate is promising. In a rather different way, it may be possible to capitalise upon an existing situation by pushing the logic of provision to its limits. The school meals service, it was argued, cannot effectively secure the welfare of children if it is provided upon a selective, means-tested basis, but may be able to do so if one utilises the potential of a compulsory educational system, by making the basis of the service free and universal. The rhetoric of 'welfare' gives opportunity for campaigns to be pursued which make it a reality. In such campaigns, alliances may be possible which cut across other interests. The very fact that the great majority of children do attend state schools, and that comprehensive schools *can* contain children from highly diverse backgrounds, opens the possibility for such alliances on issues – of which school meals might be one – where all parents would have similar interests. As Mishra notes, [2(p. 116)] one consequence of the welfare state is that it has reduced basic class cleavages in the sense that social groups (such as the old, the widowed and so on) share common interests and problems in relation to social welfare. The potential of this can be exploited in education as in other contexts.

Second: are the benefits of education inevitably confined to small numbers of individuals? Can education ever be the means of securing advantages for whole social groups, especially for hitherto disadvantaged groups? These issues follow logically from the first set, since there are many examples of education reforms which have succeeded in advancing the position of small numbers of individuals from the working classes, from ethnic minorities, and so on, while at the same time retaining the status quo as far as those groups as a whole are concerned. The extension of secondary education provides one obvious example here, as indeed does its reorganisation along comprehensive lines, both of which failed to advance the position of the working classes *per se*. Similarly, in the field of adult education, it can be argued that it has been successful in promoting an elite, but for the working class as a whole, it has had very little impact.

Education as social policy

It is of course important to acknowledge that limits are set upon the general advancement of any group through education, by the terms in which the educational system itself is constituted; that is, it is a competitive system which *requires* large numbers of people to fail. Within those limits, there is some evidence that there is potential for modifying the patterns of success or failure in relation to different groups. More privileged groups have, after all, been using the educational system to secure and maintain their own advantage for a very long time. There seems to be some evidence that certain strategies are capable of modifying these educational outcomes: for example, the widespread availability of good nursery education; or the exercise of positive discrimination in relation to girls' education. Equally, there is evidence that such strategies will not be effective unless they are applied seriously and that means, crucially, being applied in such a way that real redistribution takes place. That is, privileged groups must *lose* certain things, in order that disadvantaged groups may gain in relation to them.

Finally: can the recipients of education successfully resist its controlling features? Can they turn the situation to their own advantage? As has already been noted, when developing accounts of regulation and control in education it is important to build in the space for understanding instances where it is not successful. It is clearly the case that attempts at control do not always work very effectively. The use of teachers as agents of control sounds a neat device but has never been unproblematic, since teachers do not invariably co-operate with this. Sometimes they themselves have to be controlled, and sometimes they still find the space to pursue alternative goals in education. Similarly, the reproduction of the political order through education, it was shown in an earlier chapter, cannot be regarded as invariably successful when educational systems quite frequently are responsible for producing political radicals.

Resistance to certain features of education can be of either a negative or a positive sort. Instances of the former type occur very commonly. Through disruptive activity within the school, or simply by not attending, young people often demonstrate their reluctance to be moulded and controlled. It is possible, however, that resistance can take on a more positive character; that is an attempt not merely to avoid controls but to change the structure in which they operate, using means which may well include education itself. If dominant groups maintain their control through cultural and ideological means, then education itself can be the route to challenging that domination. As Tapper and Salter argue, there is always the possibility that subordinate groups will become conscious of the nature of the value system which legitimates their subordinate position, and will challenge it.[6(p. 66)] This means, in the terminology of Gramsci's influential discussion, establishing a counter-hegemony; which meant, for him, that workers must learn to think and act like a ruling class. Education is central to producing this, but Gramsci believed that it could not be accomplished in schools. Only through adult education, where political experience derived from the workplace could become part of political education, could a counter-hegemony be established.[7]

Gramsci's position suggests another strategy which would be endorsed by other writers: that successful creative resistance to the controlling and dominating features of education may involve activities which go beyond the formal educational system itself. Deem, for example, argues that if women are to make further gains within education, they need to develop strategies which will challenge patriarchal structures in broader social contexts.[5(p. 142)] Such strategies may involve fostering alternative forms of knowledge which facilitate challenges to the dominant forms perpetuated within the educational system. The development of alternative forms of knowledge has a very long history, as is well demonstrated by Johnson in his discussion of the tradition of working-class radicals education, and its concern to foster 'really useful knowledge'.[8]

To these three questions about the operation of social policy in and through education I have offered answers which are necessarily tentative, speculative and partial, based upon the discussion of the English educational system developed in this book. They are the kinds of questions which will repay further study, and indeed systematic research, in particular instances of education as social policy. The answers suggested here are not merely answers to academic questions but also suggest some possible political strategies for changing the direction of policy and its effects. Engaging with issues of social policy cannot be other than a political activity, even if it is given a gloss of objective neutrality. I would commend the further study and exploration of the kinds of questions raised in this final chapter to any reader who wishes to engage with education as social policy, both as an area of academic study and of political activity.

NOTES AND REFERENCES

1.   SILVER, H. (1980), *Education and the Social Condition*. Methuen: London.

2. MISHRA, R. (1977), *Society and Social Policy: Theoretical Perspectives on Welfare*. Macmillan: London.

3. GOUGH, I. (1979), *The Political Economy of the Welfare State*. Macmillan: London.

4. GLENNERSTER, H. (1979), 'Education and inequality', in D. Rubenstein (ed.), *Education and Equality*. Penguin: Harmondsworth.

5. DEEM, R. (1981), 'State policy and ideology in the education of women 1944–1980', *British Journal of the Sociology of Education*, Vol. 2, No. 2.

6. TAPPER, T. and SALTER, B. (1978), *Education and the Political Order: Changing Patterns of Class Control*. Macmillan: London.

7. ENTWISTLE, H. (1979), *Antonio Gramsci: Conservative Schooling for Radical Politics*. Routledge & Kegan Paul: London.

8. JOHNSON, R. (1979), ' "Really useful knowledge": education and working class culture, 1790–1848', in J. Clark, C. Critcher and R. Johnson (eds), *Working Class Culture: Studies in History and Theory*. Hutchinson: London.

Part three
DOCUMENTS

Document one
EDUCATION AND SOCIAL POLICY IN BRITAIN

Education has been used in this century as a vital instrument of social policy by governments of all kinds – with varying degrees of commitment or reluctance, and with different and conflicting intentions. The level of confidence in the instrument has been marked by spurts of expansion and contraction, investment and cuts, flurries of enquiry and policy-making, legislation and regulation, and the diversification of levels of types of provision. Whatever the other functions of the increasingly large and complex system of education, its history can be written in terms of social policy – the attempt to use education to solve social problems, to influence social structures, to improve one or more aspects of the social condition, to anticipate crisis. All schooling and all education have involved such 'social' dimensions, whether it be the medieval song or grammar school, the aristocratic 'grand tour', the eighteenth-century charity school or the nineteenth-century mutual improvement society of working men. It is only in this country, however, that an education system has been deliberately filled out, stage by stage, under a variety of pressures and with varying rhythms, to provide – through education – an elaborate social service, responding to expressed needs in child psychology, child development and child health; providing (or under the stronger pressures of economic policy, taking away) school meals and milk, medical inspection and dental treatment, open-air classrooms and playing fields, pre-school education, community schools and education for retirement. Although the criticism of educational isolation remains pertinent, educational policy has throughout this century been responsible (often slowly, reluctantly or half-heartedly, under threat, pressure or persuasion) to questions of health and welfare, to changes in employment or social structure, and to changing expectations by different social groups of access to education – and to privilege or power or anything else that education may imply.

Education-as-social-policy has in Britain meant overwhelmingly the State-provided and State-supported sector of education, subsuming but leaving intact the Churches' involvement in education from the 1902 Education Act onwards. It has imposed only marginal constraints on the independent, fee-paying sector of education. The English 'public school' has never become amenable to the pressures of national social policy-making, which is not, of course, to imply that it does not have social 'functions'. It was untouched by the Government-sponsored enquiries and reports during the Second World War and at the end of the 1960s.

Source: H. Silver, *Education and the Social Condition*, Methuen, London (1980) pp. 17–18.

Document two
THE PURPOSES OF EDUCATIONAL RECONSTRUCTION

EDUCATIONAL RECONSTRUCTION

'Upon the education of the people of this
country the fate of this country depends.'

I. Introduction

1.   The government's purpose in putting forward the reforms described in
this Paper is to secure for children a happier childhood and a better start in
life; to ensure a fuller measure of education and opportunity for young people
and to provide means for all of developing the various talents with which they
are endowed and so enriching the inheritance of the country whose citizens
they are. The new educational opportunities must not, therefore, be of a single
pattern. It is just as important to achieve diversity as it is to ensure equality of
educational opportunity. But such diversity must not impair the social unity
within the educational system which will open the way to a more closely knit
society and give us strength to face the tasks ahead. The war has revealed
afresh the resources and character of the British people – an enduring
possession that will survive all the material losses inevitable in the present
struggle. In the youth of the nation we have our greatest national asset. Even
on a basis of mere expediency, we cannot afford not to develop this asset to the
greatest advantage. It is the object of the present proposals to strengthen and
inspire the younger generation. For it is as true to-day, as when it was first
said, that 'the bulwarks of a city are its men'.

From: *Educational Reconstruction*. Cmd. 6458, HMSO (1943) para. 1.

Document three
EDUCATIONAL RECONSTRUCTION: MAJOR RECOMMENDATIONS

THE FOLLOWING ARE THE PRINCIPAL REFORMS PROPOSED IN THE 1943 WHITE PAPER ON EDUCATIONAL RECONSTRUCTION:

126. The changes described in this document may be summarised as follows.

A. The legislative changes proposed will include:

(a) the improvement of the facilities for the training of children below compulsory school age by the provision of nursery schools wherever they are needed;

(b) the raising of the school leaving age to 15 without exemptions, with provision for a later raising to 16;

(c) the completion of the reorganisation of the present public elementary schools, so that well-designed and equipped primary schools are available for all children up to the age of 11 and secondary schools, with varied facilities for advanced work, for all children over that age;

(d) an amendment of the existing law so as

   (i) to emphasise the position of religious instruction as an essential element of education; and

   (ii) to enable the schools provided by voluntary bodies to play their part in the proposed developments;

(e) the introduction of a system of compulsory part-time education in working hours for young persons up to the age of 18;

(f) the provision of adequate and properly co-ordinated facilities for technical and adult education;

(g) the extension of existing facilities for securing the health and physical well-being of children and young persons;

(h) the introduction of a system of inspection and registration of all independent schools which cater for children of compulsory school age;

(i) the adjustment of the present system of local educational administration to the new educational layout.

B. The changes to be effected by administrative action, include:

(a) a progressive decrease in the size of classes in primary schools;

(b) the abolition of the present Special Place examination and the adoption of other arrangements for the classification of the children when they pass from primary to secondary schools;

(c) the introduction of a common Code of Regulations applicable to secondary schools of all types, so framed as to secure that standards of accommodation and amenities generally are raised to the level of those of grammar schools;

(d) the remodelling of the curriculum of secondary schools;

(e) the further expansion of the Youth Service;

(f) the improvement of the facilities for enabling poor students to proceed to the universities;

(g) the reform of the present methods of recruiting and training teachers.

From: *Educational Reconstruction*, Cmd. 6458, HMSO (1943) para. 126.

THE 1944 EDUCATION ACT: SOME KEY SECTIONS

1.—(1) [It shall be the duty of the Secretary of State for Education and Science] to promote the education of the people of England and Wales and the progressive development of institutions devoted to that purpose, and to secure the effective execution by local authorities under his control and direction of the national policy for providing a varied and comprehensive educational service in every area.

7.   The statutory system of public education shall be organised in three progressive stages to be known as primary education, secondary education, and further education; and it shall be the duty of the local education authority for every area, so far as their powers extend, to contribute towards the spiritual, moral mental and physical development of the community by securing that efficient education throughout those stages shall be available to meet the needs of the population of their area.

8.—(a) . . . the schools available for an area shall not be deemed to be sufficient unless they are sufficient in number, character, and equipment to afford for all pupils opportunities for education offering such variety of instruction and training as may be desirable in view of their different ages, abilities, and aptitudes, and of the different periods for which they may be expected to remain at school, including practical instruction and training appropriate to their respective needs.

25.—(1)   Subject to the provision of this section, the school day in every country school and in every voluntary school shall begin with collective worship on the part of all pupils in attendance at the school, and the arrangements made therefore shall provide for a single act of worship attended by all such pupils . . .

36.   It shall be the duty of the parent of every child of school age to cause him to receive sufficient full-time education suitable to his age, abilities and aptitudes, either by regular attendance at school or otherwise.

49. Regulations made by the [Secretary of State] shall impose upon local education authorities the duty of providing milk, meals and other refreshment for pupils in attendance at schools and county colleges maintained by them; . . .

55.—(1) A local education authority shall make such arrangements for the provision of transport and otherwise as they consider necessary or as the [Secretary of State] may direct for the purpose of facilitating the attendance of pupils at schools or county colleges or at any course or class provided in pursuance of a scheme of further education in force for their area, and any transport provided in pursuance of such arrangements shall be provided free of charge.

68. [The Secretary of State may take such actions, as appear expedient if he is satisfied] that any local education authority, or the managers or governors of any county or voluntary school have acted or are proposing to act unreasonably.

76. Local education authorities shall have regard to the general principle that, in so far as is compatible with the provision of efficient instruction and training and the avoidance of unreasonable public expenditure, pupils are to be educated in accordance with the wishes of their parents.

From: Education Act 1944

Document five
BUTLER'S ASSESSMENT OF THE 1944 ACT

The Act of 1944, in common with its predecessors of 1870, 1902, and 1918, affords a classic example of what Dicey called 'our inveterate prejudice for fragmentary and gradual legislation'. It did not, as some would have wished, sweep the board clean of existing institutions in order to start afresh. On the contrary, it established a financial framework within which schools provided by the local education authorities and schools provided by the Churches could continue to live side by side. The more generous assistance which it made available to the voluntary bodies enabled the physical reorganisation of schools into primary and secondary to proceed, albeit slowly. It was therefore possible for the Act to cut right out of the educational vocabulary the word 'elementary', to which the stigma of an inferior kind of schooling for children of the poorer classes had continued to cling. Henceforth every child would have a right to free secondary education and in order that these secondary courses should become a full reality, they were to last for at least four and eventually five years. It was, however, equally important to ensure that a stigma of inferiority did not attach itself to those secondary institutions – and they were bound now to be the preponderant majority – which lacked the facilities and academic prestige of the grammar schools. Conditions in each of the different types of school, grammar, modern and technical, would therefore have to be made broadly equivalent: indeed, as my 1943 White Paper stated, 'It would be wrong to suppose that they will necessarily remain separate and apart. Different types may be combined in one building or on one site.' This forecast the comprehensive idea. Even so, equality of opportunity would remain something of an empty phrase if children entered the period of compulsory schooling from conditions of family deprivation, or left it to pursue what Churchill called blind-alley occupations. Accordingly, the Act made provision, on the one hand, for a major expansion of maintained and grant-aided nursery schools and, on the other hand, for compulsory part-time education up to the age of eighteen.

From: R. A. Butler, *The Art of the Possible*, Hamish Hamilton, London (1971) p. 123.

Document six
THE NEW SECONDARY EDUCATION

THE MINISTRY OF EDUCATION PRESENTED THE CASE FOR THREE
DIFFERENT TYPES OF SECONDARY SCHOOLS AS FOLLOWS:

Experience has shown that the majority of children learn most easily by
dealing with concrete things and following a course rooted in their own
day-to-day experience. At the age of eleven few of them will have disclosed
particular interests and aptitudes well enough marked for them to require any
other course. The majority will do best in a school which provides a good
all-round education in an atmosphere which enables them to develop freely
along their own lines. Such a school will give them a chance to sample a variety
of 'subjects' and skills and to pursue those which attract them most. It is for
this majority that the secondary *modern* school will cater.

Some children, on the other hand, will have decided at quite an early stage
to make their careers in branches of industry or agriculture requiring a special
kind of aptitude in science or mathematics. Others may need a course, longer,
more exacting, and more specialized than that provided in the modern school,
with a particular emphasis on commercial subjects, music or art. All these
boys and girls will find their best outlet in the secondary *technical* school.

Finally, there will be a proportion whose ability and aptitude require the
kind of course with the emphasis on books and ideas that is provided at a
secondary *grammar* school. They are attracted by the abstract approach to
learning and should normally be prepared to stay at school long enough to
benefit from the 'sixth form' work which is the most characteristic feature of
the grammar school.

From: Ministry of Education, *The New Secondary Education*, HMSO (1947)
p. 23.

Document seven
EDUCATION FOR GIRLS: TEACHING GIRLS TO BE WOMEN

Hitherto the tenor of this book has been analytical rather than constructive, it has stated a problem, described the dual function of women in society, the educational forces which shape her and something of the manner in which they have evolved. It is now time to make some positive suggestions for experiments that might do something to reconcile the educative process with her particular contribution to society . . .

There is need for a clearer realization of this vital influence of women as women, of the fact which Rousseau was groping to express – and for which he received such obloquy – that women civilize men and thus preserve civilization. Nor, at the risk of wearying repetition, is this a less important role than males perform. To work through others is not derogatory to human dignity, nor do the restrictions that Almighty God has imposed upon Himself to work through mortals detract from His Majesty. This mission of women is a far greater one than can ever be fulfilled by attaining the minor political or professional successes, which in the past generation they have imitatively adopted from men as a criterion of social usefulness; a tendency fostered by those who have failed to perform – not necessarily through any fault of their own – the essential feminine function in society. Indeed, my own limited experience has taught me that almost all intelligent women agree with this assumption; and that those who do not, however able and intelligent they may be, are normally deficient in the quality of womanliness and the particular physical and mental attributes of their sex. The future of women's education lies not in attempting to iron out their differences from men, to reduce them to neuters, but to teach girls how to grow into women and to re-learn the graces which so many have forgotten in the past thirty years.

From: J. Newsom, *The Education of Girls*, Faber & Faber, London (1948) pp. 108–9.

Document eight
FIFTEEN TO EIGHTEEN: THE AGENDA FOR EDUCATIONAL ADVANCE

157.   Fifteen years ago Mr. Butler's Education Act gave all children for the first time the right to free secondary education. Twelve years ago the minimum school-leaving age was raised from 14 to 15. Two further provisions of the Act affecting older children remain to be brought into force. One would add another year to compulsory school life, extending it to 16; the other would provide compulsory part-time day education until 18 for those who leave school before that age. Any review, such as ours, of the educational provision for boys and girls between 15 and 18 must almost of necessity start from these remaining provisions of the 1944 Act. When will it be possible to take these promised further steps forward? Which foot should be advanced first – the extension of compulsory full-time education, or the introduction of compulsory part-time day education? Before these can be answered, there is a preliminary question. Is it wise to go forward with any extensions of compulsion at school beyond the age when, at home, parental orders are gradually replaced by parental requests? The 1944 Act was inevitably a bold act of faith. Was it misjudged? We have now had half a generation's knowledge of keeping at school until 15 boys and girls who would not have stayed if left to themselves. Has it been a good thing? Is there anything in our experience since the war to suggest that the two further extensions of compulsion provided for by the 1944 Act were ill-conceived, and should not be brought into force? We shall later examine each measure separately. But at the outset we must state our belief that both should be confirmed in their position on the agenda of educational advance. They are important and complementary reforms, which are necessary if we are to have a satisfactory education system for the teenagers. It is not a matter of one or the other, though it must be one before the other. Both are necessary.

From: *Fifteen to Eighteen*, The Crowther Report, HMSO (1959) para. 157.

Document nine
THE CASE FOR RAISING THE SCHOOL-LEAVING AGE

201.   There is, then, a strong case on economic grounds for raising the school-leaving age; but, if this were the only reason for doing so, it might not be a sufficient reason. It is true, of course, that the country cannot afford to let so much talent go unutilised at a time when industry demands greatly increased skill and knowledge, and especially in the face of the tremendous efforts being made by other countries to develop all their human resources. There might, however, be other measures which could be taken to see that this kind of human waste was avoided. It is possible to imagine, for instance, though it would not be easy to produce, a system of financial incentives which made it so clearly worth while for a relatively able boy to carry his education to a later age than he does now, that it would, perhaps, in the end hardly be necessary to raise the school-leaving age. After all, the present encouraging growth of extended courses has taken place in spite of a wages structure which certainly does not encourage a boy to stay longer at school unless he is prepared to look very far ahead. The economic argument alone, in fact, stops a little way short of being finally conclusive. We come back, therefore, to clinch the matter, to the point from which this chapter started. Our main case is not economic at all. It rests on the conviction that all boys and girls of 15 have much to learn, and that school (in the broadest sense) and not work is the place for this. 'Secondary Education for All' will not be a reality until it is provided for all up to the age of 16. We believe that this is a duty which society owes all its young citizens just as we individually recognise it as an obligation in our own families.

From: *Fifteen to Eighteen*, The Crowther Report, HMSO (1959) para. 201.

Document ten
EDUCATION AND CHANGING SOCIAL NEEDS

THE CROWTHER REPORT ARTICULATED VARIOUS CONCERNS ABOUT
THE NEED TO PREPARE YOUNG PEOPLE FOR A CHANGING SOCIETY:

663. *Changing Social Needs*

(a)   If the family is to be as secure in the future as it has been in the past (and
we can be content with nothing less), there will have to be a conscious effort to
prepare the way for it through the educational system on a much greater scale
than has yet been envisaged.

(b)   The problem of sexual ethics is wider than marriage. Young people enjoy
a freedom of unsupervised association which is quite new and brings both gain
and loss. At the same time there is much public indecision over what is right
and wrong. Disaster often results for the young.

(c)   Juvenile delinquency and other social problems are especially marked in
certain areas in which, more even than elsewhere, the teacher has to be a social
worker. A quick turnover of teachers is to be especially avoided in these areas,
but is commonly to be found in them.

(d)   The fact that the peak age for juvenile delinquency is the last year at
school suggests that more thought ought to be given to the condition of boys'
and girls' life, both in and out of school, during the last year or so before they
reach the leaving age.

(e)   Teen-agers are especially exposed to the influence of the 'mass media' of
communication. The duty to see that this power is used responsibly is one for
the whole community, but there is specific educational responsibility to see
that the young learn how to approach the mass media with discrimination.

From: *Fifteen to Eighteen*, The Crowther Report, HMSO (1959) para. 663.

Document eleven
HALF OUR FUTURE

THE NEWSOM REPORT'S CONCERN WAS WITH PUPILS OF AVERAGE ABILITY OR BELOW, IN SECONDARY SCHOOLS:

Despite some splendid achievements in the schools, there is much unrealized talent especially among boys and girls whose potential is masked by inadequate powers of speech and the limitations of home background. Unsuitable programmes and teaching methods may aggravate their difficulties, and frustration express itself in apathy or rebelliousness. The country cannot afford this wastage, humanly or economically speaking. If it is to be avoided, several things will be necessary. The pupils will need to have a longer period of full-time education than most of them now receive. The schools will need to present that education in terms more acceptable to the pupils and to their parents, by relating school more directly to adult life, and especially by taking a proper account of vocational interests. Possible lines of development can be found in many good schools now, but experiment is required, both in the content of the school programme and in teaching methods. Finally, the schools will need strong support in their task, not least from parents, and they will need the tools for the job, in the provision of adequate staff and buildings and equipment.

From: *Half Our Future*, The Newsom Report, HMSO (1963), para. 3.

EDUCATION 'IN THE SLUMS': SPECIAL MEASURES

72.   We are clear . . . that an adequate education cannot be given to boys and girls if it has to be confined to the slums in which they live. They, above all others, need access to the countryside, the experience of living together in civilized and beautiful surroundings, and a chance to respond to the challenge of adventure. They need priority in relation to school journeys, overseas visits, and adventure courses. Clearly this is an educational matter, but it is not solely one. Children below shcool age, young workers, older people – the whole community – need to have a stake in something more than the streets in which they live.

73.   In the last four paragraphs we have been concerned with the fact that certain problems which are primarily educational have wider social implications. Whatever is decided by the educational authorities in these matters will have repercussions on other social agencies. It is equally true that decisions made in other fields – housing, for example, or in public health – will have reactions in the schools. There may well be a case, as has been suggested to us, for really short term residential provision in their own neighbourhood for boys and girls who are in especially difficult or distressing home circumstances, or who may be in danger of lapsing into serious delinquency. If this is so, the relation of such a plan to the schools is something which might be explored jointly by the services which would be involved. In the slums the need for reform is not confined to the schools. It is general.

From: *Half Our Future*, The Newsom Report, HMSO (1963) paras. 72–3.

Document thirteen
HIGHER EDUCATION AND PREPARATION FOR WORK

THE ROBBINS REPORT PLACES THE FOLLOWING AS THE FIRST AIM
OF HIGHER EDUCATION:

25. We begin with instruction in skills suitable to play a part in the general
division of labour. We put this first, not because we regard it as the most
important, but because we think it is sometimes ignored or undervalued.
Confucius said in the *Analects* that it was not easy to find a man who had
studied for three years without aiming at pay. We deceive ourselves if we claim
that more than a small fraction of students in institutions of higher education
would be where they are if there were no significance for their future careers in
what they hear and read: and it is a mistake to suppose that there is anything
discreditable in this. Certainly this was not the attitude of the past: the ancient
universities of Europe were founded to promote the training of the clergy,
doctors and lawyers; and though at times there may have been many who
attended for the pursuit of pure knowledge or of pleasure, they must surely
have been a minority. And it must be recognised that in our own times,
progress – and particularly the maintenance of a competitive position –
depends to a much greater extent than ever before on skills demanding special
training. A good general education, valuable though it may be, is frequently
less than we need to solve many of our most pressing problems.

From: *Higher Education*, The Robbins Report, Cmnd. 2154, HMSO, (1963)
para. 25.

Document fourteen
ARGUMENTS FOR DEALING WITH THE PUBLIC SCHOOLS

18.   The first solution is to declare that the problem is insoluble, and to leave the public schools as they are. This view, in different forms, is held by those at opposite ends of the political spectrum. It is held by those who detest the notion of any State interference with the public schools and who are at best lukewarm in supporting any scheme to broaden their social entry. Those who hold this view believe that the public schools exist for those who can pay the fees: that the whole point of the schools is that they should be the places where boys and girls of the same class should go – together with those who through their parents' wealth have acquired the ability to enter that class. We cannot accept this view. It is directly opposed to our terms of reference . . . To extricate the State entirely from its involvement in these schools would call for the withdrawal of all these pupils. This would be a negative act. We prefer to think of these pupils as the forerunners of a bolder measure of integration.

19.   The view that the public schools are best left alone is also held by those who disapprove of them most strongly – and by those who, having read the numerous articles and reports on the future of these schools which have appeared since the Commission was set up, have formed the opinion that integration is neither worth the money nor the effort involved. Some believe that any scheme of integration will be thwarted by the governing bodies and heads of these schools so that they will remain as socially divisive as before and worse still, more directly bolstered by State subsidies. Such people argue that the schools should be boycotted and subjected to every form of ostracism that wit can devise to strip them of their privleges. We have faced the issue of these privileges. We deal with the charitable status of the schools and the tax-avoidance schemes which undoubtedly enable many parents to afford the fees. We explore the extent to which independent schools employ more teachers than comparable maintained schools. We have suggested ways of meeting these problems; but they would be mainly negative actions unless we looked also to the integration of the schools. We do not believe that guerrilla war waged against these schools is any substitute for recognising that they are an important part of the nation's secondary education system.

28.   Our general conclusion is that independent schools are a divisive

influence in society. The pupils, the schools and the country would benefit if they admitted children from a wider social background. We recommend a scheme of integration by which suitable boarding schools would make over at least half of their places to assisted pupils who need boarding education. This change will take time, and not all schools can be brought within the integrated sector simultaneously. The details should be worked out school by school, by a body we shall call the Boarding Schools Corporation.

From: *The Public Schools Commission*, First Report, HMSO (1968) paras. 18, 19, 28.

Document fifteen
BOARDING SCHOOLS AND SOCIAL DIVISIVENESS

JOHN VAIZEY DISSENTED FROM THE OTHER MEMBERS OF THE
PUBLIC SCHOOLS COMMISSION, AND ARGUED THAT THEY HAD
AVOIDED THE REAL ISSUE OF WHETHER THE PUBLIC SCHOOLS
OUGHT TO BE ABOLISHED, BY SIMPLY PROPOSING A DIFFERENT
KIND OF RECRUITMENT:

5. *Boarding.* The main objection to private schools is that they are socially
divisive. Some of them happen to have beds. It therefore seems less revolutionary to change the bodies in the beds than to eliminate the beds. It is as
though Henry VIII had not dismantled the monasteries, but filled them with
social need cases, after an exhaustive social survey of the number of people in
the population who felt the urge for a life of contemplation in a cell. There is a
degree of confusion in attempting to 'solve' a social question by throwing out
the middle class and replacing it by a different social group . . .

13.   I know of no evidence which suggests that there is some large unrecognised area of boarding need which the local authorities are not meeting –
though there are obviously deficiencies in particular areas of need, and in
particular parts of the country, which require to be remedied through the
normal development of these services. And even if there are unrecognised
types of need, they will be brought to light by the local personal services, and
should be met by expanding the residential facilities which these services have
at their disposal. They will not be discovered by a Boarding Schools Corporation totally lacking in relevant expertise or local resources. Nor would the
public schools be suitable places in which to place all but a small minority of
such children. The Home Office evidence is incontrovertible on this point:
and it is a plain inference from this evidence that the children's services would

not want to take over the public schools even if they were abolished as educational communities, and made available simply as premises for adaptation. These services are already sufficiently embarrassed by their legacy of over-large, georgraphically isolated, Poor Law Institutions and Approved Schools.

From: *The Public Schools Commission*, First Report, HMSO (1968) pp. 221–3.

Document sixteen
GOOD PRIMARY EDUCATION AND THE DISADVANTAGED CHILD

1231.   Since the war there has been a great increase in secondary education and in further and higher education. These developments were necessary if we were to hold our own with other advanced industrial countries. We are certainly not leading an advance party. This progress, however, has been in part at the expense of primary education. We think that a higher priority in the total educational budget ought now to be given to primary schools. It is desirable in its own right: nobody ought to be satisfied with the conditions under which many of the four million primary school children are educated. It is also desirable in the interests of secondary and further education. A good deal of the money spent on older children will be wasted if more is not spent on them during their primary school years . . .

1235.   We hope we have described in the Report what good primary education is, and how robust, imaginative, sensitive and skilful the work of a good primary school pupil can be. Much of our thinking, however, has been given to considering those children to whose work none of these epithets could be applied. We know that in almost every primary school there are some such children. We know that in some districts almost every child is at a disadvantage that can only be removed by unusual excellence in the school. An outstanding trend in recent years has been the growing awareness of the importance for the individual of his family and social background. The last three reports by the Council and the Robbins report on higher education published evidence that shows how closely associated are social circumstances and academic achievement. We have been able to set on foot research which has suggested that the most vital factor in a child's home is the attitude to school, and all that goes on there, of his mother and father. The interested parent has the interested child. In contrast we have been conscious of the unfairness that dogs many boys and girls through life. The loss to them, the loss to the community that arises because of the inequality of educational opportunity, is avoidable and in consequence intolerable. We have, therefore, deliberately given their needs the first priority among our recommendations even though this may delay for a while long-overdue benefits for the greater number of children. Our proposal for the introduction of educational priority areas, a detailed plan for dealing with a situation to which the Council's last report also drew attention, is sufficiently urgent to be put forward for immediate action even in the present economic difficulties.

From: *Children and Their Primary Schools*, The Plowden Report, HMSO, (1967) paras. 1231, 1235.

POSITIVE DISCRIMINATION IN EDUCATION

151.   The many teachers who do so well in the face of adversity cannot manage without cost to themselves. They carry the burdens of parents, probation officers and welfare officers on top of their classroom duties. It is time the nation came to their aid. The principle, already accepted, that special need calls for special help, should be given a new cutting edge. We ask for 'positive discrimination' in favour of such schools and the children in them, going well beyond an attempt to equalise resources. Schools in deprived areas should be given priority in many respects. The first step must be to raise the schools with low standards to the national average; the second, quite deliberately to make them better. The justification is that the homes and neighbourhoods from which many of their children come provide little support and stimulus for learning. The schools must supply a compensating environment. The attempts so far made within the educational system to do this have not been sufficiently generous or sustained, because the handicaps imposed by the environment have not been explicitly and sufficiently allowed for. They should be.

152.   The proposition that good schools should make up for a poor environment is far from new. It derives from the notion that there should be equality of opportunity for all, but recognises that children in some districts will only get the same opportunity as those who live elsewhere if they have unequally generous treatment. It was accepted before the First World War that some children could not be effectively taught until they had been properly fed. Hence free meals were provided. Today their need is for enriched intellectual nourishment. Planned and positive discrimination in favour of deprived areas could bring about an advance in the education of children in the 1970s as great as the advance in their nutrition to which school meals and milk contributed so much . . .

17.   Positive discrimination accords with experience and thinking in many other countries, and in other spheres of social policy. It calls both for some redistribution of the resources devoted to education and, just as much, for an increase in their total volume. It must not be interpreted simply as a gloss upon

the recommendations which follow in later chapters. This would not only be a misunderstanding of the scheme; it would destroy all hope of its success. For it would be unreasonable and self-defeating – economically, professionally and politically – to try to do justice by the most deprived children by using only resources that can be diverted from more fortunate areas. We have argued that the gap between the educational opportunities of the most and least fortunate children should be closed, for economic and social reasons alike. It cannot be done, unless extra effort, extra skill and extra resources are devoted to the task.

From: *Children and Their Primary Schools*, The Plowden Report, HMSO (1967) paras. 151,152, 173.

Document eighteen
EDUCATIONAL PRIORITY AREAS: SOME CONCLUSIONS

Our major conclusions from the four English E.P.A. action-research projects are that:
(1) The educational priority area, despite its difficulties of definition, is a socially and administratively viable unit through which to apply the principle of positive discrimination.
(2) Pre-schooling is the outstandingly economical and effective device in the general approach to raising educational standards in E.P.A.s.
(3) The idea of the community school, as put forward in skeletal outline by Plowden, has now been shown to have greater substance and powerful implications for community regeneration.
(4) There are practical ways of improving the partnership between families and schools in E.P.A.s.
(5) There are practical ways of improving the quality of teaching in E.P.A. schools.
(6) Action-research is an effective method of policy formation and practical innovation.
(7) The E.P.A. can be no more than a part, though an important one, of a comprehensive social movement towards community development and community redevelopment in a modern urban industrial society.

From: *Educational Priority*, Vol. 1, HMSO (1972) p. 180.

Document nineteen
THE 'PROBLEM' OF EDUCATING IMMIGRANT CHILDREN

It is misleading and damaging to all concerned to talk in generalisations about immigrant children. There is too frequently a tendency to regard 'immigrant child' as synonymous with 'problem'. The immigrant child, whether coloured or not, does not necessarily present problems, and this kind of automatic reaction is to be deprecated. Too many, seeing the amount of educational backwardness which exists among immigrant children, wrongly suppose that this derives from some inherent or genetic racial inferiority . . . Nevertheless, for a number of reasons – such as the bewilderment they often experience on changing from one educational environment to another – and the frequently unreliable initial assessment of their potential – a large proportion of immigrant pupils find their way into lower streams and remedial classes of our schools – and the number who secure a place in selective schools, in areas still served by them, is disturbingly small . . . They may thus experience a more complex form of deprivation than the native-born child as they stand bewildered between two cultures. Not only, however, may their difficulties be greater – they are also different – need different responses, requiring sensitivity and care based on understanding. Their education must involve social, cultural and emotional adjustments of a special kind.

From: *The Education of Immigrants*, Education Survey No. 13, Department of Education and Science (1971) pp. 4–5.

The problem of how immigrants' children should be dealt with in the educational system has entered national debates about education in the form of the following questions:

1. Is there overt discrimination in the form of a deliberate denial of opportunities to immigrant children on grounds of race?
2. Should statistics of immigrant numbers and immigrant performance be kept officially as a basis for educational planning?
3. Should immigrant children be spread evenly through the education system, particularly through a programme of dispersal from the inner city to suburban schools?
4. Do West Indian and Asian children achieve less than their indigenous peers in selection tests and examinations?
5. Do immigrants face special problems in schools or do they have problems because they are part of a large category of disadvantaged children?
6. How can non-English-speaking children be assimilated into the school system?
7. What provision should be made for the education of the children of immigrants in their own language and culture?
8. How should funds be provided to overcome the disadvantages of immigrants and, more widely, of all the 'disadvantaged'?

We shall now record the main points which have been made in the debate around these questions, but before we do that we must make an important preliminary observation. This is that there was no planning at all for the absorption of immigrants' children into the educational system. Had there been, in a society which valued the notions of equality of opportunity and equality of outcome for all of its citizens, then the question would have been how to overcome the manifest disadvantages of the children of immigrants by providing them with the linguistic and other skills necessary for them to compete equally at school, and by giving special consideration to the problems which these children might face as a result of living uneasily between two cultures and as a result of migrating from one social system to another. Instead the problems mentioned arose *ad hoc*, decisions were often taken in panic, and the very way the debate was structured, almost regardless of the answers given to the eight questions, fostered racism.

From: J. Rex and S. Tomlinson, *Colonial Immigrants in a British City*, Routledge & Keegan Paul (1979) pp. 162–3.

Document twenty-one
THE GREAT DEBATE: SCHOOL AND WORK (1)

THE PRIME MINISTER – (JAMES CALLAGHAN'S) SPEECH AT RUSKIN COLLEGE, WHICH INITIATED THE 'GREAT DEBATE', INCLUDED THE FOLLOWING COMMENTS:

I am concerned on my journeys to find complaints from industry that new recruits from the schools sometimes do not have the basic tools to do the job that is required.

I have been concerned to find that many of our best trained students who have completed the higher levels of education at university or polytechnic have no desire or intention of joining industry. Their preferences are to stay in academic life (very pleasant, I know) or to find their way into the civil service. There seems to be a need for a more technological bias in science teaching that will lead towards practical applications in industry rather than towards academic studies . . .

The goals of our education, from nursery school through to adult education, are clear enough. They are to equip children to the best of their ability for a lively, constructive place in society and also to fit them to do a job of work. Not one or the other, but both . . .

The balance was wrong in the past. We have a responsibility now in this generation to see that we do not get it wrong in the other direction. There is no virtue in producing socially well-adjusted members of society who are unemployed because they do not have the skills. Nor at the other extreme must they be technically efficient robots. Both of the basic purposes of education require the same essential tools. These are to be basically literate, to be basically numerate, to understand how to live and work together, and have respect for others and respect for the individual.

From: *Times Educational Supplement*, 22 October 1976.

Document twenty-two
THE GREAT DEBATE: SCHOOL AND WORK (2)

1.3   There is a wide gap between the world of education and the world of work. Boys and girls are not sufficiently aware of the importance of industry to our society, and they are not taught much about it. In some schools the curriculum has been overloaded, so that the basic skills of literacy and numeracy, the building blocks of education, have been neglected. A small minority of schools has simply failed to provide an adequate education by modern standards. More frequently, schools have been over-ambitious, introducing modern languages without sufficient staff to meet the needs of a much wider range of pupils, or embarking on new methods of teaching mathematics without making sure the teachers understood what they were teaching, or whether it was appropriate to the pupils' capacities or the needs of their future employers.

7.5   Young people need to reach maturity with a basic understanding of the economy and the activities, especially manufacturing industry, which are necessary for the creation of Britain's national wealth. It is an important task of secondary schools to develop this understanding, and opportunities for its development should be offered to pupils of all abilities. These opportunities are needed not only by young people who may have careers in industry later but perhaps even more by those who may work elsewhere, so that the role of industry becomes soundly appreciated by society in general.

From: *Education in Schools: a Consultative Document*, Cmnd. 6869, HMSO (1977).

THE CASE AGAINST CONTRACTING PUBLIC PROVISION OF HIGHER EDUCATION

NEIL KINNOCK, SPEAKING FOR THE LABOUR PARTY, ATTACKED THE VIEW THAT PUBLIC FINANCING OF HIGHER EDUCATION SHOULD BE REDUCED IN FAVOUR OF THE OPERATION OF A FREE MARKET IN ITS PROVISION:

[The system which the government] appears to want is one in which access to and provision in higher education should be reduced. University places should be available only to those who pursue knowledge for its own sake. The great yoke of publicly-provided opportunities should be lifted from the necks of our oppressed citizenry and replaced by a privatised university system . . .

If such a system were brought fully into operation, presumably it would satisfy the right hon. Gentleman's perceptions of liberty and his definition of utility. We shall fight and defeat his ideas just as surely as previous generations fought and defeated such ideas when they were laid across those generations' roads to freedom. The right hon. Gentleman thinks of himself and is thought of as a lover of liberty, but the liberty in which he believes requires that people are freed from certain communal obligations and must therefore seek and secure their liberties with minimal communal assistance. The right hon. Gentleman bases his views on the imagined equity and dispassion that he believes exist in the market place. All the legions of history march against that view of liberty. The story of the advancement of the common people in this country and in other countries is one of the expansion of public provision and the retreat of purchased private privilege. Public provision might be the enemy of freedom for the right hon. Gentleman, but it is freedom to me, and I shall tell the right hon. Gentleman why.

Public provision has been the means of my personal emancipation and the emancipation of thousands of my contemporaries and of those who have come from similar backgrounds in the generations following mine.

From: *Parliamentary Debates (Commons)*, Sixth series, Vol. 13, Cols. 299–300.

Document twenty-four
DEFENDING THE 1944 SETTLEMENT

R. A. BUTLER, SPEAKING IN THE HOUSE OF LORDS DEBATE ON THE 1980 EDUCATION ACT, EXPLAINS WHY HE FOUND IT NECESSARY TO INTERVENE TO DEFEND THE 1944 SETTLEMENT:

My objective is what? It is not political. It is to retain the continuity of national policy regarding education throughout the greater part of this century. When I spoke on Second Reading I was able to say that the vital clauses reserving to the Secretary of State powers – particularly Section 89 of the 1944 Act, to which the noble Baroness referred, and the other section to which she referred – have seldom been used. But they illustrate that the pillars of the settlement of 1944 have been preserved by this Act. The noble Baroness has already acknowledged this.

It seems very peculiar, but this question of transport was, if not an integral part – as I said in my Second Reading speech -- at any rate a vital part of the concordat or settlement of 1944. Why was that? It simply was that the denominations and all those partners involved in that settlement were given that assurance that their children would be taken to school. I agree with some things that the noble Baroness said. The three-mile limit derives from 1870 and the Act of Mr. Foster. If I were summoned to a conference one day to look at it I would not mind taking part, provided my noble friends on the other side of the House and the denominations and local authorities were brought into it. But at present it is the law of the land, although it dates from 1870. These extra charges are going to upset not just the noble Duke, the Duke of Norfolk, who might perhaps be held to represent the Roman Catholics, but also the Anglican community, the Free Church Federal Council and the National Union of Teachers.

With all those people I made a settlement – some were laymen and some were churchmen – and the fact is that this was agreed.

From: *Parliamentary Debates (Lords)*, Vol. 406, 13 March 1980, Col. 1220.

THE EFFECTS OF PUBLIC EXPENDITURE CUTS ON SCHOOLS

72.   To put it in a nutshell, many LEAs and schools are surviving financially by doing less; but they are often obliged to take the less in the form that comes easily to hand rather than shaping it to match educational priorities. This means, in some cases, a general retrenchment in which most services, schools and pupils are affected to some degree. But it is clear that some things are more vulnerable than others. Subjects that require expensive specialist books or materials and equipment for practical work, and which are taken by relatively few pupils, are particularly at risk. Remedial teaching, courses for academically less able pupils and additional work with the very able, are less easy to justify and provide when provision for the majority is under pressure. Except in those LEAs with well organised policies of positive discrimination, schools and pupils in deprived and disadvantaged areas are adversely affected by a combination of factors including old and deteriorating buildings, sharp falls in pupil numbers, reductions in specialist help for pupils with learning difficulties, cuts in ancillary staff, such as nursery assistants and classroom helpers, and the absence of alternative sources of funding from, and support within, the community.

73.   Schools are turning increasingly to parents and the local community for financial and other help. Some schools have a long tradition of raising funds to pay for educational visits and desirable but expensive items of equipment. Funds are now frequently used to provide basic materials and equipment. This trend is leading to marked disparities of provision between schools serving affluent and poor areas.

From: *Report by Her Majesty's Inspectors on the effects of local authority expenditure policies on the education service in England, 1981*, DES, (1982) paras. 72–3.

PROMOTING CHILDREN'S WELFARE: SCHOOL MEALS AND HEALTH SERVICES

. . . the continued existence of malnutrition, and the fact that more than 300,000 children are still given free meals, show that much poverty still persists. It seems from our surveys that the schools themselves consider the School Health Service to be highly successful. Its job is widely understood and accepted. Its staff is highly trained, even though some, like the school doctors, have no special preparation for work with school children. Its responsibility, much more advisory than therapeutic, is to ensure that children function normally and live and grow in harmony with their environment. It is primarily a preventive service, and it does not compete with the general practitioners or hospital services.

From: *Children and Their Primary Schools*, The Plowden Report, HMSO (1967) para. 206.

SCHOOL FEEDING: THE DEMANDS OF LABOUR WOMEN

The fight for the implementation of the Feeding of School Children Act is a recurring theme throughout branch reports of the Women's Labour League. In Leicester, for instance, in 1908, Miss Bell of the National Executive reported on two large demonstrations which were organised and a petition signed by over 1,000 women which was sent to the council. But the council's reply was to agree that meals for needy children should be organised but to entrust the work to charitable bodies instead of paying for the service out of the rates. Central London, Jarrow, Leeds, St Pancras and Westminster branches took similar action that year and throughout the next few years this pressure was kept up throughout the country. The Annual Conference passed resolutions in 1909, 1910, 1911, 1912, and 1913 urging the government to make the provision of school meals compulsory instead of permissive, to abolish the halfpenny rate limit on the service and to permit authorities to feed the children during school holidays . . .

During the First World War, though most authorities cut down their arrangements for feeding school children, as a result of the full employment of wartime, there were certainly much smaller number of necessitous children, reported *Labour Woman*. But now there was a class of children for whom the education authorities had to provide meals, whose parents were not poor and were willing enough to pay; these were the children whose mothers were employed in war work and were unable to cook dinner for their children and were even compelled to lock their children out all day. So the Labour women's campaign became one for school meals for all, not just for the needy, an objective which was not to be fully achieved until the Second World War.

From: S. Ferguson, 'Women and the social services', in L. Middleton (ed.), *Women in the Labour Movement*, Croom Helm (1977) pp. 41–2.

THE WORK OF EDUCATION WELFARE OFFICERS

[Their] duties can be grouped under two main headings.

28.   The first concerns the functions undertaken by education welfare officers in regard to the whole range of problems which have the effect of preventing children from deriving benefit from their education. These are essentially problems which involve the education welfare officer in personal contact with parents and children, teachers and the staffs of the education and social services departments. They are:
(a) non-attendance and truancy, involving all those functions connected with school attendance and court proceedings;
(b) various types of physical and mental handicap, which entail appropriate referral, follow-up and after-care;
(c) material handicaps calling for assistance in securing grants for school meals, clothing and maintenance, and liaison with all types of social agency;
(d) parental attitudes, which involve conveying information about official policy and decisions, and advice as to the availability of educational resources, etc;
(e) relationships between the school, the community and the home requiring liaison between school and home, teacher and parent, and groups within the community;
(f) behaviour and progress, calling for liaison with appropriate specialists such as education guidance officers.

29.   The second main group of functions cannot be sharply distinguished from the first because in practice the two may well overlap. Thus a routine call to check the number of children in a family likely to require school places in the following year may uncover problems which call for urgent attention and concern. With this reservation they can be listed as follows:

(a) routine arrangements for the placement for children in school, including keeping of extra-district records;
(b) assisting in selection for places in nursery schools and classes on a basis of

social priority;
(c) arranging school transport;
(d) checking and maintaining census records in regard to children;
(e) assistance in revision of catchment areas and siting of new schools.

From: *The Role and Training of Education Welfare Officers*, The Ralphs Report, Local Government Training Board (1973) paras. 28, 29.

THE CASE FOR SOCIAL WORK IN SCHOOLS

The schools' interest in social work arises from their need to identify and help families with difficulties that lead to poor performance and behaviour of their children in school. Construed narrowly, these responsibilities mean that an education authority must prevent unnecessary absence from school and deal with problems that obviously prevent attendance, for example, inadequate clothing. Construed more positively, they call for social work amounting to general family case work, supported by specialist services equipped to deal with the more serious physical, environmental and psychological problems. Teachers are responsible for establishing a good understanding between the school and parents. There will, however, be difficult cases beyond the competence, time or training of the head or class teacher. These should be the responsibility of trained social workers, collaborating closely with the schools, readily available to teachers, and capable of securing help quickly from more specialised social services.

From: *Children and Their Primary Schools*, The Plowden Report, HMSO (1967) para. 243.

Document thirty
PROFESSIONALS' VIEWS ON SCHOOLS ATTENDANCE

[It seems that there are] differences in the way teachers and social workers view each other's role. Social workers claim that the school represses the individual child whereas teachers believe that social workers do not take a wide enough view and are too eager to make excuses for an individual child or his family. In particular the difference is apparent in relation to the enforcement of school attendance, which in itself stems from a different interpretation of the desirability of compulsory school attendance. In recent years compulsory attendance has been attacked on a number of fronts, and of course as this is the original rationale for the role of education welfare officers it is only natural that officers take a view to that of teachers on this issue, and it is this more than anything else which distinguishes their role from that of the orthodox social worker.

From: K. MacMillan, *Education Welfare*, Longman, London (1977) p. 101.

Document thirty-one
EDUCATION WELFARE AND SOCIAL SERVICES: THE CASE FOR INTEGRATION

However, we have concluded that social work in schools should be the responsiblity of the social service department because we consider the arguments for this course are even stronger than those outlined above. First and foremost, it is essential to consider and, if necessary, deal with a child in his total environment which includes his family and neighbourhood as well as his school. Social workers within the social service department will more readily achieve this objective and deal with the whole range of family problems, including families where there are children under as well as over school age. Second, a separate social work service in the education department would perpetuate the present system of fragmented *ad hoc* social work services largely operating in isolation. Third, to be completely effective the school social worker needs to be a member of a community based area team on which he can call for support and consultation or for extra resources in dealing with particular problems. Fourth, there are advantages for the individual school in having a link with the social service department through a social worker in the school, since the department will include services which may directly or indirectly affect its pupils, for example, the care of deprived children. Fifth, a better career structure, including wider opportunities for in-service training and for promotion, can be offered to workers in a unified service. We attach considerable weight to this consideration. The skill and understanding of the social workers concerned are crucial; and there must be enough social workers. We think there is a better chance of achieving this if the social workers are part of the social service department. Lastly, the ability of these workers to win the confidence of schools, parent and education departments, will depend on the quality of the service they offer.

From: *Report of the Committee on Local Authority and Allied Personal Social Services*, Seebohm Report, Cmnd. 3703 (1968) para. 226.

Document thirty-two
DILEMMAS OF TEACHERS' INVOLVEMENT IN CHILDREN'S WELFARE

. . . the whole question of child care and preventive work is an area of difficulty and confusion for the teaching profession. Not being strictly education, it has not been accepted as essential to the professional tasks of teachers. The whole question of the teacher's *in loco parentis* role, the ethics of intervening in family or personal problems, the use of the support service, none of these questions have really been thought through. When a child is in trouble or danger, is the teacher's task to teach? Is it to act like a parent? To care? To intervene? To delegate? Where should the balance be struck between these alternatives? These questions have not been sorted out within the profession, nor in teacher education. Many courses do not discuss them at all. Young teachers often have no opportunity to work out their role about such questions until they are faced with a child in need, when they have to act one way or the other, often with nobody to share the problem . . .

From: K. Fitzherbert, 'Strategies for prevention', in Craft, M. (ed.), *Linking Home and School*, 3rd edn, Harper & Row (1980) pp. 356–7.

Document thirty-three
WELFARE VERSUS THE MORAL ORDER

THE STUDY OF THE RESPONSE OF SCHOOLS AND EDUCATION
AUTHORITIES TO PREGNANT PUPILS PROVIDES A GOOD EXAMPLE OF
THE TENSION BETWEEN PROMOTING THE WELFARE OF INDIVI-
DUALS AND SECURING THE MORAL ORDER:

111.   Sometimes the school sees a conflict between the welfare of an individual pregnant girl and the interests of their other students. This dilemma was
described to us as 'a difficult tight-rope between trying to maintain moral
standards in the school and consequently not accepting such occurences as
normal, and at the same time helping the girl. But the utmost care should be
taken to ensure that the school's moral standards are not prejudiced. If it
appeared that a school regarded a pregnancy as a part of normal school life,
immense harm could be done.'

112.   We received no evidence to show that the presence of an obviously
pregnant girl has a contagious effect on other girls in the school. In fact the
reverse could well be true – other girls could be deterred from pregnancy by
observing the realities of a pregnant friend's situation. Moreover, the
emotional and social value to a girl of a continuing link with school and
ordinary schoolgirl life during pregnancy was widely stressed in our evidence,
as without this link a girl is likely to suffer from loneliness, isolation and
boredom. In addition, although attitudes towards work may change and
examinations may no longer appear relevant, evidence from America suggests
that those girls who do remain at school during pregnancy are more likely to
continue their education successfully afterwards.

From: *Pregnant at School*, National Council for One Parent Families, London
(1979) paras. 111–12.

PASTORAL CARE: WELFARE OR CONTROL?

The aims of pastoral care are often vague, and tend to be expressed in the most general terms. Typically, the school is assumed to have some sort of welfare role, where the function of pastoral care is seen as supporting the individual child who is a casualty of some aspect of the social environment. Schools rarely see themselves as part of this environment . . . .

In some schools the emphasis is on therapeutic aims, and they claim to provide the means. But in this case problems are defined from an individual and pathological standpoint and solutions are seen in terms of client adjustment, aims typical of much counselling practice. Although this provides for some young people, it is alien to and inappropriate for the majority.

This diversity and lack of clarity of aims helps to account for the way in which in a significant number of schools the more pressing preoccupations of teachers' administration, discipline, containment and control, take over the functioning of many pastoral systems. Consequently, despite their expressed welfare aims, the aims are too weak and vague to prevent the systems becoming little more than teachers functioning in extended disciplinary-administrative roles.

That this was the true nature of pastoral systems in their schools was clearly the view of many of the young people I talked to. Though most conceded that there were a minority of teachers who showed some real concern for them, their view was perhaps best summarized by the boy who, when asked why his school had a house system, replied: 'This is a very big school, and it makes it easier to punish us in small groups.'

This leads to the second problem – the failure to involve young people in the development of systems which purport to be there for their benefit. In almost all cases in my experience, the development of pastoral care has been teacher generated and planned, while what counts as a problem is also decided by teachers. The views and feelings of the young people have rarely been sought, and where they have, it has been in the form of a token gesture by the schools rather than a genuine wish to involve them.

From: P. Lang, 'It's easier to punish us in small groups', *Times Educational Supplement*, 6 May 1977, p. 17.

Document thirty-five
CITIZENSHIP RIGHTS AND EDUCATIONAL PROVISION

. . . I propose to divide citizenship into three parts. . . I shall call these parts, or elements, civil, political and social. The civil element is composed of the rights necessary for individual freedom . . . By the political element I mean the right to participate in the exercise of political power . . . By the social element I mean the whole range from the right to a modicum of economic welfare and security to the right to share to the full in the social heritage and to live the life of a civilised being according to the standards prevailing in the society. The institutions most closely connected with it are the educational system and the social services. . . .

[The example of education] illustrates my earlier point about the balance between individual and collective social rights. In the first phase of our public education, rights were minimal and equal. But, as we have observed, a duty was attached to the right, not merely because the citizen had a duty to himself, as well as a right, to develop all that is in him – a duty which neither the child nor the parent may fully appreciate – but because society recognised that it needed an educated population. . . .

[Since] 1944, individual rights have ostensibly been given priority. Competition for scarce places is to be replaced by selection and distribution into appropriate places, sufficient in number to accommodate all, at least at the secondary school level. In the Act of 1944 there is a passage which says that the supply of secondary schools will not be considered adequate unless they 'afford for all pupils opportunities for education offering such variety of instruction and training as may be desirable in view of their different ages, abilities and aptitudes'. Respect for individual rights could hardly be more strongly expressed. Yet I wonder whether it will work out like that in practice.

If it were possible for the school system to treat the pupil entirely as an end in himself, and to regard education as giving him something whose value he could enjoy to the full whatever his station in after-life, then it might be possible to mould the educational plan to the shape demanded by individual needs, regardless of any other considerations. But, as we all know, education to-day is closely linked with occupation, and one, at least, of the values the pupil expects to get from it is a qualification for employment at an appropriate level. Unless great changes take place, it seems likely that the educational plan will be adjusted to occupational demand.

From: T. H. Marshall, *Citizenship and Social Class*, Cambridge University Press (1950) pp. 10–11, 62–4.

Document thirty-six
CITIZENSHIP AND INEQUALITY

The starting point of [Marshall's] analysis here is the paradox that the growth of citizenship – which has to do with equality – has coincided with the development of capitalism, a system of inequality. However, the paradox is more apparent than real for, as Marshall observed, citizenship has to do with equality of status as a member of a community and not with equality in any other sense. Thus equal status as a citizen is quite compatible with inequality in other aspects, for example material rewards, resulting from the operations of the market and other structures of capitalism . . . Neither the primary objectives nor the consequences of state welfare are egalitarian in the sense of reducing class inequality. As Marshall pointed out, with the social services the redistribution of incomes and life-chances tends to be mainly horizontal (within classes) rather than vertical (between classes). Far from reducing class inequality, citizenship creates an equality of conditions in certain respects in order that a structure of social inequality may be built all the more securely. It provides 'the foundation of equality on which the structure of inequality could be built'. In this sense the welfare state makes inequality more acceptable and legitimate.

From: R. Mishra, *Society and Social Policy*, Macmillan, London (1977) pp. 22–3.

Document thirty-seven
THE W.E.A SPIRIT

IN HIS PERSONAL ACCOUNTS OF THE ORIGINS OF THE WORKERS'
EDUCATIONAL ASSOCIATION, ALBERT MANSBRIDGE DESCRIBES
WHAT HE CALLS 'THE W.E.A. SPIRIT':

The power of the movement lay in the fact that it inspired its members, and
those with whom it came into contact, to give of their highest and best,
because to do so was the way of life. As we have seen over and over again, the
objects to which knowledge and training were to be applied were never
thought about. Education was recognised as a force enabling man to develop
to the furthest limits of his powers. All the time the Association was confident
that every true cause, particularly that of justice for the labourer, would
benefit in proportion to the increase in the number of those who had made
themselves into finer and purer men . . .

The genesis of the Association was due to the lamentable situation which
had risen in English life owing to the neglect of education for the people. In
this matter the ordinary working man was disinherited; but because there are
so many working men it was easy to secure their full representation without
making a class appeal. There never was a single occasion upon which the ideals
expressed were not in harmony with the spirit of labour. The scholars and
others who joined the movement were as men watching all the time how they
could assist and forward the wishes of the majority. Not that they for one
moment abrogated their rights in a democratic body, but always there was the
manifest desire to perceive and understand the spirit and needs of those
engaged in manual toil. Yet because scholarship is a vital force the fusion of it
with the experience of life and labour produced a greater wisdom than could
have been the case if scholars had been absent or quiescent. That is indeed the
whole case for the Association.

From: A. Mansbridge, *An Adventure in Working Class Education*, Longmans,
Green & Co., (1920) pp. 54–5.

76.   Most teachers and parents would agree with us about general objectives. Skills, qualities of character, knowledge, physical well-being, are all to be desired. Boys and girls need to be helped to develop certain skills of communication in speech and in writing, in reading with understanding, and in calculations involving number and measurement: these skills are basic, in that they are tools to other learning and without some mastery of them the pupils will be cut off from whole areas of human thought and experience. But they do not by themselves represent an adequate minimum education at which to aim. All boys and girls need to develop, as well as skills, capacities for thought, judgement, enjoyment, curiosity. They need to develop a sense of responsibility for their work and towards other people, and to begin to arrive at some code of moral and social behaviour which is self-imposed. It is important that they should have some understanding of the physical world and of the human society in which they are growing up.

77.   Our pupils, because some of them acquire skills slowly, and others only with the utmost difficulty, may be in danger of spending their whole time at school in continual efforts to sharpen tools which they never have opportunity enough to use. They may be kept busy, and yet never have their minds and imaginations fully engaged; and leave school very ill-equipped in knowledge and personal resources . . .

328.   An education which is practical, realistic and vocational in the sense in which we have used these words, and which provides some ground in which to exercise choice, is an education that makes sense to the boys and girls we have in mind. It should also make sense to the society in which they live and which provides their education. But if their education could be completely described in these words it would be sadly lacking. An education that makes complete sense must provide opportunity for personal fulfilment – for the good life as well as for good living. This is not, of course, a matter for a series of lessons. It is a quality to be sought, not a subject to be taught. One of the elements involved is that which shines out when the only possible answer to the question 'why are you taking so much trouble to do this properly', is 'because I

enjoy doing it'. This situation may well arise in the course of a hobby but it may also be found in parts of school work. Wherever it occurs, it is something to be fostered – doing something worth while for its own sake is a principal aim not only of education but of life. It is within the reach of clever and stupid alike.

From: *Half Our Future*, The Newsom Report, HMSO (1963) paras.76, 77, 328.

THE CASE FOR PROVIDING ADULT EDUCATION

7. The grounds for justifying public expenditure are not the same for all sectors of education, nor even for the whole range of further education. The need for basic education is now so well established that full-time attendance at school is legally enforced upon all young people in this country to the age of sixteen and avenues to many of the more responsible employments depend on full-time education continuing for several years beyond this minimum. Since the connection between the amount of, and success in, initial education and the style of life consequent upon it is so clear, initial education can easily be justified in material terms. Education for industry and commerce tends to find its justification, by natural transfer, in the economic importance of the process of production and marketing. Thus, because initial education and education connected with employment both have such an obvious pay-off in terms of production and consumption, these forms of education are immediately recognised as worthy of expenditure.

8. In fact these easily measurable effects of education are only a few of the benefits it confers. Education is concerned with developing the ability of individuals to understand and to articulate; to reason and to make judgments; and to develop sensitivity and creativity. Initial education is designed for these purposes too, but it would be surprising if individual development were completed and curiosity satisfied by the age of sixteen or even twenty-six. Indeed, we recognise that initial schooling is not completely successful for everyone. Many of those who have had the least schooling, and these form the great majority of the population, may have made only partial use of such opportunities as were then available to them; and a larger number have rejected as irrelevant to their felt needs much of the early education they were offered. If individuals are to be given the chance to develop their talents and abilities to the full and to meet with understanding the impact of rapidly changing patterns of employment and the stresses of a rapidly changing society, they require access to education in adult life as their needs emerge. There is no reason to expect that these will always be tied closely to some aspect of occupational training. This Report is therefore concerned with opportunities for men and women to continue to develop their knowledge,

skills, judgment and creativity throughout adult life by taking part, from time to time, in learning situations which have been set up for the purpose as part of the total public provision of education. This is what we mean when we employ the phrase 'adult education' in these pages.

From: *Adult Education: a Plan for Development*, The Russell Report, HMSO (1973) paras. 7–8.

Document forty
THE 'SOCIAL PURPOSE' OF ADULT EDUCATION

We have already seen that in the sphere of education society has a positive duty of the most binding kind towards each of its members as an individual. Clearly, the discharging of its obligations towards individuals, which it owes to them in virtue of various general moral principles which we have already noted, in itself constitutes an amply sufficient reason for making regular and substantial provision for adult education. However, many people have also considered adult education to be something which a wise society ought in any case to promote because of the unique contribution which it can make to the wellbeing of society itself. Traditionally, and rightly, British adult educators have attached great importance to what they have usually called the 'social purpose' of adult education . . .

No one, I think, would seriously wish to dispute that adult education can in many ways make a notable contribution, perhaps an indispensable contribution, to the remedying of many specific social problems and to the general betterment of our social life – for example, in helping to create better industrial relations, helping to alleviate racial and religious conflicts, helping to improve the quality of family life, helping to smooth the transition between work and retirement, helping to promote higher standards of health and hygiene, helping to reduce environmental pollution, and in countless other ways helping to make the world an altogether better place to live in.

From: R. K. W. Paterson, *Values, Education and the Adult*, Routledge & Kegan Paul, London (1979) pp. 254–5.

THE CASE FOR EDUCATIONAL MAINTENANCE ALLOWANCES

5. Section 81 of the Education Act 1944 empowers the Minister to make regulations 'for the purpose of enabling pupils to take advantage without hardship to themselves or their parents of any educational facilities available to them'. Since 1945, regulations made under that section of the Act have empowered local education authorities in England and Wales, at their discretion, to provide EMAs to pupils who remain at school beyond compulsory age.

6. In 1957 the Minister of Education set up a Working Party under the chairmanship of Mr. T. R. Weaver (Sir Toby Weaver), who was then a senior official in the Ministry of Education, 'to consider . . . the effects of educational maintenance allowances paid in respect of pupils remaining at school over the compulsory school age . . . and whether any changes should be made in the existing arrangements'. The resultant 'Weaver Report' of 1957 was a landmark in the history of EMAs. We shall refer to its findings later in our Report, but at this stage, we are concerned only to record the philosophy which inspired them:

> We wish to emphasis that in our deliberations we have had one object only: to seek the means of enabling pupils to remain at school and to take full advantage of the educational opportunities provided for them without themselves undergoing hardship and without causing hardship to their parents. (Extract from para. 11 of the *Report of the Working Party on Education Maintenance Allowances*, published by the Ministry of Education, 1957).

7. It has been put to us in the course of our inquiry that this philosophy may have become outdated; that the relationship between the 16 to 18 year-old and his parents has changed in the last decade; that young people of this age today are readier to handle their own affairs and that it would be more realistic to regard EMAs as the means of enabling 16 to 18-year-olds to maintain themselves while at school . . . Alternatively it was put to us that parents should no longer be expected to make sacrifices towards providing their children's voluntary education; that all parents, irrespective of strict financial need,

should be reimbursed for the cost of maintaining their children at school once the age of compulsion had passed . . .

8.   We do not accept either viewpoint. We agree that 16 to 18 year-olds today make many more decisions about their ways of life than they once did and, in our recommendations, we recognise this change; but we do not regard them as having the right of independent choice where their education is concerned any more than they enjoy, as minors, independence in the eyes of the law; nor should they look upon the EMAs as a substitute for wages.

9.   We are equally sure that nothing we recommend should tend to undermine the responsibility of parents for bringing up their children. The concern of Government should be to make sure that financial help is available when it is needed.

10. We endorse the words of the 1944 Act: the purpose of EMAs is 'to enable pupils to take advantage without hardship to themselves or their parents of any educational facilities available to them'.

From: *Educational Maintenance Allowances in the 16–18 Years Age Group*, House of Commons Expenditure Committee, Session 1973–74, H.C. 306, HMSO (1974).

Document forty-two

TRAVELLING TO SCHOOL: A PROBLEM OF ACCESS TO EDUCATION

THE CHILD POVERTY ACTION GROUP PRODUCED A STUDY WHICH SHOWED THE IMPORTANCE OF FREE SCHOOL TRANSPORT AS A MEANS OF ENSURING THAT ALL CHILDREN HAVE EFFECTIVE ACCESS TO SCHOOLING. WHERE FREE TRANSPORT IS NOT AVAILABLE, CHILDREN AND PARENTS FACE A VARIETY OF PROBLEMS:

First, some children are missing school because their parents cannot afford bus fares every day. This was a particular problem in one area of Cardiff where parents were organising themselves to campaign against the rapidly increasing costs. In Bracknell, some parents were economising by arranging communal taxis for their school children.

Second, parents were sending their children to school late and telling them that they must not stay for any after-school activities. This was happening in Bracknell, where adult fares are charged up to 9.15 a.m., and in Harlow, where the reduced rate ends at 4 p.m.

Third, parents felt that their choice over their children's education was being eroded by their poverty. Children in Mitcham transfer to a high school of their choosing at 13 years but can expect no help with bus fares if there are vacancies in another high school nearer home.

Fourth, many children are exposed to physical dangers when travelling to and from school. One governor in Hatfield reported that one-third of the children from an estate which her school serves have to negotiate two very busy and dangerous roads on their 2 mile journey to school. New towns present particular problems where families have moved home before adequate facilities have been built. In one part of Harlow parents must choose between sending their children by foot along 2.7 miles of lonely roads, or paying £1.20 a week for each child's fares. At the time of the survey this had been the case for one year, and it was unlikely that the nearby school would be completed within the next year. A much-needed primary school in the area had not been started, and children have a two mile journey each day through a busy main road underpass and along a lonely dark cycle track.

From: J. Tunnard. *Taken for a Ride*, Child Poverty Action Group (1976) p.11.

SPECIAL EDUCATIONAL NEEDS

1.4   We hold that education has certain long-term goals, that it has a general point of purpose, which can be definitely, though generally, stated. The goals are twofold, different from each other, but by no means incompatible. They are, first, to enlarge a child's knowledge, experience and imaginative understanding, and thus his awareness of moral values and capacity for enjoyment; and secondly, to enable him to enter the world after formal education is over as an active participant in society and a responsible contributor to it, capable of achieving as much independence as possible. The educational needs of every child are determined in relation to these goals. We are fully aware that for some children the first of these goals can be approached only by minute, though for them highly significant steps, while the second may never be achieved. But this does not entail that for these children the goals are different. The purpose of education for all children is the same; the goals are the same. But the help that individual children need in progressing towards them will be different. Whereas for some the road they have to travel towards the goals is smooth and easy, for others it is fraught with obstacles. For some the obstacles are so daunting that, even with the greatest possible help, they will not get very far. Nevertheless, for them too, progress will be possible, and their educational needs will be fulfilled, as they gradually overcome one obstacle after another on the way.

From: *Special Educational Needs*, The Warnock Report, HMSO (1978).

Document forty-four
THE RHETORIC OF NEEDS IN SPECIAL EDUCATION

Needs are relative, historically, socially and politically. The important point is that some groups have the power to define the needs of others, and to decide what provision shall be made for these predetermined needs. The unproblematic acceptance of 'special need' in education rests upon the acceptance that there are foolproof assessment processes which will correctly diagnose and define the needs of children. But the rhetoric of special needs may have become more of a rationalisation by which people who have power to define and shape the system of special education and who have vested interests in the assessment of, and provision for, more and more children as special, maintain their influence and interests. The rhetoric of special needs may be humanitarian, the practice is control and vested interests.

From: S. Tomlinson, *A Sociology of Special Education*, Routledge & Kegan Paul, London (1982) p. 75.

THE NEEDS OF SECONDARY-SCHOOL PUPILS

THE TABLE BELOW WAS CONSTRUCTED IN THE COURSE OF A STUDY OF FOUR COMPREHENSIVE SCHOOLS IN THE MID-1970S. IT SUMMARISES TEACHERS' VIEWS OF THE NEEDS OF SECONDARY SCHOOL PUPILS.

Table 1.1 The needs of secondary school pupils

Institution-specific	*Future-specific*	*Maturation-specific*
Needs related to:	*Needs related to:*	*Needs related to:*
The sense of having a place in the school as an institution security identity belonging	**Learning** opportunity and motivation to acquire and practise social, intellectual and physical skills	**Knowledge** general education specialist education education for leisure and for citizenship
The peaceful and smooth running of the school as a social and work environment attendance monitoring containment control enjoyment motivation for school work	**Moral development** moral guidance **Physical development** health monitoring health education **Emotional development** emotional support and counselling appreciation of wider	**Guidance** education guidance career guidance personal guidance

Institution-specific	Future-specific	Maturation-specific
Needs related to:	*Needs related to:*	*Needs related to:*
The education and social purposes of the school accommodation amenities equipment	social context of pupils' school life	
Life support access to health care access to food		

From: D. Johnson, *et al.*, *Secondary Schools and the Welfare Network*, Allen & Unwin, London (1980), p.16.

Document forty-six
WORKING-CLASS FAILURE IN SCHOOL: TWO CONTRASTING EXPLANATIONS

All of the research work described in this book has this common starting point, the evidence of school failure related to the social circumstances of groups of children. But the precise explanation of failure and prescription for action differ greatly. The variety of approach may be illustrated by contrasting two extreme models.

The dominant interpretation of failure has placed the emphasis on the inadequacies of a child's home; the origin of the child's difficulties at school and his failure to match up to recognized criteria of attainment lie in the deficiencies of his early educational experiences. Accordingly the model predicts that the way to improve the child's performance is to introduce an early educational programme which compensates for these deficiencies. This model is the most often associated with the policy of 'positive discrimination'. It argues that a superficial equality of access to education does not take into account that some children are at a disadvantage before they start. Consequently the road to true equality is through providing extra education for the disadvantaged groups. Many of the recommendations of the Plowden report are argued in these terms.

The alternative interpretation is that the deficiencies lie in the school, which does not provide an appropriate environment for the children, by virtue of its failure to adopt teaching methods and educational goals which are relevant to the children's experience. Adopting a sociological perspective, this model views the culture of both the working-class and middle-class home as equally valid and having a contribution to make in education; neither is deficient, but they are different. The middle-class child succeeds at school only because the educational experiences and values of the school accord with those of his home. The 'equality' sought by advocates of compensatory education is all too often a middle-class uniformity. The alternative model argues that the greatest change must be in the schools and teachers who must develop goals and methods which appeal to the children's experiences and are sensitive to the life circumstances of their families.

From: M. Woodhead, *Intervening in Disadvantage*, NFER, Slough (1976), pp. 15–16.

BLAMING THE VICTIM

WILLIAM RYAN HAS CHALLENGED THE 'SOCIAL PATHOLOGY' AP-
PROACH TO SOLVING SOCIAL PROBLEMS, BY ARGUING THAT MUCH
OF IT ENTAILS 'BLAMING THE VICTIM' FOR HIS OR HER SITUATION.

Consider some victims. One is the miseducated child in the slum school. He is
blamed for his own miseducation. He is said to contain within himself the
causes of his inability to read and write well. The shorthand phrase is 'cultural
deprivation' which, to those in the know, conveys what they allege to be inside
information: that the poor child carries a scanty pack of cultural baggage as he
enters school. He doesn't know about books and magazines and newspapers,
they say. (No books in the home: the mother fails to subscribe to *Reader's
Digest*.) They say that if he talks at all – an unlikely event since slum parents
don't talk to their children – he certainly doesn't talk correctly . . . In a word
he is 'disadvantaged' and 'socially deprived', they say, and this, of course,
accounts for his failure (*his* failure, they say) to learn much in school.

I have been listening to the victim-blamers and pondering their thought
processes for a number of years. That process is often very subtle. Victim-
blaming is cloaked in kindness and concern, and bears all the trappings and
statistical furbelows of scientism; it is obscured by a perfumed haze of
humanitarianism. In observing the process of Blaming the Victim, one tends
to be confused and disoriented because those who practice this art display a
deep concern for the victims that is quite genuine. In this way, the new
ideology is very different from the open prejudice and reactionary tactics of
the old days. Its adherents include sympathetic social scientists with social
conscience in good working order, and liberal politicians with a genuine
commitment to reform.

[The folklore of cultural deprivation] is used in an ideological fashion to
preserve the core of the *status quo* in urban education – to forestall any
questioning about the fundamental problems of recruiting and training
teachers, achieving racial integration, and, in particular, governing the school
system. Waving this banner, educationists can advocate Head Start, smaller
classes, More Effective Schools, 'scatteration' to the suburbs by one-way
busing, teaching machines, or Swahili – almost anything that involves

changing or manipulating or treating the *child*. They fight to the death any proposal that implies there might be anything at all wrong with the teachers or the teaching, and resist any exploration of, or intrusion into, the monopolistic control of public education by the teaching profession, particularly if it implies participation in decision-making by laymen from the community.

From: W. Ryan, *Blaming the Victim*, Orbach & Chambers, London, (1971) pp. 3–4, 6, 34–5.

DEPRIVED OR DIFFERENT? WORKING-CLASS CULTURE IN SCHOOLS

The clearest statement of the difference view in this country is Keddie's (1973) introduction to a collection of papers on the myth of cultural deprivation. The thrust of the argument is that what counts as the curriculum, ability and success in school is socially constructed; that is there is no absolute *a priori* requirement for the ingredients of the curriculum or for assessing competence in school. The procedures we use are relative both to a particular group and to a particular historical period . . . Calling someone culturally deprived can free us of any responsibility; our hands are clean and it becomes the child's fault that he is not making our grade. From this the argument progresses in a well-rehearsed manner; the label cultural deprivation assumes that if mainstream values do not prevail in the world of the child he is assumed less educable; failure is located within the home; it becomes an individual trouble rather than a social issue. Our task as educators should be to learn his culture before we can begin to communicate our own.

There is a tendency within Keddie's position to be over romantic about the lot of the deprived. She agrees with Wax and Wax that it is dangerous to assume that those who lack material benefits are necessarily deficient in their culture. This may well be true, but from this position it is easy to argue that there is little point in ending the degradation and squalor to which we commit the poor. There may well be virtue to be gained in heaven through living in an overcrowded, damp house which lacks basic amenities, in having such a low command over society's resources that it is near impossible to exercise control over the immediate environment. But why should it always be the poor who learn the moral lessons from economic hardship, whose inner resources are strengthened through adversity? The relativist approach adopted by Keddie attacks the irritants in the system when it is the basic structure that is at fault.

. . . We are confronted by a dilemma; much of what passes as education is of limited value even to the successful and, as Keddie suggests, even less so to the disadvantaged; however the existing curriculum has a purchasing power in the currency of external examinations. To reform the curriculum of the disadvantaged without changing the criteria of external validation for all is to place the inhabitants of the slum at a further disadvantage by excluding them from access to a path to some of society's rewards. . .

I am advocating two strategies. One is to increase social justice in all our social institutions. This means the pursuit of long-term policies of positive discrimination, of the development of a genuine system of comprehensive education, of sorting out the priorities for educational advance with the goal of social justice uppermost. But immediate action must also be taken to ensure that the poor in the system *now* get all the help and resources necessary to obtain those rewards which society values.

From: P. Robinson., *Education and Poverty*, Methuen, London (1976) pp. 44–6.

Document forty-nine
EDUCATION IS NOT A SOCIAL CURE-ALL

IN A MINISTERIAL SPEECH IN 1980, DR RHODES BOYSON (PARLIA-
MENTARY UNDER-SECRETARY FOR EDUCATION AND SCIENCE)
ARGUED THAT THE POTENTIAL OF USING EDUCATION AS SOCIAL
ENGINEERING HAS BEEN OVER-STATED.

'Education as a means of social engineering is not a new but a Victorian
concept,' Dr. Boyson said. 'We have to realise, however, that while education
can teach people to read and write, and advance knowledge, it is not a social
cure-all.'

'Some of the disillusion with the achievements of education is due to
education being asked to do too much. The expectations were too wide. It is
time Victorian-based Utopian ideas for education were abandoned and
energies concentrated on seeing that education is really effective in achieving
educational objectives – objectives which are in themselves important enough
in our society.'

The Victorians had expected too much from education. 'Certainly education can make an important contribution to economic well-being but it cannot
guarantee this by itself and, just as important, without strong support from
the family education cannot by itself uphold values and social discipline, far
less transform society', Dr. Boyson said.

From: DES Press Release, 15 October 1980.

PREPARATION FOR LEADERSHIP AND ACCESS TO ELITE EDUCATION

THE PUBLIC SCHOOLS COMMISSION REFLECTED A RANGE OF VIEWS ON THE CONTRIBUTION OF INDEPENDENT SCHOOLS TO THE PREPARATION OF THE NEXT GENERATION OF BRITAIN'S LEADERS:

99.   Some have expressed a more extreme view to us. Britain, they say, cannot flourish without leaders, and leadership could not flourish without the public schools. Public school headmasters are among those who blush for the philosophical, historical and sociological naîveté that such a proposition enshrines. Have other nations without such a system of education – the Israelis, the Japanese, the Swedes – no leaders? Have we no other source of leaders? The Robbins Report is only one of the more recent studies to demonstrate the abundant reserves of talent in this country. Much of this talent is only gradually beginning to surmount the handicaps imposed, first, by home circumstances and, secondly, by a restrictive system of secondary schooling. Justice and efficiency both demand that nobody of character and ability should be denied the chance of achieving professional competence which is the prerequisite of leadership. Our country would prosper more if greater efforts were made to attain this ideal.

From: *The Public Schools Commission*, First Report, HMSO (1968) para. 99.

Document fifty-one
RAWLS' THEORY OF JUSTICE AND THE PROVISION OF EDUCATION

Justice, according to Rawls, concerns rules for distributing socially valued goods and services. It is based on the principle of fairness that governs natural situations. If, for example, five people have to share an asset (say, a pie, or a piece of land), if none of the people have a special right, then the rule must be that each should obtain an equal share. Justice, fairness and equality are, therefore, inseparable in this concrete example. However, complex societies do not always present such explicit opportunities for applying the rule of fairness. If inequalities arise, as they seem to in every society, what then should be the guiding rule? This is the most novel part of Rawls' theory for it is here that he introduces the 'difference principle' which stands the conventional liberal and meritocratic notion of inequality on its head. The social ideal according to Rawls . . . is that 'All social primary goods – liberty and opportunity, income and wealth; and the bases of self-respect – are to be distributed equally unless an unequal distribution of any or all of these goods is to the advantage of the least favoured.'

The 'evolutionary liberal' and the 'meritocratic' models are, therefore, rejected since they attempt to establish a natural aristocracy which is based on undeserved endowments, be they from social or biological inheritance or from good fortune. Neither is the answer to be found in tinkering with an unfair system, as dictated by the 'compensatory' model. The aim of Rawls is to equalize not opportunity but results or outcomes . . .

The 'difference principle' has two aspects of relevance to policy. The main one is the principle of 'redress' for individuals who are disadvantaged. In this connection Rawls suggests that greater resources might be spent on the education of the less rather than the more intelligent, at least over a certain time of life, say, the earlier years of school. This is obviously similar to a compensatory model but it is derived from a principle of fairness that regards education as 'good' in its own right, not as an instrument of social engineering. The poor have a right to more education because they have less of everything else. The second implication for social policy is that talents are to be defined as a 'common asset'.

Education, both as a 'good' in itself and in its effects on the welfare and the wealth of a society, should according to Rawls be distributed according to the principle of inequality in favour of the *least* advantaged.

From: W. Tyler, *The Sociology of Educational Inequality*, Methuen, London (1977) pp. 117–18.

Document fifty-two
EQUALITY OF EDUCATION OPPORTUNITY: THE DEMISE OF A CRUCIAL CONCEPT

At the centre of the politico-social disputes over education has been the concept of equal opportunity – a concept handled so incautiously in the 1950s and 1960s and productive of so much uncertainty and disillusion in the 1970s . . . The concept of equal opportunity had for a long time attracted and held some of the political middle ground, but by the 1970s was crumbling somewhat in the hands of the hesitant left, abandoned by the middle as economic expansion turned to stagnation and decline, and attacked from the left flank as a concept incompatible with that of equality itself. It turned out by the end of the 1970s that people either did not understand it, had over-estimated it, had been disillusioned by the research or the rhetoric, could not longer wait for it, or did not want it.

Equal opportunity in or through education has been a popular if ambiguous slogan, and a much analysed perspective. Since inequality has been a continuous and tangible part of our experience, and at the heart of approaches to education-as-social-policy, the issue of equal opportunity is also crucial for our discussion of the social condition. It has been *the* educational issue of post-Second World War Britain, Europe, the United States, and beyond.

From: H. Silver, *Education and the Social Condition*, Methuen, London (1980) pp. 33–4.

Document fifty-three
EQUALITY OF OPPORTUNITY: MERITOCRACY IN SOCIAL POLICY

Equality has so far acted as the main inspiration to all left wing radicals. Tawney, Laski, Crosland, Titmuss, Miliband and Strachey differ on many points but they agree on one fundamental issue: they aspire to a more egalitarian society. There are many brands of equality. This is why it has united such diverse socialist thinkers. The brand that has been incorporated in social policy is equality of opportunity, i.e. the belief that every individual has a right to such services and circumstances as will enable him to fulfil his abilities. This is a meritocratic view of equality. The emphasis is on equality of competition rather than equality of results. It is the direct offspring of individualism humanised by the efforts of the welfare state. As such it is the product of a constellation of values that represents a compromise between laissez-faire and equality of results. It is a step forward from nineteenth-century philosophy because it accepts and welcomes government intervention and because it makes for a society stratified on the basis of achievement rather than ascription.

The period since the end of the last war has made equality of opportunity the central value of social policy. Educational policies, particularly, were shaped to enable every child to compete with other children on an equal footing. If the educational race was fair then the outcome of the race was also fair, it was argued.

From: V. George and P. Wilding, *Ideology and Social Policy*, Routledge & Kegan Paul, London (1976) p. 129.

POSITIVE DISCRIMINATION: A LIMITED STRATEGY?

Put most broadly positive discrimination is a strategy for reducing inequality that is aimed at the most deprived. It may benefit them by augmenting the economic resources made available, or by increasing their access to political power. What it avoids is means tested benefits for individuals.

There is an obvious limitation in any strategy against inequality which makes the deprived its target, since the deprived are but one side of the coin. On the other side are the wealthy. The relative position of the deprived cannot be improved without affecting that of other people. Thus positive discrimination may mean only redistribution within the working class, from the less poor to the very poor. Or it may provide help that is irrelevant without structural change. Positive discrimination policies should not be adopted in isolation from other measures; and outside a general programme for redistribution will only amount to tokenism.

From: H. Glennerster and S. Hatch, (eds), *Positive Discrimination and Inequality*, Fabian Research Series 314 (1974) p. 2.

Document fifty-five
A POSITIVE ACTION PROGRAMME FOR GIRLS AND SCIENCE

THE NCCL HAS SUGGESTED THE FOLLOWING PROPOSALS FOR EN-COURAGING GIRLS TO STUDY SCIENCE, BASED UPON THE EX-PERIENCE OF THE GIRLS IN SCIENCE AND TECHNOLOGY PRO-GRAMME IN MANCHESTER.

a. Recognise real sex differences; ignore imaginary ones. There is some evidence that girls have better verbal skills than boys and prefer work which has a clear practical application; there is evidence, too, that boys are better at abstract work and at answering multiple-choice questions. There is no convincing evidence, on the other hand, to suggest that boys are naturally more suited to studying physics – although many people imagine that this is so.

b. Value girls' qualities.

c. Avoid open-ended teaching. Possibly because girls have less confidence than boys in their ability to do science, they may be less responsive to open-ended, discovery methods of teaching. Guided discovery methods may be better suited to their needs.

d. Provide supporting classroom atmosphere. It is not enough simply to treat girls the same as boys: while competitive, individualistic work may suit boys, girls may prefer a more friendly, relaxed atmosphere.

e. Make examples relevant to girls' lives.

f. Discuss social implication of science.

g. Stress practical application of theory.

h. Reduce conceptual difficulty. Science is generally seen as being concerned with 'things', whereas girls are typically more interested in 'people' and may be discouraged by an impersonal, mechanistic approach to science. Strategies (e) to (g) will help to reduce conceptual difficulties.

i. Use books and teaching materials which include females.

j. Use structured or essay type exam questions. As mentioned above, girls achieve better results with these than with multiple-choice questions.

k. Amalgamate domestic science and natural science.

l. Reduce freedom to drop science. Girls may enjoy it later on in their school careers if they do not drop it at an early age – especially if special steps are taken to encourage their interest.

m. Employ more women to teach physical science.

n. Institute remedial classes for special and scientific skills. Research in the US suggests that girls develop inferior spatial skills mainly because they are encouraged to play with different kinds of toys from those with which boys play. If they are given extra help to compensate for their lack of experience, they quickly improve.

o. Examine timetabling. Do the range of options discourage girls from pursuing science?

p. Improve careers advice in third year.

q. Invite women scientists to visit school. Attractive role models are important.

r. Discuss women scientists.

s. Combact sex-stereotyping in school generally.

t. Try single-sex classes.

From: S. Robarts, *Positive Action for Women: the Next Step*, National Council for Civil Liberties (1981) pp.79-80.

SCHOOL CURRICULUM AND NATIONAL NEEDS

BARONESS YOUNG, ONE OF THE DES MINISTERS, MADE A SPEECH IN 1980 WHICH DEVELOPS THE THEME OF 'NATIONAL NEEDS' COMMON TO A NUMBER OF MINISTERIAL SPEECHES IN THE SAME PERIOD.

Schools needed to take national considerations into account in planning their curricula, and it was right for the Government to take the lead in giving a view as a means of guiding and assisting schools, Baroness Young, Minister of State said today . . .

The Minister realised that the question of national needs and who should determine them had caused anxiety. She said: 'Some have suggested that Governments will take too narrow a view of national needs, perhaps confined to economic and industrial needs: and, by implication, that they will not take sufficient account of the needs of individual pupils.

'I believe that these anxieties are unfounded. Of course, the needs of each individual pupil are central to the purposes of education; but these needs must include adequate preparation for the world in which each school leaver is going to live . . .

'Economic and industrial concerns are of course of the highest importance. But there are many other considerations. There is, for example, the challenge of a new generation of technology which will affect our home as much as our working life.

'There is also the changed position of women in our society: a clear example of a national need is the need for educational provision to be equally available both to boys and to girls. Curricular provision in schools, and in higher and further education, needs to be equally available for both; and the girls themselves need to be able to recognise the opportunities open to them in areas which have traditionally been regarded as male preserves . . .'

From: DES Press Release, 21 October 1980.

Document fifty-seven
PREPARING FOR THE SOCIAL RELATIONS OF PRODUCTION

The Correspondence Principle

> In the social production which men carry on they enter into definite relations which are indispensible and independent of their will; . . . The sum total of these relations of production constitutes . . . the real foundation on which rise legal and political superstructures, and to which correspond definite forms of social consciousness.

> Karl Marx, Contribution to
a Critique of Political
Economy, (1857).

The educational system helps integrate youth into the economic system, we believe, through a structural correspondence between its social relations and those of production. The structure of social relations in education not only inures the student to the discipline of the work place, but develops the types of personal demeanor, modes of self-preservation, self-image, and social-class identifications which are the crucial ingredients of job adequacy. Specifically, the social relationships of education – the relationships between administrators and teachers, teachers and students, students and students, and students and their work – replicate the hierarchical division of labor. Hierarchical relations are reflected in the vertical authority lines from administrators to teachers to students. Alienated labor is reflected in the student's lack of control over his or her education, the alienation of the student from the curriculum content, and the motivation of school work through a system of grades and other external rewards rather than the student's integration with either the process (learning) or the outcome (knowledge) of the educational 'production process'. Fragmentation in work is reflected in the institutionalized and often destructive competition among students through continual and ostensibly meritocratic ranking and evaluation. By attuning young people to a set of social relationships similar to those of the work place, schooling attempts to gear the development of personal needs to its requirements.

From: S. Bowles and H. Gintis, *Schooling in Capitalist America*, Routledge & Kegan Paul, London (1976), p. 131.

Document fifty-eight
TRUANCY AND THE SOCIAL WORK RESPONSE

234.   It is now widely appreciated that the main object should be to prevent persistent truancy by dealing with the underlying causes at the earliest stages. Truancy, frequent and unexplained absences (which may be connived at by parents), and school phobia are now recognised as symptoms of personal behavioural difficulties or family disturbance, misfortune or distress as well as possible signs of a child's unhappiness in the school situation. If left unattended the position may well deteriorate to the point where the only alternative is to take legal proceedings, to enforce the removal of the child from his home for a short or long period. Although in some cases removal from home may become necessary in the social or educational interests of the child, every effort should be made to avoid such a drastic step . . .

235.   All serious cases of truancy, which can so often be associated with or lead into delinquency, should be investigated by the social worker attached to the school who would have a duty to keep both the school and the education department informed and to make recommendations if necessary, for example, for a change of school. In the interests of the children involved, it would be essential to have close co-operation between the education department and the social service department over problems of non-attendance. We think that it ought to be a statutory requirement that the head of the social service department be responsible for all social investigations arising from non-attendance at school.

From: *Committee on Local Authority and Allied Personal Social Services*, The Seebohm Report, Cmnd. 3703, HMSO (1968), para. 234–5.

Document fifty-nine
REASONS FOR CANING

THE FOLLOWING LIST, DOCUMENTING THE REASONS FOR ADMINI-STERING CORPORAL PUNISHMENT, WAS COMPILED FROM THE PUNISHMENT BOOK OF A BRITISH COMPREHENSIVE SCHOOL IN 1981.

Table 4: Analysis of offences

Offence	No. of entries
Fighting/bullying	122
Missing detention	75
Swearing/cheek/insolence to staff	70
Vaguely-described misbehaviour	68
Truancy	56
Horseplay-type offences	55
Smoking	27
Disruption/disturbance of lessons, etc.	26
Stealing	23
Vandalism/damage to property	22
Spitting	15
Riding motorbike	7
Missing assembly	5
Lying	5
Refusal to accept punishment	5
Gambling	2
Lateness	2
Spoiling artwork	2
Failure to do imposition	2
Failure to bring report form/note	2
In girls' toilets	2
Two detentions in one week	1
Throwing stones at staff	1
Altering own report	1

Offence	No. of entries
Writing a disgusting and insulting document	1
Not stated	7
Total	604

From: Society of Teachers Opposed to Physical Punishment, *A Quarter of a Million Beatings*, STOPP, (1981).

EDUCATION FOR FAMILY LIFE

'What after all, do we have an educational system for, unless to train the younger generation in the way we think it should go?' So writes Barbara Wootton. In marriage and family life there is general agreement on the way we think the younger generation should go. It is the way which many people desire for themselves – a happy and enduring marriage and bringing up of a small family in a home of their own. We already know clearly some of the factors which militate for or against this almost universal aim. Why do we not teach these lessons plainly?

Our ineffectiveness arises first from the failure of society to accord prime importance to parenthood and family life . . .

Sex education, while important, is by no means the most important education for marriage and family life. The most fundamental form of education lies in the training of children in kindness, co-operation and sharing, for these basic attitudes, learned in the first few years of life, are essential to happy marriage . . .

It could be argued that perhaps too much attention has been concentrated on sexual mechanics rather than on personal relationships and responsibilities. This has made some parents look askance at sex education, fearing that it may merely stimulate curiosity and experimentation among their sons and daughters if sex is explained in purely animal terms without reference to emotions, commitments or responsibilities . . . Strong steps should be taken to ensure that teachers are properly trained to stress the responsibilities of sex rather than its biology . . .

Boys and girls should be taught that a pre-marital pregnancy is a serious matter which is best avoided by refraining from intercourse; . . .

Schoolchildren, and this particularly applies to working-class girls, should be persuaded that it is better for people not to marry too early; they will then have a better chance of success and a much better chance of getting a home of their own.

They should be told that it is of supreme importance whom you marry. Far too many working-class girls, in particular, want the status of being a married woman, with the achievement of a double bed and a pram, and find in some willing and convenient young man a means to this end. To be discriminating in judging people, and to take time over it, is one of the most important lessons. There is also need for education about the proper time for having a baby in order to give the child the best start in life; this is again bound up with the achievements of a home of one's own and often means waiting for perhaps three years of marriage.

From: A. J. Brayshaw, *Public Policy and Family Life*, Policy Studies Institute, (1980).

BIBLIOGRAPHY OF RELEVANT OFFICIAL REPORTS

Reports are given in order of publication

Consultative Committee to the Board of Education (1926) *The Education of the Adolescent*, The Hadow Report. HMSO: London.

Consultative Committee to the Board of Education (1938) *Secondary Education*, The Spens Report. HMSO: London.

Secondary Schools Examinations Council (1943) *Curriculum and Examinations in Secondary Schools*, The Norwood Report. HMSO: London.

Board of Education (1943) *Educational Reconstruction*, Cmd. 6458. HMSO: London.

Ministry of Education (1947) *The New Secondary Education*. HMSO: London.

Ministry of Education (1954) *Early Leaving*, A Report of the Central Advisory Council for Education. HMSO: London.

Ministry of Education (1958) *Secondary Education For All: A New Drive*, Cmnd. 604. HMSO: London.

Ministry of Education (1959) *Fifteen to Eighteen*, Report of the Central Advisory Council for Education, The Crowther Report. HMSO: London.

Committee of the Secondary Schools Examinations Council (1960) *Secondary School Examinations Other Than G.C.E.*, The Beloe Report. HMSO: London.

Ministry of Education (1963) *Half Our Future*, A Report of the Central Advisory Council for Education, The Newsom Report. HMSO: London.

Department of Education and Science (1966) *A Plan for Polytechnics and Other Colleges*, Cmnd. 3006. HMSO: London.

Department of Education and Science (1967) *Children and Their Primary Schools*, A Report of the Central Advisory Council for Education, The Plowden Report. HMSO: London.

275

Department of Health and Social Security (1968) *Report of the Committee on Local Authority and Allied Personal Social Services*, The Seebohm Report, Cmnd. 3703. HMSO: London.

House of Commons Select Committee on Education and Science (1968) *H.M. Inspectorate*. HMSO: London.

Public Schools Commission (1968) First Report, and (1970) Second Report. HMSO: London.

Department of Education and Science (1971) *The Education of Immigrants*, Education Survey 13. HMSO: London.

Department of Education and Science (1972a) *Education: A Framework for Expansion*, Cmnd. 5174. HMSO: London.

Department of Education and Science (1972b) *Teacher Education and Training*, The James Report. HMSO: London.

Halsey, A. H. (1972) *Educational Priority*, The Halsey Report. HMSO: London.

Department of Education and Science (1973a) *Adult Education: A Plan for Development*, The Russell Report. HMSO: London.

Department of Education and Science (1973b) *School Transport*, The Hodges Report. HMSO: London.

House of Commons Select Committee on Race Relations and Immigration (1973) *Education Vol. 1*, Session 1972–3. HMSO: London.

Department of Health and Social Security (1974) *Report of the Committee of Enquiry into the Care and Supervision Provided in Relation to Maria Colwell*. HMSO: London.

House of Commons Expenditure Committee (1974) *Education Maintenance Allowances in the 16–18 Years Age Group*, H. C. 306.

Department of Education and Science (1975) *Nutrition in Schools*, Report of the Working Party on the Nutritional Aspects of School Meals. HMSO: London.

Department of Education and Science (1975a) *The School Health Service 1908–74*. HMSO: London.

Department of Education and Science (1975b) *Curricular Differences for Boys and Girls*, HMI Education Survey No. 21. HMSO: London.

Department of Education and Science (1975a) *A Language for Life*, The Bullock Report. HMSO: London.

House of Commons Expenditure Committee (1976) *Tenth Report: Policy Making in the Department of Education and Science*. HMSO: London.

Department of Education and Science (1977a) *The Growth of Comprehensive Education*, Report on Education No. 87. DES: London.

Bibliography of relevant official reports

Department of Education and Science (1977b) *Education in Schools: A Consultative Document*, Cmnd. 6869. HMSO: London.

Department of Education and Science (1977c) *How the Department of Education and Science is Organised*. DES: London.

Department of Education and Science (1977d) *A New Partnership for Our Schools*, The Taylor Report. HMSO: London.

Department of Health and Social Security/Welsh Office (1977) *Working Together for Children and Their Families*. HMSO: London.

Education in Schools: A Consultative Document (1977), Cmnd. 6869. HMSO: London.

Scottish Education Department (1977) *Truancy and Indiscipline in Schools in Scotland*, The Pack Report. HMSO: London.

Her Majesty's Inspectorate (1978a), *Behavioural Units*. HMSO: London.

Her Majesty's Inspectorate (1978b) *Truancy and Behavioural Problems in Some Urban Schools*. HMSO: London.

Special Educational Needs (1978) The Warnock Report. HMSO: London.

Department of Education and Science (1979) *Local Authority Arrangements for the School Curriculum*. HMSO: London.

Department of Education and Science (1980b) *Girls and Science*, HMI Series, Matters for Discussion No. 13. HMSO: London.

Department of Education and Science (1980c) *A View of the Curriculum*, HMI Series, Matters for Discussion No. 11. HMSO: London.

Department of Education and Science (1980d) *Special Needs in Education*, Cmnd. 7996. HMSO: London.

Department of Education and Science (1982a) *Pupils and School Leavers: Future Numbers*, Report on Education No. 97. DES: London.

Her Majesty's Inspectorate (1982b) *The Effects of Local Authority Expenditure Policies on the Education Service in England, 1981*. DES: London.

SELECT BIBLIOGRAPHY

ASSOCIATION OF DIRECTORS OF SOCIAL SERVICES (1978) *Social Work Services for Children in School*. ADSS: London.

BACON, W. (1978) *Public Accountability and the Schooling System*. Harper & Row: London.

BANKS, O. (1955) *Parity and Prestige in English Secondary Education*. Routledge & Kegan Paul (RKP): London.

BARKER, R. (1972) *Education and Politics 1900–1951: A Study of the Labour Party*. Clarendon: Oxford.

BARON, G. and HOWELL, D. (1974) *The Government and Management of Schools*. Athlone Press: London.

BARTON, L., MEIGHAN, R. and WALKER, S. (eds) (1980) *Schooling, Ideology and the Curriculum*. Falmer Press: Lewes.

BELL, R. and GRANT, N. (1977) *Patterns of Education in the British Isles*. Allen & Unwin: London.

BENN, C. and SIMON, B. (1970) *Half Way There*, McGraw Hill: London.

BERNBAUM, G. (ed.) (1979) *Schooling in Decline*. Macmillan: London.

BEST, R., JARVIS, C. and RIBBINS, P. (1980) *Perspectives on Pastoral Care*. Heinemann: London.

BURGESS, R. (ed.) (1982) *Exploring Society*. British Sociological Association: London.

BYRNE, E. M. (1974) *Planning and Educational Inequality*. NFER: Slough.

CENTRE FOR CONTEMPORARY CULTURAL STUDIES (1981) *Unpopular Education: Schooling and Social Democracy in England since 1944*. Hutchinson: London.

CORBETT, A. (1978) *Much Ado About Education*, 4th edn. Macmillan: London.

CORRIGAN, P. (1979) *Schooling the Smash Street Kids*. Macmillan: London.

CRAFT, M., RAYNOR, J. and COHEN, L. (eds) (1980) *Linking Home and School*, 3rd edn. Harper & Row: London.

DALE, R., ESLAND, G., FERGUSSON, R. and MCDONALD, M. (eds) (1981) *Education and the State*, Vol. 1, Schooling and the National Interest: Vol. 2, Politics, Patriarchy and Practice. Falmer Press: Lewes.

DAVID, M. E. (1980) *The State, the Family and Education*. RKP: London.

DAVIES, B. (1978) *Universality, Selectivity and Effectiveness in Social Policy*. Heinemann: London.

DEAN, J., BRADLEY, K., CHOPPIN, B. and VINCENT, D. (1979) *The Sixth Form and its Alternatives*. NFER: Slough.

DEEM, R. (1976) *Women and Schooling*. RKP: London.

DEEM, R. (ed.) (1980) *Schooling for Women's Work*. RKP: London.

DEEM, R. (1981) 'State policy and ideology in the education of women 1944–1980', *British Journal of the Sociology of Education*, Vol. 2, No. 2, pp. 131–44.

DOCKING, J. W. (1980) *Control and Discipline in Schools: Perspectives and Approaches*. Harper & Row: London.

ENTWISTLE, H. (1979) *Antonio Gramsci: Conservative Schooling for Radical Politics*. RKP: London.

FENWICK, I. (1976) *The Comprehensive School 1944–1970*. Methuen: London.

FENWICK, K. and MCBRIDE, P. (1981) *The Government of Education*. Martin Robertson: London.

FINN, D., GRANT, N. and JOHNSON, R. (1977) 'Social democracy, education and the crisis', in Centre for Contemporary Cultural Studies, *On Ideology*. Hutchinson: London.

FITZHERBERT, K. (1977) *Child Care Services and the Teacher*. Temple-Smith: London.

FLUDE, M. and AHIER, J. (1974) *Schools, Educability and Ideology*. Croom Helm: London.

FOWLER, G., MORRIS, V. and OZGA, J. (eds) (1973) *Decision-Making in British Education*. Heinemann/OU: London.

FULTON, O. (ed.) (1981) *Access to Higher Education*. Society for Research into Higher Education: Guildford.

GALLOWAY, D. (1981) *Teaching and Counselling: Pastoral Care in Primary and Secondary Schools*. Longman: London.

GOSDEN, P. (1976) *Education in the Second World War: A Study in Policy and Administration*. Methuen: London.

HALSEY, A. H., HEATH, A. F. and RIDGE, J. M. (1980) *Origins and Destinations: Family, Class and Education in Modern Britain.* Clarendon: Oxford.

HENCKE, D. (1978) *Colleges in Crisis.* Penguin: Harmondsworth.

HOPKINS, A. (1978) *The School Debate.* Penguin: Harmondsworth.

JAMES, P. (1980) *The Reorganisation of Secondary Education.* NFER: Slough.

JENNINGS, R. (1977) *Education and Politics: Policy-Making in Local Education Authorities.* Batsford: London.

JOHNSON, D., RANSOM, E., PACKWOOD, T., BOWDEN, K. and KOGAN, M. (1980) *Secondary Schools and the Welfare Network.* Allen & Unwin: London.

JONES-DAVIES, C. and CAVE, G. (1976) *The Disruptive Pupil in Secondary School.* Ward Lock: London.

KARABEL, J. and HALSEY, A. (1977) *Power and Ideology in Education.* OUP: New York.

KIRP, D. (1979) *Doing Good by Doing Little: Race and Schooling in Britain.* University of California Press: Berkeley.

KOGAN, M. (1971) *The Politics of Education.* Penguin: Harmondsworth.

KOGAN, M. (1973) *County Hall: The Role of the Chief Education Officer.* Penguin: Harmondsworth.

KOGAN, M. (1975) *Educational Policy-Making.* Allen & Unwin: London.

LAWTON, D. (1980) *The Politics of the School Curriculum.* RKP: London.

LOVETT, T. (1975) *Adult Education, Community Development and the Working Class.* Ward Lock: London.

MACFARLANE, E. (1978) *Sixth-Form Colleges: The 16–19 Comprehensives.* Heinemann: London.

MACMILLAN, K. (1977) *Education Welfare.* Longman: London.

MURPHY, J. (1971) *Church, State and Schools in Britain 1800–1970.* RKP: London.

NEWELL, P. (1972) *A Last Report? Corporal Punishment in Schools.* Penguin: Harmondsworth.

PETERS, R. (1976) *The Role of the Head.* RKP: London.

PRATT, J. and BURGESS, T. (1974) *Polytechnics: A Report.* Pitman: London.

REAGAN, D. (1977) *Local Government and Education.* Allen & Unwin: London.

ROBINSON, P. (1976) *Education and Poverty.* Methuen: London.

ROGERS, R. (1980) *Crowther to Warnock.* Heinemann: London.

RUBENSTEIN, D. (ed.) (1979) *Education and Equality*. Penguin: Harmondsworth.

RUBENSTEIN, D. and SIMON, B. (1969) *The Evolution of the Comprehensive School 1926–1972*. RKP: London.

RUTTER, M. and MADGE, N. (1977) *Cycles of Disadvantage*. Heinemann: London.

RUTTER, M. MAUGHAN, B., MORTIMORE, P. and OUSTON, J. (1979) *Fifteen Thousand Hours: Secondary Schools and their Effects on Children*. Open Books: London.

SALTER, B. and TAPPER, T. (1981) *Education, Politics and the State*. Grant McIntyre: London.

SARAN, R. (1973) *Policy-Making in Secondary Education*. OUP: Oxford.

SILVER, H. (1973) *Equal Opportunities in Education*. Methuen: London.

SILVER, H. (1980) *Education and the Social Condition*. Methuen: London.

SIMON, B. (1965) *Education and the Labour Movement 1870–1920*. Lawrence & Wishart: London.

TAPPER, T. and SALTER, B. (1978) *Education and the Political Order: Changing Patterns of Class Control*. Macmillan: London.

TOMLINSON, S. (1981) *Educational Subnormality*. RKP: London.

TOMLINSON, S. (1982) *A Sociology of Special Education*. RKP: London.

TUNSTALL, J. (1974) *The Open University Opens*. RKP: London.

TURNER, B. (1974) *Truancy*. Ward Lock: London.

WHITE, R. (1980) *Absent With Cause: Lessons of Truancy*. RKP: London.

WHITE, R. and BROCKINGTON, D. (1978) *In and Out of School: The ROSLA Community Education Project*. RKP: London.

WHITFIELD, R. (1979) *Education for Family Life: Some New Policies for Child Care*. Hodder & Stoughton: London.

WILLIS, P. (1977) *Learning to Labour: How Working Class Kids Get Working Class Jobs*. Saxon House: London.

WILSON, B. (ed.) 1975) *Education, Equality and Society*. Allen & Unwin: London.

WOODHEAD, M. (1976) *Intervening in Disadvantage*. NFER: Slough.

WRIGHT, N. (1977) *Progress in Education*. Croom Helm: London.

YOUNG, M. and WHITTY, G. (eds.) (1977) *Society, State and Schooling*. Falmer Press: London.

INDEX